The Philosophy of Reid as Contained in the "Inquiry Into the Human Mind on the Principles of Common Sense"

g.i. 1.7.5

90

H. Carr, C.L.B.

H. Carr, C. L. B.

Series of Modern Philosophers.

Edited by E. Hershey Sneath, Ph.D.

DESCARTES by Prof. H. A P. TORREY of the University of Vermont.*

SPINOZA by Prof. GEO S. FULLERTON of the University of Pennsylvania *

LOCKE by Prof. JOHN E. RUSSELL of Williams College *

BERKELEY by ex-President NOAH PORTER of Yale University.

HUME by Prof. H. AUSTIN AIKINS of Trinity College, N C

REID by E HERSHEY SNEATH of Yale University.*

KANT by Prof JOHN WATSON of Queen's University, Canada.*

HEGEL by Prof. JOSIAH ROYCE of Harvard University.

* Those marked with an asterisk are ready

HENRY HOLT & CO., Publishers,

NEW YORK.

Series of Modern Philosophers

Edited by E. Hershey Sneath, Ph.D.

THE

PHILOSOPHY OF REID

AS CONTAINED IN THE

"INQUIRY INTO THE HUMAN MIND

ON THE PRINCIPLES OF

COMMON SENSE"

WITH INTRODUCTION AND SELECTED NOTES

BY

E. HERSHEY SNEATH, PH.D.

Instructor in Philosophy in Yale University

NEW YORK

HENRY HOLT AND COMPANY

1892

PREFACE.

AFTER careful consideration, it seemed better to me, and, at the same time, to be consistent with the idea of the "Series" of which this book is a member, to present Reid's Philosophy in an edition of the "Inquiry," rather than in a book of extracts taken from the "Inquiry" and the "Intellectual Powers." The substance of Reid's Philosophy is contained in his theory of perception and his doctrine of common sense. Herein, too, lies his historical significance. The "Inquiry" contains all that is essential for an understanding of Reid's views on these subjects, and presents it in a comparatively brief form. By omitting Secs. IX–XIX (pp. 199–287), which can be easily spared, the subject-matter will be brought within the limits prescribed by the "Series." The sections referred to above will be found interesting, especially when studied in connection with Berkeley's famous "Theory of Vision,"—hence their retention. The text of this edition is taken from Sir Wm. Hamilton's seventh edition of Reid's Works (Edinburgh, 1872). The most important notes of Hamilton, as well as his Index, abridged, have been retained. The "Inquiry" affords an inviting field for criticism, but the limits of the Introduction forbade my entering upon it.

E. H. S.

CONTENTS.

PAGE
BIOGRAPHICAL SKETCH.................................. 1
BIBLIOGRAPHY.................................. 7
RELATION OF REID'S PHILOSOPHY TO ITS PHILOSOPHICAL ANTECEDENTS.................................. 11
THE INFLUENCE OF REID'S PHILOSOPHY UPON SUBSEQUENT PHILOSOPHIC THOUGHT.................................. 47

AN INQUIRY INTO THE HUMAN MIND.

DEDICATION.................................. 65

CHAPTER I. INTRODUCTION.

Section I. The Importance of the subject, and the Means of prosecuting it.......................... 70
II. The Impediments to our knowledge of the mind.. 72
III. The Present State of this part of philosophy. Of Descartes, Malebranche, and Locke......... 76
IV. Apology for those philosophers............. ... 80
V. Of Bishop Berkeley; the "Treatise of Human Nature"; and of Scepticism................ 81
VI. Of the "Treatise of Human Nature".......... . 84
VII. The system of all these authors is the same, and leads to Scepticism... 86
VIII. We ought not to despair of a better........ 87

CHAPTER II. OF SMELLING.

Section I. The Order of proceeding. Of the medium and organ of Smell.......................... 89
II. The Sensation considered abstractly............ 90
III. Sensation and Remembrance, natural principles of Belief.................................. 92

PAGE

Section IV. Judgment and Belief in some cases precede Simple Apprehension.......................... 95
V. Two Theories of the Nature of Belief refuted. Conclusions from what hath been said........ 96
VI. Apology for metaphysical absurdities. Sensation without a sentient, a consequence of the theory of Ideas. Consequences of this strange opinion.................................. 99
VII. The conception and belief of a sentient being, or Mind, is suggested by our constitution. The notion of Relations not always got by Comparing the related ideas......................... 105
VIII. There is a quality or virtue in bodies, which we call their Smell. How this is connected in the imagination with the sensation.................. 109
IX. That there is a principle in human nature, from which the notion of this, as well as all other natural virtues or causes, is derived.......... 111
X. Whether in Sensation the mind is Active or Passive.................................. 116

CHAPTER III. OF TASTING.............................. 118

CHAPTER IV. OF HEARING.

Section I. Variety of Sounds. Their place and distance learned by Custom, without reasoning........ 122
II. Of Natural Language........................ 124

CHAPTER V. OF TOUCH

Section I. Of Heat and Cold.............................. 129
II. Of Hardness and Softness...................... 131
III. Of Natural Signs.............................. 135
IV. Of Hardness, and other Primary Qualities....... 139
V. Of Extension.................................. 141
VI. Of Extension.................................. 144
VII. Of the existence of a Material World........... 148
VIII. Of the Systems of Philosophers concerning the Senses.................................. 156

PAGE

CHAPTER VI. OF SEEING.

Section I. The excellence and dignity of this faculty........ 162
II. Sight discovers almost nothing which the Blind may not comprehend. The reason of this.... 164
III. Of the Visible Appearances of objects........... 169
IV. That Colour is a quality of bodies, not a sensation of the mind............................... 173
V. An inference from the preceding................ 177
VI. That none of our sensations are Resemblances of any of the qualities of bodies................ 181
VII. Of visible Figure and Extension................ 187
VIII. Some Queries concerning Visible Figure answered.................................. 192
IX. Of the Geometry of Visibles................ 199
X. Of the Parallel Motion of the eyes.............. 211
XI. Of our seeing objects Erect by inverted images.. 215
XII. The same subject continued.. 222
XIII. Of seeing objects Single with two eyes.......... 238
XIV. Of the laws of vision in Brute animals........... 246
XV. Squinting considered hypothetically............. 249
XVI. Facts relating to Squinting..................... 261
XVII. Of the effect of Custom in seeing objects Single.. 265
XVIII. Of Dr. Porterfield's account of single and double vision.................................. 272
XIX. Of Dr. Brigg's theory, and Sir Isaac Newton's conjecture on this subject.................. 276
XX. Of Perception in general............. 287
XXI. Of the Process of Nature in perception.......... 297
XXII. Of the Signs by which we learn to perceive Distance from the eye......... 303
XXIII. Of the Signs used in other acquired perceptions... 316
XXIV Of the Analogy between Perception, and the credit we give to Human Testimony.......... 320

CHAPTER VII. CONCLUSION.

Containing Reflections upon the opinions of Philosophers on this subject.................... 338

INDEX.. 363

BIOGRAPHICAL SKETCH.

Dugald Stewart truly says, that the life of Thomas Reid "was uncommonly barren of those incidents which furnish materials for biography." His life was spent in comparative quiet and retirement, and was, therefore, not replete with varied incident. He was born April 26th, 1710, at Strachan, Kincardineshire, Scotland. His father was the Rev. Lewis Reid, a highly respected clergyman, who was descended from a succession of ministers of the Church of Scotland. His mother, Margaret Gregory, belonged to a family somewhat distinguished in Scotland for their scientific attainments. Early in life Reid was sent to the parish school of Kincardine where he spent two years. From the parish school he went to Aberdeen, where he received instruction in the classics. When about twelve or thirteen years of age he entered Marischal College. Here he was instructed in Philosophy by Dr. George Turnbull, who undoubtedly exerted a great influence upon his philosophical thinking.* He graduated from college in 1726. Receiving an appointment of librarian to the University, he continued his connection with it until 1736. During

* Dr. McCosh says that Turnbull exercised a greater influence upon Reid's thinking "than all other masters and writers" combined. "The Scottish Philosophy," pp. 95-106.

this period he devoted much of his time to the study of Mathematics. Resigning his office in 1736, he visited England in company with his friend, John Stewart, who afterward held the chair of Mathematics in Marischal College. They visited London, Oxford and Cambridge, where they were introduced to many noted literary men. In 1737, having been presented "to the living of New-Machar," by King's College, Aberdeen, he entered upon his clerical work. The early part of his ministerial life in this parish was signalized by an intense hostility to him on the part of his parishioners. This was occasioned specially by the aversion which his people had to the law of patronage. Furthermore, he was accustomed, because of his modesty, to preach the sermons of Drs. Tillotson and Evans instead of his own. This practice was very offensive to the people. However, despite his unpopularity, through his fidelity to the interests of his parish, and his amiability of disposition, he soon ingratiated himself into the good will and affections of the people. In 1740, he was married to his cousin, Elizabeth Reid, daughter of Dr. George Reid, a London physician. His wife proved a great help to him in his work at New-Machar. While living here, "the greater part of his time," says Dugald Stewart, "was spent in the most intense study; more particularly in a careful examination of the laws of external perception, and of the other principles which form the groundwork of human knowledge."* In 1748, his first publication appeared. It was in the form of an Essay, published in the "Transactions" of the Royal Society of London, and

"Collected Works," vol. x, p. 251.

was entitled, "An Essay on Quantity, occasioned by reading a Treatise in which Simple and Compound Ratios are applied to Virtue and Merit." The "Treatise" to which Reid alludes was Hutcheson's "Inquiry into the Origin of our Ideas of Beauty and Virtue." In this "Treatise," Hutcheson made use of mathematical forms in illustrating moral subjects. Whether he meant to apply mathematical reasoning to such subjects may be doubted. Reid, however, was aware of the fact that Pitcairn and Cheyne had applied this form of reasoning to medicine, and he felt constrained to write an essay showing what rendered a subject capable of mathematical treatment.

In 1752, he was elected Professor of Philosophy, in King's College, Aberdeen. Shortly after his removal to Aberdeen, the "Aberdeen Philosophical Society" was founded, principally through his endeavors. It included among its members such men as Campbell, Gerard, Beattie and John Gregory.* While connected with this society, he read papers which contained the essential principles of the "Inquiry." In 1764, he published the "Inquiry into the Human Mind on the Principles of Common Sense." Reid's speculations on the subjects treated in the "Inquiry" were really begun in 1739, on the appearance of Hume's "Treatise of Human Nature." In the "Inquiry" Reid attempts to refute the scepticism of Hume by attacking the "theory of ideas" on which he thought this scepticism to be founded. Being thus directed against the sceptical philosophy of Hume,

* Cf. McCosh, "The Scottish Philosophy," pp. 227–9, for an account of this society.

he was desirous of subjecting his manuscript to Hume's perusal, so as not to misrepresent his philosophy in any particular. He was enabled to do this through the kind services of Dr. Blair, a mutual friend. After perusing it carefully, Hume wrote to Reid the following complimentary words: "By Dr. Blair's means I have been favored with the perusal of your performance, which I have read with great pleasure and attention. It is certainly very rare that a piece so deeply philosophical is wrote with so much spirit, and affords so much entertainment to the reader."* In 1763, Reid was called to the Professorship of Moral Philosophy, in the University of Glasgow, to succeed Adam Smith, who had resigned. He accepted the call, removing to Glasgow the following year. In the University he lectured on the intellectual and active powers of man, and on natural jurisprudence and politics. Many of his colleagues were able men and they proved to be a great inspiration to him. During his connection with the University, he published "An Account of the Logic of Aristotle," as an appendix to Lord Kame's "Sketches of the History of Man." In 1781, he retired from the professorship, for the purpose of devoting his attention to the completion of his philosophical works. In 1785, he published the "Essays on the Intellectual Powers of Man,"—a more elaborate treatment of the powers of the mind than is contained in the "Inquiry." In 1788, he published the "Essays on the Active Powers of the Human Mind," advocating one form of Intuitional Ethics. This was the last work of his published during his lifetime.

* Stewart's "Collected Works," vol. x., p. 256.

Reid remained an active student almost till death. Among the most important efforts of the closing years of his life, were several papers written probably for a literary society in Glasgow. These were entitled, "Some Observations on the Modern System of Materialism," and "A Free Discussion of the Doctrines of Materialism and Philosophical Necessity." One thing marred the serenity of these closing years. It was the death of his wife, with whom he had lived fifty-two years. Only one daughter, Mrs. Carmichael, of a large family of children, was still living. She was a great solace to him in his old age. On the 7th of October, 1796, after a brief illness, he died.

As a man, Reid was modest, sober, sincere, and devout. He was modest almost to diffidence. Indeed, Dugald Stewart expresses doubt as to whether Reid's modesty would have permitted him to publish the "Inquiry," had he not been encouraged to do so by his friends. His soberness and earnestness are manifest both in his life and writings. Something of his devout character may be learned from a confession and re-dedication of himself to the service of God, during his wife's illness, in the sixth year of their marriage. It is a most penitent and pathetic confession of dereliction of duty, and a most solemn pledge of a more devoted service to God.*

As a philosophical thinker, Reid, if not profound, was, at least, deeply earnest and original. Cousin thought him to be a man of genius. He says: "Yes, Reid is a man of genius, and of a true and powerful

* Cf. McCosh, "The Scottish Philosophy," pp. 199–200.

originality; so we said in 1819, and so we say in 1857, after having held long converse with mighty systems, discovered their secret, and taken their measure."* McCosh says: "He has not the mathematical consecutiveness of Descartes, the speculative genius of Leibnitz, the sagacity of Locke, the *spirituel* of Berkeley, or the detective skill of Hume; but he has a quality quite as valuable as any of these, even in philosophy; he has in perfection that common sense which he so commends."† Sober earnestness and originality seem to be his merits as a philosophical thinker. His earnestness is manifest in his anxious endeavor to establish the reality of knowledge, and thus to save philosophy from nihilistic scepticism. His originality is manifest in his breaking away from the "theory of ideas" which he had accepted on authority, and establishing philosophy upon a new basis.

* Quoted by McCosh, "The Scottish Philosophy," p. 193.

† Ibid., pp. 192–3.

BIBLIOGRAPHY.

I. On the Life of Reid.

Dugald Stewart, "Account of the Life and Writings of Thomas Reid, D.D.," "Collected Works," ed. by Hamilton, Edinburgh, 1854-60, vol. x, ch. v. Published also in "The Works of Thomas Reid, D.D.," ed. by Hamilton, Edinburgh, 1872, vol. i, pp. 1–35. Cf. Notes A, B, C, D, E, F, of Hamilton, appended to this account.

James McCosh, "The Scottish Philosophy," New York, 1874, Art. xxvi.

II. The Works of Reid.

Complete Works *in English:* "The Works of Thomas Reid, D.D., now fully collected, with Selections from his Unpublished Letters. Preface, Notes, and Supplementary Dissertations, by Sir William Hamilton, Bart.," etc., 7th ed., Edinburgh, 1872, 2 vols. *In French:* "Œuvres Complètes de Thomas Reid, par M. Th. Jouffroy, avec des Fragments de M. Royer Collard," Paris, 1828–9, 6 tomes.

For information concerning various editions of individual works of Reid, cf. N. Porter, "Ueberweg's History of Philosophy," translated by Geo. S. Morris, New York, 1871–3, vol. ii, Appendix I, pp. 396–7.

III. Books of Reference.

In English: J. Priestley, "Examination of Dr. Reid's Inquiry," etc., London, 1774.

Dugald Stewart, "Collected Works," ed. by Hamilton, Edinburgh, 1854-60, vols. i, pp. 108–13; v, pp. 101–13.

Th. Brown, "Inquiry into the Relation of Cause and Effect," 3d ed., Edinburgh, 1818. "Lectures on the Philosophy of the Human Mind," Hallowell, 1829, especially lectures xxvi, xxvii.

Sir Wm. Hamilton, "Lectures on Metaphysics," ed. by Mansel and Veitch, Edinburgh and London, 1870, vol. i, Appendix I (B), vol. ii, lectures xxi–xxiii. Also, "Preface, Notes and Supplementary Dissertations," in his edition of Reid's "Works," referred to above.

J. F. Ferrier, "Reid and the Philosophy of Common Sense," "Blackwood's Magazine," 1847; the same in Lectures, ed. by Grant and Lushington, London, 1866, vol. ii, pp. 407–59.

J. Walker, Notes in his abridged edition of Reid's "Intellectual Powers of Man," Philadelphia, 1850.

A. C. Fraser, "Essays in Philosophy," Edinburgh, 1856, Essays II and III.

J. McCosh, "The Scottish Philosophy," New York, 1874, pp. 192–227, "Realistic Philosophy," New York, 1887, vol. ii, pp. 173–81.

Thomas E. Webb, "The Veil of Isis," Dublin and London, 1885, pp. 123-62.

A. Seth, "Scottish Philosophy," Edinburgh and London, 1885. Article on Reid, "Encyclopædia Britannica," 9th ed., vol. xx.

In French: Royer Collard, "Fragments de Royer Collard," Jouffroy's translation of Reid's Works.

V. Cousin, "Philosophie Ecossaise," Paris, 1846, pp. 185–281.

Thomas Jouffroy, Preface to his "Œuvres Complètes de Thomas Reid," Paris, 1828–9.

A. Garnier, "Critique de la Philosophie de Thomas Reid," Paris, 1840.

J. P. A. Remusat, "Mélanges," Paris, 1842.

L. Peisse, Preface to "Fragments de Philosophie," 1840.

In German: M. Kappes, "Der Common Sense bei Thomas Reid," Munich, 1890.

E. Koenig, "Die Entwickelung des Causalproblems von Cartesius bis Kant," Leipzig, 1888.

IV.

Consult also the following writers on the History of Philosophy: J. D. Morrel, "History of Modern Philosophy," 2d ed., London, 1847, vol. i, pp 281–94.

N. Porter, "Ueberweg's History of Philosophy," translated by Geo. S. Morris, New York, 1871–3, vol. ii, Appendix I, pp. 394-403.

F. D. Maurice, "Moral and Metaphysical Philosophy," London, 1873, vol. ii, pp. 580–6.

G. H. Lewes, "Biographical History of Philosophy," New York, 1883, vol. ii, pp. 618–629.

Falckenberg's "Geschichte der Neueren Philosophie," Leipzig, 1886, pp. 180–82.

J. E. Erdmann, "History of Philosophy," ed. by W. S. Hough, London and New York, 1890, pp. 271–4.

RELATION OF REID'S PHILOSOPHY TO ITS PHILOSOPHICAL ANTECEDENTS.

REID'S philosophy, like every other system of philosophy, cannot be thoroughly understood without taking into consideration its relation to preceding philosophic thought. It was one of two movements in the world of philosophy awakened by the scepticism of Hume—the Philosophy of Common Sense, and the Critical Philosophy of Kant. Reid had been a disciple of Berkeley, virtually accepting the Idealism of that acute thinker. But when he saw what he thought to be the logical outcome of Berkeley's philosophy, as manifested in the scepticism of Hume, he was somewhat alarmed, and began to suspect the validity of "the principles commonly received with regard to the human understanding." * After careful examination, he came to the conclusion that Hume's scepticism was the legitimate outcome of the "theory of ideas," *i. e.*, the theory of perception, upon which it was founded. In his letter, dedicating the "Inquiry" to James, Earl of Findlater and Seafield, he says: "For my own satisfaction, I entered into a serious examination of the principles upon which this sceptical system is built; and was not a little surprised to find that it leans with its whole weight upon a hypothesis which is ancient indeed, and hath been very generally

* "Works," vol. i, I. P., p. 283.

received by philosophers, but of which I could find no solid proof. The hypothesis I mean is, that nothing is perceived but what is in the mind which perceives it. That we do not really perceive things that are external, but only certain images and pictures of them imprinted upon the mind, which are called *impressions and ideas.*" * This theory he ascribed to all preceding philosophy—both ancient and modern. In regard to Descartes, Malebranche, Locke, Berkeley, and Hume, he says: "The system of all these authors is the same, and leads to scepticism." "Descartes no sooner began to dig in this mine, than scepticism was ready to break in upon him. He did what he could to shut it out. Malebranche and Locke, who dug deeper, found the difficulty of keeping out this enemy still to increase: but they labored honestly in the design. Then Berkeley, who carried on the work, despairing of securing all, bethought himself of an expedient:—By giving up the material world, which he thought might be spared without loss, and even with advantage, he hoped, by an impregnable partition, to secure the world of spirits. But, alas! the 'Treatise of Human Nature' wantonly sapped the foundation of this partition, and drowned all in one universal deluge." † It was the sceptical outcome of this "theory of ideas" which awakened Reid from his serene repose in authority, just as later it awakened Kant from his dogmatic slumber, and he resolved to make a new inquiry into "this subject," independent of authority; for, said he: "I thought it unreasonable, upon the authority of philosophers, to admit a hypothesis which, in my opinion, overturns all

* "Works," Inq., p. 96. † Ibid., p. 103.

philosophy, all religion and virtue, and all common sense—and, finding that all systems concerning the human understanding which I was acquainted with, were built upon this hypothesis, I resolved to inquire into this subject anew, without regard to any hypothesis." * Since, then, the special task of Reid was an examination of the "theory of ideas," it may be well for a thorough appreciation of his task, to briefly survey the development of modern philosophy from Descartes to Reid, with special reference to the "theory of ideas."

The scepticism into which modern philosophy had issued, prior to Reid, seems to have been the result of its peculiar subjective tendency. This tendency characterized it from the beginning. Descartes' sceptical method forced him back upon the authority of consciousness. His starting-point in philosophy was universal doubt.† But this very fact of doubt led him to the recognition of a fact that had to be accepted—his own existence. Because, he reasoned, though I doubt everything, doubt, at least, remains. Doubt, however, is a form of thought. Hence the formula:—*cogito, ergo sum.*‡ Now, it is possible to think myself devoid of everything but thought; hence I must conclude that I am a being, the very essence of which is thought.§ Thus we arrive at a knowledge of mind. But what of our knowledge of an external world? He inferred from the existence of clear and distinct ideas of things in the

* "Works," Inq., p. 96.
† "First Meditation."
‡ "Second Meditation."
§ Ibid.

mind, the objective reality of things which occasioned them—that these ideas were images or copies of things existing without the mind.* In short, his theory of perception is representative perception. However, this vicarious or representative character of ideas is only *inferential* with Descartes. He falls back upon the veracity of God, (whose existence and veracity are known to us through our innate idea of God †) for the trustworthiness of our knowledge of the external world.‡ We see, then, in both the sceptical method of Descartes, and also in his theory of representative perception the subjective tendency referred to above.

Turning to Malebranche we find in his teaching, also, this subjective trend manifested. He says, material things are known to us only under the forms of ideas.§ As to the origin of these ideas, we are informed that they are not originated by the mind from itself—because of its inability.‖ Neither are they given to us by things themselves.¶ How, then, do we come into possession of them? Malebranche answers: through the mind's union with God, who possesses within Himself ideas representing all things created by Him. God, by His presence, is united to the finite mind—He being the "place of spirits" just as "space is the place of bodies." This union makes it possible for the mind to see in God that

* "Sixth Meditation."

† "Third and Fourth Meditations.'

‡ "Sixth Meditation."

§ "De la Recherche de la Verité," lvr. iii, pt. ii, ch. 1.

‖ Ibid., ch. 3.

¶ Ibid., ch. 2.

which represents things, viz., ideas.* It is thus that "we see all things in God."

In the philosophy of Locke we find the same element of subjectivity. He wrote his famous "Essay on Human Understanding" with the purpose of explaining the origin, certainty and extent of knowledge. After explaining away all innate ideas,† Locke endeavored to show how we come into possession of ideas. He assumes that the mind in its original condition is like a blank sheet of paper, or a *tabula rasa.*‡ Whence, then, come its ideas? The source of ideas is experience—sensation and reflection.§ Having thus given the source of our ideas, he divides them into two kinds, simple and complex. A simple idea contains in it nothing but a uniform appearance or conception in the mind, and is not distinguishable into different ideas. These constitute the material of all knowledge. Complex ideas are formed by the mind by combining and uniting simple ideas.‖ Locke then proceeds to make another distinction between our ideas, by pointing out the objective character of some, and the subjective character of others. He, of course, assumes the existence of an external world of corporeal bodies. Now, that which in a body occasions an idea in the mind, he calls a quality. There are some qualities in bodies which cause ideas in the mind which are exact likenesses or resemblances of these qualities. The idea in the mind is a copy of the quality in the body. These qualities are called primary

* "De la Recherche de la Verité," lvr. iii. pt. ii, ch. 3.

† "Essay," bk. i, chs. 2, 3, 4.

‡ "Essay," bk. ii, ch. 1.

§ Ibid., bk. ii., ch. 1.

‖ Ibid., ch. 2.

or original qualities of matter, viz., extension, solidity, figure, motion, number, etc. But there are other ideas in the mind which have no resemblance to the qualities in the bodies which cause them. To this class belong most of the ideas of sensation, viz., colors, sounds, tastes, smells, etc. These do not resemble their causes. The qualities which cause such ideas in us are the secondary qualities of bodies.*

Locke then proceeds to the explanation of the idea of substance, and it is important to note his remarks on this point, because of the positions taken by Berkeley and Hume afterward. This idea, according to Locke, is not derived from sensation and reflection, as simple ideas are derived. Its origin is as follows: We frequently recognize a certain combination of simple ideas, and we cannot conceive them as self-subsisting, so we are wont to provide a substratum for them as a ground of subsistence, and as a cause of their existence, which we call substance. However, although substance is an abstract idea, he believed in its objective reality.†

After this consideration of the sources and kinds of ideas the mind has, we are prepared to hear Locke's conception of knowledge. Knowledge is simply "conversant about our ideas." It is, "nothing but the perception of the connection and agreement or disagreement and repugnancy of any of our ideas." Things are not known immediately by the mind, but through the intervention of ideas. How far, then, is knowledge real? Only "so far as there is a conformity between our ideas and the reality of things." But what

* "Essay," bk. ii, ch. 8. † Ibid., bk. ii, ch. 23.

shall be our criterion in determining this conformity? As Locke himself asks: "How shall the mind, when it perceives nothing but its own ideas, know. that they agree with things themselves?" He answers this question by telling us that there are two kinds of ideas of which we may have assurance of their agreement with things. First, we have simple ideas, which are affections of the mind produced by external things, "operating on the mind in a natural way." Hence these ideas cannot be fictions, but, being produced in this way, they "carry with them all the conformity which is intended or which our state requires." The second kind of ideas to which he refers in this connection, is complex ideas. These being formed by the mind itself, and not, with the exception of the ideas of substances, being intended to represent anything external, cannot mislead us.*

We see, then, in what Locke says in regard to knowledge, a recognition of its subjectivity. He admits that the mind does not have an immediate knowledge of things. It only knows them "by the intervention of ideas." He gives no other than a practical reason for the correspondence of ideas and things. In this recognition of the subjective character of our knowledge he certainly anticipated Berkeley, as Reid suggests. He even anticipated Hume, and his taking refuge in a practical reason was doubtless more for the purpose of avoiding scepticism than idealism. Even for the assumption of the existence of an external world of corporeal substances, involved in his theory of perception, he really gives us no warrant of a speculative character. This, too, he ulti-

* "Essay," bk. iv, chs. 1, 4.

mately rests on practical grounds; apparently, also, for the purpose of escaping scepticism.

It was this subjectivity of knowledge as involved in Locke's "theory of ideas," and the idealism and scepticism which were ultimately developed from it, which attracted Reid's attention, and impelled him to examine this theory, hoping to be instrumental in its overthrow, and to establish knowledge on a firm foundation. We must, then, trace this subjective tendency as manifested in the philosophy of Berkeley, and then in the scepticism of Hume, which awakened the reactionary philosophy of Reid.

Berkeley's problem, as Prof. Fraser suggests, was an inquiry into the real meaning of substance and cause as external. In answering the first part of the question, the real meaning of material substance, he endeavored to show that the doctrine of substance as advocated by the philosophers, involved a contradiction. He claimed that the objects of knowledge are ideas, which ideas, of course, exist in the mind. Knowledge is concerned only with ideas. Now, when we ask what is meant by the existence of sensible things, it is evident "that their esse is percipi." All that really is meant by the existence of a thing is that it is seen, touched, etc.,—in short, that it is perceived. To speak of something existing independent of a mind perceiving it is unintelligible and impossible. So-called things are objects perceived by sense, "and what do we perceive besides our own ideas or sensations? and is it not plainly repugnant that any one of these, or any combination of them, should exist unperceived?" The being of things, then, consists in their being perceived. Ideas cannot be images of substantial things, because an idea can only be like an idea, and things to be perceived must be ideas, and, if not, there is no sense in saying an idea is like something of which we can know nothing.*

Berkeley then discusses the subject of primary and secondary qualities, in which discussion he apparently had Locke in mind. He objects to the distinction made by Locke, affirming our knowledge of primary qualities to be just as subjective as our knowledge of secondary qualities; extension, solidity, figure, etc., are ideas in the mind just as colors, odors, etc., are ideas; and, as ideas can only resemble ideas, and, as they exist only in the mind, extension, figure, etc., cannot exist in an unthinking external substance. The very "notion" of matter, then, involves a contradiction.†

But if there be no external material substance—if there be no world of corporeal substances—how are we to account for the existence of our ideas? They must have a cause. This brings us to the consideration of the second part of Berkeley's question, the nature of the originating cause. This cause, he says, cannot be an idea, for all ideas are "visibly inactive." "There is nothing of power or agency in them," and hence an idea cannot be a cause. In the second place, the cause cannot be a material substance, for we have seen there is no such thing. What, then, is the cause? The cause of the ideas must be an "incorporeal active substance or spirit." But it is not my spirit which originates them, because the ideas of sense are not originated by me—

* "Principles," §§ 4, 6, 8, 10. † Ibid., § 15.

they are not produced by my will. The Will or Spirit which does originate them Berkeley infers to be God.*

In our knowledge of spirit we seem to be conversant with something more than ideas. He tells us we have no idea of a spirit and can have none. However, he says, we have a "notion" of spirit. We have also a "notion" of other spirits and of relations. "We comprehend our own existence by inward feeling or Reflection, and that of other spirits by Reason (inference). We may be said to have some knowledge or *notion* of our own minds, of spirits and active beings, whereof in a strict sense we have not ideas. In like manner we know and have a *notion* of relations between things or ideas, which relations are distinct from the ideas or things related, inasmuch as the latter may be perceived by us without our perceiving the former."† The preceding quotation is important as showing Berkeley's deviation from the position taken in the beginning of the "Principles," where he affirmed ideas to constitute the objects of our knowledge (see § 1). Here he recognizes another object of knowledge in "notions." Reid suggests that Berkeley took refuge in the "notion" because of an aversion to scepticism.‡

Thus we see that Berkeley, beginning with Locke's doctrine of ideas as the only objects of knowledge, carried it so far as to reject his arbitrary assumption as to the objective character of certain ideas, existing as qualities of a substratum called substance, which substratum is also an unwarrantable assumption, thus

* "Principles," §§ 25, 26, 29. † Ibid., § 89, cf. also § 27.
‡ "Works," Inq., p. 207.

resolving the world of material things into a world of ideas. In all of this the subjectivity heretofore referred to is still more manifest than in the preceding systems considered. In the philosophy of Hume, which we are now to consider, we shall see the culmination of this subjective tendency in scepticism.

In the "Treatise on Human Nature" Hume argues as follows:—

"All perceptions of the human mind resolve themselves into two distinct kinds, which I shall call impressions and ideas." By impressions, he means, "sensations, passions, and emotions." By ideas, he means, "the faint images of these in thinking and reasoning." Ideas, then, are images of impressions.* Every simple impression has its corresponding idea, and every simple idea has its corresponding impression, and he holds to the general proposition, "*That all our simple ideas, in their first appearance, are deriv'd from simple impressions, which are correspondent to them, and which they exactly represent.*"†

As to the division of impressions and ideas Hume said, that they could be divided into two classes—simple and complex. Simple impressions and ideas admit of no distinction and are inseparable. Complex ideas are distinguishable into parts. Complex ideas include ideas of substances, modes and relations. "The idea of a substance as well as that of a mode, is nothing but a collection of simple ideas that are united by the imagination, and have a particular name assigned them, by

* "Treatise on Human Nature," ed. by Green and Grose, London, 1886, vol. 1, p. 311.

† Ibid., p. 314.

which we are able to recall, either to ourselves or others, that collection."* Since we have no simple idea of substance, derived from an impression of sense, Hume joined with Berkeley in refusing to affirm the objective existence of material substance.

He then takes up the question of knowledge. Here he makes quite an effort to provide for that synthesis which knowledge implies. He finds this synthetic power in imagination, with its principles of association. In knowledge the imagination deals with seven different kinds of relations: "Resemblance, identity, relations of time and place, proportion in quantity or number, degrees in any quality, contrariety, and causation."† These relations may be divided into two classes, the one depending upon the ideas compared: the other relations are "such as may be changed without any change in the ideas." Resemblance, contrariety, degree, proportion belong to the first class. They arise out of the very nature of the ideas, and certainty can only arise with these as objects of knowledge, but the knowledge is purely subjective. It can never transcend perceptions. Hume says that in the other class of relations it seems as though we are carried beyond our perceptions, but in this we are deceived. Neither identity, nor time, nor space carries us beyond perceptions.‡ But how is it with causation? Here we seem to have assurance of conclusions which extend beyond the impressions of sense.§ Hence this relation must be carefully examined, and this examination on the part of Hume constitutes

* "Treatise," pp. 312, 313, 321, 324.
† Ibid., p. 372.
‡ Ibid., pp. 375, sq.
§ Ibid., pp. 376-7.

the principal merit of his philosophy. When we believe in the existence of an object we have simply an idea of the object—and no additional idea, and belief is distinguished from incredulity simply in its superior liveliness and vigor. The vividness of an idea and belief are one and the same. Now, when an impression is vivid it gives its vividness to the ideas associated with it by resemblance, contiguity or causation.* Now, how are we to explain our belief in causation? This idea we gain from experience. Experience presents us with objects in constant conjunction, and thus produces in us "a habit of surveying them in that relation, that we cannot without a sensible violence survey them in any other."† But whence the belief of necessary connection implied in the relation of cause and effect? This may be accounted for by a propensity, born of custom, to pass from the impression or idea of an object to the idea of the object which usually attends it. "When any object is presented to it, it immediately conveys to the mind a lively idea of that object which is usually found to attend it, and this determination forms the necessary connection of these objects."‡ In brief, we mean by causation simply this: that when two objects have been constantly conjoined (in experience), the presence of one determines the mind to form the idea of the other, and this determination is the result of habit or custom. Hence this relation of cause and effect, which at first seemed to carry us beyond impressions, does not really do so, but resolves itself into a propensity, begotten of

* "Treatise," pp. 394-400, *sq.* † Ibid., p. 424.
‡ Ibid., pp. 450-68.

custom, to pass from the impression or idea of an object to the idea of that object which usually attends it. The causal relation between things and ideas involved in the theory of Locke, Hume regarded as a mere assumption which experience did not justify. "The mind," he says, "has never anything present to it but the perceptions, and cannot possibly reach the experience of their connection with objects. The supposition of such a connection is, therefore, without any foundation in reasoning." The ultimate realities, then, with which the mind has to deal are individual, unreferable impressions, and from such impressions we cannot infer the existence of external material objects. Here we see idealism pure and simple.

But he did not rest content with a denial of the reality of an external world; he also denied the reality of the soul. "Since all our perceptions are different from each other, and from everything else in the universe, they are also distinct and separable, and may be considered as separately existent, and may exist separately, and have no need of anything else to support their existence." * Hence there is no necessity of a self as a substratum or subject of our perceptions. Proceeding upon his original thesis, that the perceptions of the mind are resolvable into impressions and ideas—ideas being mere images of impressions—he says: "If any impression gives rise to the idea of self, that impression must continue invariably the same, through the whole course of our lives; since self is supposed to exist after that manner. But there is no impres-

* "Treatise," p. 518.

sion constant and invariable. Pain and pleasure, grief and joy, passions and sensations succeed each other, and never all exist at the same time. It cannot, therefore, be from any of these impressions, or from any other, that the idea of self is derived, and consequently *there is no such idea.*" * Hume thinks we have no more an idea of a thinking substance as the support of perceptions than we have of an external substance as the support of qualities, and Berkeley in rejecting the one ought to have rejected the other.†

To make his scepticism complete, Hume impeaches the veracity of reason: (1) Because it leads to conclusions different from those of the senses; (2) Because it is so frequently found to be fallible. (3) Because each judgment must be tested by other judgments "containing uncertainty," and these in turn by other judgments containing uncertainty, and so on *ad infinitum.* Nihilistic scepticism is the fruit of Hume's endeavors.‡

Thus, in our brief historical survey of modern philosophy down to Hume, we find it culminating in scepticism. The subjectivity which characterizes it from the beginning peculiarly paves the way toward the conclusion. It was against this scepticism that Reid recoiled. Repugnant as it was to him, and, as before stated, believing it to be "inlaid" in all modern philosophy, and traceable to the theory of perception which he believed to be common to these systems,§ he determined to make a new inquiry into the subject, with the pur-

* "Treatise," p. 533.

† Ibid., pp. 517–18.

‡ Ibid., p. 472, *sq.*

§ "Works," Inq., pp. 96, 103, 106.

pose of refuting this theory of perception, and placing philosophy upon a new basis, by substituting a new theory of perception, and a new philosophical organon in the principle of common sense.

In inquiring anew into this subject, Reid adopted a particular method. The "Inquiry" especially bears the marks of its age. Like other systems of philosophy, it is affected by the "Zeit-Geist." It is not often, if ever, that we have a purely closet philosophy—a philosophy produced absolutely independent of the spirit of the age. Consciously or unconsciously speculation is affected by the subtle influences of the intellectual and moral atmosphere in which it is brought forth. This influence of the spirit of the age upon Reid's philosophy may be seen in the method which he adopts—the experimental or inductive method. The results of an application of this method in the study of physical phenomena, by such men as Newton, were wonderful. Reid, who was an earnest student of physics, was greatly impressed by the validity and fruitfulness of this method, and he came to the conclusion that it was the only method which should be employed in the investigation of the phenomena of the mind, and determined to apply it. All through the "Inquiry" the steadfastness of his purpose is manifest. Dugald Stewart truly remarks, that "the influence of the general view opened in the 'Novum Organon' may be traced in almost every page of his writings: and, indeed, the circumstance by which these are so strongly and characteristically distinguished, is that they exhibit the first systematical attempt to exemplify in the study of human nature the same plan of investigation which conducted Newton to the properties of light and to the law of gravitation." *

Having thus stated the aim and method of Reid's philosophy, let us proceed to an exposition of the same. And, first, let us consider the theory of perception, which he urged in opposition to the "theory of ideas."

His theory of perception has both negative and positive aspects. In its negative aspect, it is a denial of (1) the particular form of perception which Reid ascribed to all preceding philosophy. This particular form Reid conceived to be, as Hamilton suggests, that the object before the mind in perception is "always a *tertium quid* numerically different both from the object existing and from the subject knowing."† This is the theory which Reid felt called upon to deny—the calling into question of which he deemed to be the special merit of his own philosophy.‡ (2) In its negative aspect, Reid's theory of perception is a denial that we attain our knowledge of external objects by an act of reasoning.

In denying the theory of ideas his argument runs as follows: §

1. The theory is in direct opposition to the universal sense of men uninstructed in philosophy. When a plain man sees the sun and moon he does not doubt that there are objects far distant from himself, and not merely ideas in his mind. If he asks whether there are no substantial beings called sun and moon, the answer which he will

* "Collected Works," vol. x, p. 259.

† Works, Inq., Note, p. 106.

‡ Ibid., p. 88.

§ Cf. "Works," Inq., pp. 201-11 and especially I. P., pp. 298-309.

get from the philosophers will differ. Locke and his predecessors will answer, that there are such beings, but they never appear to us in person, but only by ideas— which are their representatives in our minds, and all we know of them must be gained from these ideas. Berkeley and Hume would say, that there are no such substantial beings. That is simply a prejudice of the vulgar. Berkeley would say that nothing exists but ideas and minds, and these things are simply ideas in our minds. Hume would say, only ideas exist, and the mind is simply a series of ideas bound together by a few relations. To the plain man this must, of course, be opposed to "the dictates of common understanding."

2. Those who advocate the "theory of ideas" have, as a rule, assumed the existence of the ideas, and have regarded their existence as unquestionable. The few arguments which they have incidentally offered in their behalf have been "too weak to support the conclusion." Locke, for example, says we are conscious of such ideas. But, says Reid, we are not conscious of them. All we are conscious of, are the operations of the mind, such as perceiving, remembering, etc., and not of the objects of such operations. And thus he quotes others, endeavoring to show the assumptive character of their positions, and the weakness of their "incidental arguments."

3. Although there is a unanimous agreement among philosophers on the subject of the existence of ideas, there seems to be a pronounced disagreement among them with respect to everything else concerning the ideas. This ought not to be, if they are a reality, for of all things they ought to be most easily accessible to knowledge. Some hold that they are self-existent; others, that they

exist in the Divine mind. Some hold that they exist in our minds; others, that they exist in the brain or sensorium. Some hold that they are innate, or, at least, a part of them; others, that they are all adventitious. Some, that they are gained through the senses; others, that they are derived from sensation and reflection. As to how they arise, some think the mind originates them; others, that they are occasioned by external causes: still others, that they are produced by God acting upon the mind. And so on, in regard to other features of the ideas there is this wide disagreement. This, as has been suggested, ought not to be, if ideas really exist, for they ought to be very accessible to knowledge.

4. Ideas do not improve our knowledge of the various operations of the mind. They were, doubtless, brought forward for this purpose. "This power of perceiving ideas is just as inexplicable as any of the powers explained by it."

5. The consequences of this theory are such as to prejudice every man against it who has a due regard for the common sense of mankind. Aside from the peculiarities and absurdities which flow from the theory as seen in ancient philosophy, we see in modern philosophy consequences which are enough to prejudice mankind against it. It has led to the attempts of trying to prove the existence of material things. And who does not see that philosophy must make a very ridiculous figure in the eyes of sensible men while it is employed in mustering up metaphysical arguments to prove that there is a sun and a moon, an earth and a sea? It has led to such paradoxes as, "that the secondary qualities of body are not qualities of body at all, but sensations of the

mind: That the primary qualities of body are resemblances of our sensations: That we have no notion of duration, but from the succession of ideas in our minds: That personal identity consists in consciousness; so that the same individual thinking being may make two or three different persons, and several different thinking beings make one person: That judgment is nothing but a perception of the agreement or disagreement of our ideas." But these consequences are tolerable when brought into comparison with those which we find in Berkeley and Hume. Here we have the negation of the world of matter and the world of mind, and nothing is left us but ideas. A general scepticism is the result. These are the "noble fruits" which this "theory of ideas" has brought forth. Such consequences, so startling to common sense, must cause a reaction against the theory.

In the second place, Reid denies that we attain to a knowledge of external objects by an act of reasoning. He depends mainly upon the strength of his own theory of perception for an overthrowal of this doctrine.

Having thus considered the negative aspects of Reid's theory of perception let us proceed to a consideration of its positive aspects.

The following are the main features of his theory:

I. Sensation.

1. A sensation is a simple, inexplicable affection of the mind. "It appears to be a simple and original affection or feeling of the mind, altogether inexplicable and unaccountable." *

2. Sensations exist only in the mind. They do not

* "Works," Inq., p. 105.

exist in material things—not even in our own bodies. "The sensations of touch, of seeing, and hearing, are all in the mind, and can have no existence but when they are perceived." *

3. Sensations are antecedent to perceptions. The "sensation is followed by the perception of the object."†

II. Perception.

1. *Perception defined.* Sensation naturally suggests a "notion" or "conception" of, together with a belief in the existence of, an object. This is perception. "But I think it appears, from what hath been said, that there are natural suggestions: particularly that sensation suggests the notion of present existence and the belief that what we perceive or feel does now exist, . . . and that our sensations and thoughts do also suggest the notion of a mind, and the belief of its existence, and of its relation to our thoughts. . . . And in like manner . . . certain sensations of touch, by the constitution of our nature, suggest to us extension, solidity and motion."‡ In the "Intellectual Powers," we find Reid essentially agreeing with his definition of perception given in the "Inquiry." He says: "If, therefore, we attend to that act of our mind which we call the perception of an external object of sense, we shall find in it these three things:—*First,* Some conception or notion of the object perceived; *Secondly,* a strong and irresistible conviction and a belief of its present existence; and

* "Works," Inq., pp. 159, 105, 187; I. P., pp. 229, 310.

† Ibid., pp. 186, 187; I. P., p. 320.

‡ Ibid., Inq., p. 111.

Thirdly, that this conviction and belief are immediate, and not the effect of reasoning." In other words: Sensations are attended by certain original "suggestions" and beliefs, and this constitutes perception.

2. *Perception illustrated.* This theory of perception will be more intelligible to us if we examine Reid's doctrine of "suggestion" as we find it illustrated in his treatment of the so-called secondary and primary qualities of body. Reid agreed with Locke in regard to the essential distinction between the secondary and primary qualities, which Berkeley and Hume had endeavored to remove.* The two points of distinction to which he directs attention, are: (1) The ease with which we distinguish between the sensation and its external correlate in the case of secondary qualities as compared with primary qualities. (2) The sensations in the case of secondary qualities only suggest a power or quality of the object as a cause; whereas, in the case of the primary qualities, the sensation also suggests the nature of the cause. Now, in the treatment of the secondary and primary qualities, as above stated, we may see Reid's theory of perception, as sensation attended by original suggestions and beliefs, fully illustrated.

(*a.*) In the case of secondary qualities, take, for example, the secondary quality—smell. On this point Reid makes the following remarks: "The smell of a rose signifies two things: *First*, a sensation, which can have no existence but when it is perceived, and can only be in a sentient being or mind. *Secondly*, it signifies some power, quality, or virtue, in the rose, or in efflu-

* "Works," Inq., p. 123; I. P., p. 314.

via proceeding from it, which hath a permanent existence, independent of the mind, and which, by the constitution of nature, produces the sensation in us. By the original constitution of our nature we are both led to believe that there is a permanent cause of the sensation, and prompted to seek after it: and experience determines us to place it in the rose." * That is, sensations of smell and, as he elsewhere suggests, those of taste, sound, etc., suggest to us qualities in objects as the causes of these sensations. Thus sensations attended by suggestions are perception so far as the secondary qualities are concerned. As Hamilton interprets Reid on this point: "In a sensation (proper) of the secondary qualities, as affections in us, we have a perception (proper) of them as properties in objects and causes of the affections in us." †

(*b.*) In the case of primary qualities his theory of perception as sensations attended by original "suggestions" and beliefs is still more marked. Take, for example, the sense of touch. Here we are liable to confound the sensation and the quality of body from which it arises. The sensation is only a "sign" of a quality in the external body: but we are wont to pass quickly from the "sign" to the thing signified without making a distinction. There is, nevertheless, a distinction. The sensation has no similitude to the quality known as hardness in the external object. How, then, do we come to have the "conception" and "belief" (perception) of the objective reality of what we call hardness in body? For certainly we have such a perception. This "conception

* "Works," Inq., p. 114.

† Ibid., Note D, p. 884.

and belief," Reid answers, comes to us in the following manner: "By an original principle of our constitution a certain sensation of touch both suggests to the mind the conception of hardness, and creates the belief of it: or, in other words, that this sensation is a natural sign of hardness."* Now what is true of hardness is also true of softness, roughness, smoothness, figure and motion. "All these," says Reid, "by means of corresponding sensations of touch, are presented to the mind as real external qualities; the conception and belief of them are invariably connected with the corresponding sensations, by an original principle of human nature."† The same thing is true in regard to extension and figure. Our perception of extension and figure is a natural suggestion attending sensations of touch. "Extension, therefore, seems to be a quality suggested to us, by the very same sensations which suggest the other qualities above mentioned (*i. e.*, other primary qualities). When I grasp a ball in my hand, I perceive it at once hard, figured and extended. The feeling is very simple, and hath not the resemblance to any quality of body. Yet it suggests to us three primary qualities perfectly distinct from one another, as well as from the sensation which indicates them. When I move my hand along the table, the feeling is so simple that I find it difficult to distinguish it into things of different natures: yet, it immediately suggests hardness, smoothness, extension and motion—things of very different natures, and all of them as distinctly understood as the feeling which sug-

* "Works," Inq., p. 121. † Ibid., Inq., p. 123.

gests them." * It is apparent from the above quotations concerning both the secondary and primary qualities that what Reid means by perception is sensations attended by original "suggestions" in the form of "notions" or "conceptions" and beliefs. When he uses the terms "sign" and "signify," he means simply that the sensation is a "sign" of a quality in the external thing; and what he means by this, is that the sensation suggests a "notion" or "conception" of, and belief in the existence of, that quality. The "notion" and "conception" are "suggestions" attending sensations, immediately inspired by the constitution of our nature. The "belief" in the existence of the quality or object attending sensations is also immediately inspired by our constitution. Perception, then, according to Reid, is, as was suggested in the beginning, sensations attended by certain original suggestions and beliefs. Or, to put the definition more nearly in his own language: perception is the "notion" or "conception" of an object, together with a belief in its existence; which "notion" and belief are originally "suggested" or "inspired" by the constitution of our nature, on the occasion of a sensation arising in the mind.

The foregoing is the substance of Reid's theory of perception as we find it developed in both the "Inquiry" and the "Intellectual Powers." Two questions very naturally suggest themselves here: 1. Was Reid right in attributing the "theory of ideas" to preceding philosophy? In regard to this question there is a difference of opinion. Such critics of Reid as Priestley, †

* "Works," Inq., pp. 124-5.

† "Remarks on Reid, Beattie, and Oswald," 2d ed., § 3, p. 30.

Brown,* and Webb † think that Reid seriously erred in his interpretation of the large majority of previous systems of philosophy. On the other hand, Hamilton ‡ comes to Reid's defense, and, while admitting him to be mistaken in several instances, regards him, especially in respect to modern philosophy, to have good grounds for ascribing this theory to his predecessors. To discuss this question would require a survey of the entire history of philosophy, which, of course, cannot be done here. If, however, the reader desires to determine the correctness of Reid's interpretation, I will be pardoned in once more calling attention to the fact that Reid's conception of the "theory of ideas" was not what is ordinarily understood by representative perception. The theory which he ascribes to his predecessors is, that in perception there is an image or "idea" existing between the mind perceiving and the existing object—*numerically different from both.* 2. From all that is said upon the subject, what are we to understand Reid's theory of perception really to be? Is it the theory of immediate or intuitive perception—a direct gaze upon extra-mental, substantial objects; or, is it some form of representative perception, only one form of which, viz., the *tertium quid* form, it is claimed by some, he really combated? Concerning this question, it must be admitted that it is an exceedingly difficult task to determine precisely what Reid's theory of perception is. This difficulty is the result not only of the looseness of his presentation of the subject,

* "Philosophy of the Human Mind," lecs. xxvi, xxvii.

† "The Veil of Isis," pp. 125–162.

‡ "Metaphysics," lecs. xxi, xxii.

but also of his failure to fully think the subject through. By some, and doubtless by the majority of scholars who have given Reid's philosophy thoughtful consideration, he is supposed to advocate the theory of immediate perception. So emphatically do they affirm this to be his theory, that they regard it, in connection with his doctrine of common sense, to determine his historical position or significance. By others, and for very good reasons, he is supposed to teach some form of representative perception. This form, to use the terminology of Hamilton, may be called egoistical representationism, *i. e.*, the object before the mind in perception is a subjective representative object, which subjective object is a modification of the mind. And, as there are two forms of egoistical representationism, the form which is ascribed to Reid is: *that the subjective object is really identical with the perceptive act, but logically distinguished from it,* "being simply the perceptive act itself, considered in one of its relations, to wit, to the immediate object, the reality represented, and which, in and through that representation alone, is objectified to consciousness and perceived."* As has been suggested, those who ascribe some form of representative perception to Reid, have good grounds for doing so. His use of "notion," "conception," "suggestion," etc., certainly is favorable to an interpretation of his teachings in favor of some form of mediate, rather than immediate, perception. On the other hand, there are good reasons for believing that he meant to teach the doctrine of immediate or intuitive perception. Sir Wm. Hamilton has, with characteristic thoroughness, careful-

* "Works," Note C, p. 818.

ly selected and arranged the evidence to be found in both the "Inquiry" and the "Intellectual Powers" bearing on each view of Reid's theory of perception. An examination of this evidence will put us in a better position to come to some conclusion on this disputed point.* Following the order of Hamilton, the following is the substance of the leading arguments in favor of egoistical representationism in the form stated above.†

1. Reid's doctrine of primary qualities implies it. He teaches that the primary qualities of body are suggested through certain sensations. They are suggestions, or conceptions, immediately arising in the mind, we know not how—by a natural magic as it were—on occasion of certain sensations. If the primary qualities are nothing more than suggestions, or conceptions "inspired by a means unknown," then they are only representations of it knows not what, blindly determined by the mind. Perception is simply the consciousness of these conceptions or suggestions, hence our knowledge of the external world would certainly not be immediate. The immediate object before the mind would be a conception or suggestion and not an extra-mental object. Hence Reid must be considered an advocate of representative perception. (Inq., pp. 122, 123, 128, 183, 188; I. P., pp. 258, 318, 320.) This argument, somewhat overdrawn by Hamilton, seems to me to be one of the strongest arguments in favor of Reid's theory being that of egoistical representationism: because in his teaching, concerning the primary qualities, the mind has naught but sensations accompanied by "suggestions"

* "Works," Note C, pp. 819-24. † Ibid., Note C, p. 820-2.

or "conceptions" to deal with. Hamilton, who believes Reid to hold the theory of immediate perception, makes a plea for his view in regard to this point by saying, we must not hold Reid too rigidly to what he says in the "Inquiry" on the subject of "suggestion," as he does not mention it in the "Intellectual Powers," which would seem that he was doubtful of its tendency. But this plea, to my mind, has little force, because, in the first place, Reid did not retract the doctrine of "suggestion" in the "Intellectual Powers;" and, in the second place, although he does not use the word "suggestion" in the "Intellectual Powers," his theory of perception in both the "Inquiry" and "Intellectual Powers" is essentially the same.

2. Intuitive perception implies that a knowledge and belief of the existence of an external world is given in perception, and there is no need of resorting to "natural magic," "inspiration," etc., to explain that knowledge and belief, as Reid really does. In the case of cosmothetic idealism, whose theory of perception is representative perception, in which "the mind is determined to represent to itself the external world, which, *ex hypothesi*, it does not know, the fact of such representation can only be conceived possible through some hyperphysical agency." Now, the rationale of Reid's theory of perception—"natural magic," "inspiration," "infused faith," etc.,—rather makes a representationist than a presentationist out of him. (Inq., 122, 188; I. P., 257.)

There is certainly some force in the above argument, and in the "Intellectual Powers," Reid, in a measure, approaches the Cartesian doctrine of a *Deus ex machina* in his remarks on perception. (See I. P., p. 257.) Even Hamilton admits this. (See note, p. 257, of Reid's "Works," also Note C, p. 821.)

3. Reid equalizes perception and imagination. He speaks of imagination as a faculty of immediate knowledge. Now all will admit that in an act of the imagination the external object is known only mediately, in a representative way. Hence Reid must have meant by ascribing to the faculty of imagination immediate knowledge, that its knowledge is not representative in the *tertium quid* sense, as advocated by the "theory of ideas," but that it is really mediate in the sense in which we ordinarily speak of the images of the imagination being representative. If this be so, in the case of the imagination, then when Reid equalizes perception and imagination by attributing to both of them immediate knowledge, he must use the word immediate in the case of perception, just as he uses it in the case of imagination, viz., immediate in opposition to mediate as advocated by the *tertium quid* theory, but nevertheless mediate in the true sense. Or, as Hamilton states the argument: "In calling imagination of the past, the distant, etc., an immediate knowledge, Reid, it may be said, could only mean by immediate, a knowledge effected not through the supposed intermediation of a vicarious object, numerically different from the object existing and the mind knowing, but through a representation of the past, or real, object in and by the mind itself; in other words, that by mediate knowledge he denoted a non-egoistical, by immediate knowledge an egoistical, representation. This being established, it may be further argued—that in calling perception an immediate knowledge, he, on the

same analogy, must be supposed to deny, in reference to this faculty, only the doctrine of non-egoistical representation. This is confirmed by his not taking the distinction between perception as a presentative, and memory, for instance (*i. e.*, recollective imagination), as a representative cognition : which he ought to have done, had he contemplated, in the former, more than a faculty, through which the ego represents to itself the non-ego, of which it has no consciousness—no true objective and immediate apprehension." * (Inq., p. 106; I. P., pp. 226, 233, 292, 293, etc.)

Hamilton tries to lessen the force of this argument by saying that it merely "proves that Reid's perception *may be* representative, not that it actually is so."† However, when taken in connection with the preceding arguments, it at least shows that the logical implication of Reid's presentation of his theory of perception is representationism.

4. Reid, in some instances, seems to make perception the result of inference, so that the remote cause is the object perceived, and, hence, not the immediate object of perception. Hence perception cannot be immediate. (Inq., p. 125; I. P., 259, 260, 309, 326, 328.)

This argument has weight. Reid seems to teach that perception is the result of inference, thus making it mediate instead of immediate. However, it must be taken into consideration, that there are other passages in which he expressly denies that perception is the result of inference. (I. P., 259, 260, 309, 326, 328.)

There are several minor arguments favoring this inter-

* "Works," Note C, pp. 821–822.

† Ibid., p. 822.

pretation of Reid, but they are hardly of sufficient importance to be noticed here.* On the other hand, let us state the evidence favoring the interpretation of Reid's theory of perception as immediate perception.†

1. "Knowledge and existence only infer each other when a reality is known itself or as existing." That is, knowledge and existence are only convertible when there is a knowledge of reality in itself. It is only under such conditions that we can say that the reality "is known because it exists, and exists since it is known." This is what constitutes an immediate perception. Now Reid's teaching is in harmony with the above position. He says: "It seems admitted as a first principle, by the learned and unlearned, that what is really perceived must exist, and that to perceive what does not really exist is impossible." (I. P., p. 274.)

2. All philosophers agree that the idea or representative object is immediately apprehended, and that as thus apprehended it exists necessarily. Now if Reid affirms that external objects are perceived not less immediately he must be regarded as holding the theory of immediate perception. This he affirms. (I. P., 263, 272, 274, 289, 446.)

3. All admit that mankind at large believe that the external reality is the immediate object of perception. Mankind, in general, take the "common-sense" view of the world—*i. e.*, they believe in the existence of a world of substantial "things," which "things" are immediately perceived. Only philosophers affirm the contrary.

* Reid's "Works," Note C, pp. 821-2.

† Ibid., pp. 822-3.

Now Reid affirms himself to be on the side of mankind in general—or, as he suggests, on the side of the vulgar, in this respect. (I. P., 275, 284, 298, 299, 302.)

This argument certainly has great force. Reid refers frequently to the view of the "vulgar," which is the belief that in perception we gaze immediately upon an external world of "things," and then places himself on the side of the "vulgar." (See above references.)

4. Reid affirms, that in self-consciousness we have an immediate knowledge of the modifications of self: and adds, that in perception we have knowledge just as immediate of the qualities of the "not-self." (I. P., 263, 269, 373.)

Thus runs the evidence in favor of both interpretations. It is apparent at once that there are good grounds for holding either view. Sir Wm. Hamilton and most interpreters, for the reasons above mentioned, think that Reid really held the theory of immediate perception. Brown, Webb, and Ferrier think his theory was a theory of representative perception—egoistical representationism. When the doctors disagree, who shall decide? It is quite evident, from a consideration of the above evidence, that it is not well to dogmatically affirm either view. My own opinion is, that Reid *meant* to teach natural realism, with its theory of immediate perception; but his presentation of the subject is so loose, owing to a looseness of language and a failure to fully think the subject through, as to afford good grounds for supposing him to teach cosmothetic idealism, with its theory of egoistical representationism. This is the only way that Reid can be saved from self-contradiction.

Let us now proceed to the second feature of Reid's philosophy—his doctrine of common sense. Not only did Reid oppose to scepticism his theory of immediate perception, to subvert the "theory of ideas," on which he supposed this scepticism to be based; but he also established his organon of common sense as authority for the acceptance of certain fundamental principles which this scepticism denied. Reid used this term in a rather ambiguous way, and often in such a way as to mislead the reader as to his real meaning. Especially careless is he in the use of the term in the "Inquiry,"* where he lays himself open to an interpretation which is really opposed to his real meaning—particularly as indicated in the "Intellectual Powers."† Reid is sometimes supposed to mean by common sense, the undeveloped belief of the masses, which he would oppose to the reasonings of philosophers. Again, he is supposed to mean by the term "good sense,"—sound understanding. Even Kant was misled in thus interpreting Reid.‡ Sometimes he is thought to mean the voice of the majority, or universal assent. But, while his carelessness lays some of his remarks open to such interpretations, a critical study of his works reveals the fact, that what he really means by the *principles of common sense* is, the *self-evident principles of reason;* and what he means by *common sense* is the *faculty of such principles;* or, reason judging self-evident truth. This is quite evident from the following statements, taken both from the "Inquiry" and the "Intellectual Powers":—

* p. 101. † p. 425.

‡ "Prolegomena," pp. 4–6.

"If there be certain principles, as I think there are, which the constitution of our nature leads us to believe, and which we are under a necessity to take for granted in the common concerns of life, without being able to give a reason for them; these are what we call the *principles of common sense;* and what is manifestly contrary to them is what we call absurd." * "It is absurd to conceive that there can be any opposition between reason and common sense. It is indeed the firstborn of reason: and, as they are commonly joined together in speech and in writing, they are inseparable in their nature We ascribe to reason two offices, or two degrees. The first is to judge of things self-evident; the second to draw conclusions that are not self-evident from those that are. The first of these is the province, and the sole province, of common sense: and, therefore, it coincides with reason in its whole extent, and is only another name for one branch or one degree of reason." † The self-evident principles of reason, then, are what Reid means by common-sense principles; and by common sense he means reason declaring self-evident truth. It will appear, also, from the above citations, that the criteria of common-sense principles, with Reid, are, necessity and self-evidence.

Reid, however, was very unfortunate in his classification of these principles. He places on the list of common-sense principles, truths which are nothing more than mere generalizations of experience. His loose classification has had considerable to do in bringing condemnation upon his philosophy. ‡

* "Works," Inq,, p. 108.

† "Ibid., I. P., p. 425.

‡ Ibid., I. P., pp. 434-468.

The historical significance of Reid's philosophy, then, lies in calling into question the "theory of ideas" on which the scepticism of Hume is founded, and in opposing to it the theory of immediate perception, and the organon of common sense.

* "Works," I. P., pp. 441–461.

THE INFLUENCE OF REID'S PHILOSOPHY UPON SUBSEQUENT PHILOSOPHIC THOUGHT.

CONTEMPORANEOUS with Reid, and influenced by him, were James Oswald * and James Beattie,† also exponents of the doctrine of common sense. Both adhered more slavishly to the doctrine than Reid. Oswald, in his "Appeal," virtually uses the same argument which is used by Reid, so far as the validity of so-called fundamental truths is concerned. Common sense discerns and vouches for all fundamental truths. It is reason declaring self-evident truth. Now just as common sense declares self-evident truth in other departments of thought, so it declares primary truths in the domain of morals and religion. In endeavoring to strengthen the argument from common sense he makes use of the *reductio ad absurdum*. Beattie's "Essay" was called forth specially by the scepticism of Hume. In it, with Reid, he opposes the affirmations of common sense to scepticism. He holds to the validity of so-called primary truths. Our ground for accepting them is their

* "An Appeal to Common Sense in behalf of Religion," London, 1766–72.

† "Essay on the Nature and Immutability of Truth in Opposition to Sophistry and Scepticism," 4th ed., London, 1773.

own self-evidence. So that his doctrine is essentially the same as Reid's.

The real successor of Reid was Dugald Stewart.* He, too, is in substantial harmony with the views of Reid.

1. He agrees with him in regard to the method which ought to be adopted in studying the phenomena of the human mind—the inductive method.†

2. In his theory of perception he is in substantial agreement with Reid. He regards perception as the "notion" of an object, which notion and belief are instinctively suggested or inspired on the occasion of sensation.‡ Like Reid, he doubtless *meant* to teach immediate perception, but, unfortunately, did not succeed much better than Reid in clearing his doctrine of those inconsistencies and ambiguities which render the theory capable of a two-fold interpretation. That is, although he doubtless meant to teach the theory of immediate perception common to natural realism, his presentation of the subject involves egoistical representationism.

3. With respect to his doctrine of common sense, we find him also in substantial agreement with Reid. However, Stewart did not like the term—"the principles of common sense," thinking it open to serious objections, because of its associations and ambiguity. For this term he substituted the expression: "the fundamental laws of human belief." These laws he considered "the constituent elements of reason." This doctrine he emphasized just as much as Reid did, and he saw in it

* "Collected Works," ed. by Hamilton, Edinburgh, 1854-60.

† Ibid., vol. ii, Int., §§ 1 and 2.

‡ Ibid., vol. ii, ch. 1.

the only true organon for philosophy, and the antidote for scepticism.*

Dr. Thomas Brown,† was also, to a certain extent, a disciple of Reid. Influenced, however, by the teachings of Hartley, and the sensationalism of the French Ideologists, he, in a measure, deviated from some of the positions of the Scottish School. This is especially manifest in his analysis and classification of the phenomena of the mind. Reid and Stewart being emphatically opposed to sensationalism, did not carry their psychological analysis as far as they doubtless would have done, had not sensationalism been such a bugbear to them. Brown, however, was not to be so easily frightened, and he carried his analysis to a greater simplification. He tried to unite some of the positions of the Sensational School with certain positions of the Scottish School.

1. His method was that of the Scottish School, viz., the inductive method. He insisted upon applying the method adopted by physical science.‡

2. The result of an application of this method was a reduction of the number of original faculties to which Reid and Stewart held, and the resolving of all mental phenomena into modifications of the mind itself.§

3. His theory of perception differs from the theory of Reid and Stewart. It is egoistical representationism, *i. e.*,

* "Collected Works," vol. iii, ch. 1.

† "Lectures on the Philosophy of the Human Mind," Hallowell, 1829.

‡ Ibid., lecs. ix, x, xi.

§ Ibid., lecs. xvi, xvii.

the object before the mind in perception is not an extra-mental, material object, but a mental object, which object is merely a modification of the mind itself." *

4. On what authority, then, do we believe in an external world? Brown answers: through the intuitive principle of causation, we are led to infer the existence of an external world. On occasion of certain sensations arising in the mind, we infer an extra-mental reality as their cause, which external cause he affirmed to be an extended, material object. †

Brown, then, retreats from natural realism with its doctrine of immediate perception, and goes over to cosmothetic idealism, with its doctrine of mediate perception—affirming, however, the existence of an external, material world on the strength of the causal principle.

In Sir William Hamilton‡ we have the ablest exponent and special defender of the Scottish realism. To fully appreciate his philosophy, as Dr. McCosh suggests, we must bear in mind the influence of four men upon his thinking: Aristotle, Reid, Kant, and Jacobi. Our interest here extends only to the influence exerted upon his philosophical thinking by Reid. This is manifest in his theory of perception and his doctrine of common sense.

1. His theory of perception is intuitive or immediate

* "Lectures on the Philosophy of the Human Mind," Hallowell, 1820, lecs. xxv-xxvii.

† Ibid.

‡ "Lectures on Metaphysics," Edinburgh and London, 1870; Cf. also Reid's "Works," Notes and Dissertations.

perception.* The mind gazes immediately upon extra-mental reality. He differs from Reid, however, in excluding from the objects immediately known, objects which are not in correlation to the bodily organism. According to Hamilton, the objects which the mind immediately perceives in sense-perception are the organism, and the extra-bodily objects in correlation to the organism, *i. e.*, extra-bodily objects in their resistance to our locomotive or muscular energy.† The grounds on which he bases the theory of immediate perception are, positively, the testimony of consciousness,‡ and, negatively, the sceptical consequences which he regards to be the inevitable result of a denial of this theory.§

2. Reid's influence upon Hamilton is very marked indeed in his doctrine of common sense. Hamilton made an elaborate attempt not only to establish the legitimacy of the argument from common sense, and to point out the criteria of common-sense principles, but also to vindicate the use of the term "common sense." The propriety of using the term "common sense" he tries to establish by an appeal to the history of philosophy. He traces the use of the word "from the dawn of speculation to the present day," finding it in use by nearly every philosopher. This historical survey evinces a patience and erudition which are simply remarkable.

* "Metaphysics," vol ii, lecs. xxiv-xxviii, also Reid's "Works," Note D.

† Ibid. See in Note D other differences of a minor character, pp. 882-6.

‡ Ibid.

§ Reid's "Works," Note A.

In the works of one hundred and six writers, he finds witnesses to the legitimacy of the term "common sense." Among these writers are numbered the greatest names in philosophy. As to the meaning and authority of common sense he says:

Demonstration, if proof be possible at all, must ultimately rest upon certain fundamental propositions which must be accepted. These propositions are more on the order of facts, feelings, beliefs, than cognitions, because of their inexplicable character. Nevertheless, Hamilton calls them cognitions. Now, if they must be accepted, the question arises as to the authority for accepting them. The answer to this is: they must be accepted because they are the conditions *sine quâ non* of knowledge, and to impeach them is to impeach the data of consciousness. To show that a denial of a certain proposition would impeach the integrity of an original datum of consciousness, is to argue from common sense. "Limiting, therefore, our consideration to the question of authority: how, it is asked, do these primary propositions—these cognitions at first hand—these fundamental facts, feelings, beliefs, certify us of their own veracity? To this the only possible answer is—that as elements of our mental constitution—as the essential conditions of our knowledge—they *must* by us be accepted as true. To suppose their falsehood, is to suppose that we are created capable of intelligence, in order to be made the victims of delusion: that God is a deceiver, and the root of our nature a lie. But such a supposition, if gratuitous, is manifestly illegitimate. For, on the contrary, the data of our original consciousness must, it is evident, *in the first instant?* be presumed true. It is only if proved false, that their authority can, *in consequence of that proof*, be, in the second instance, disallowed. Speaking, therefore, generally, to argue from common sense is simply to show, that the denial of a given proposition would involve the denial of some original datum of consciousness: but as every original datum of consciousness is to be presumed true, that the proposition in question, as dependent on such a principle, must be admitted."*

But still it may be urged: Why trust the deliverances of consciousness? To this question Hamilton replies: "If, therefore, it can be shown on the one hand, that the deliverances of consciousness must philosophically be accepted, until their certain or probable falsehood has been positively evinced: and if, on the other hand, it cannot be shown that any attempt to discredit the veracity of consciousness has ever yet succeeded: it follows that, as philosophy now stands, the testimony of consciousness must be viewed as high above suspicion, and its declarations entitled to demand prompt and unconditional assent."†

In regard to the first point it must be acknowledged that, at least, in the first instance, the veracity of consciousness must be accepted. We may not gratuitously assume that Nature works "in counteraction of herself." Unless there are reasons to the contrary, it is not to be supposed that our faculty of knowledge is "an instrument of illusion."

But, secondly, even though in the outset the veracity of the deliverances of consciousness must be admitted,

* "Works," Note A, p. 743. † Ibid., p. 745.

"it still remains competent to lead a proof that they are undeserving of credit." The question, however, arises as to how this is to be accomplished. This can only be done (1) by showing, inasmuch as there are quite a number of these primary data, that they immediately contradict each other, or (2) that they are indirectly contradictory, inasmuch as conclusions derived from them, and for which they are responsible, are mutually contradictory. This would prove the inconsistency of consciousness with itself, and, of course, as a consequence, its inconsistency with the unity of truth. But such contradiction or inconsistency, says Hamilton, has never yet been established. "No attempt to show that the data of consciousness are (either in themselves, or in their necessary consequences) mutually contradictory, has yet succeeded: and the presumption in favor of the truth of consciousness and the possibility of philosophy has therefore, never been redargued. In other words, an original, universal, dogmatic subversion of knowledge has hitherto been found impossible." * We must, then, accept the primary deliverances of consciousness as true, and the argument from common sense which shows that a denial of a certain proposition discredits an original datum of consciousness must be regarded as legitimate.

The essential marks which distinguish these original or fundamental cognitions or convictions from those which are derived, are four, viz., incomprehensibility, simplicity, necessity and absolute universality, and comparative evidence and certainty. A conviction is incomprehensible when it is merely given in consciousness

* "Works," Note A, p. 746.

that its object is, and not why or how it is. A cognition or belief is simple when it is not compounded of other cognitions or beliefs. A cognition or belief is necessary or universal (these are coincident) when it is impossible to think it false. By comparative evidence and certainty is meant, quoting from Aristotle, "If we know and believe through certain original principles, we must know and believe these with *paramount* certainty, for the very reason that we know and believe all else through them." These four marks, then, incomprehensibility, simplicity, necessity and absolute universality, and comparative evidence and certainty, constitute the essential characters by which original cognition or beliefs are known.* Common-sense principles, then, are incomprehensible, simple, necessary, and absolutely universal principles, which if an attempt be made to prove or disprove them would involve a resort to principles "neither more evident nor more certain."

Hamilton made no such attempt as that of Reid's to classify, or to make a list of, these principles. However, he emphatically pronounces the immediate perceptions of self and of an extra-mental world of extended objects to be common-sense principles, for they are primary data of consciousness.

Our interest here in Hamilton's philosophy, as before suggested, does not extend beyond his theory of perception and his doctrine of common sense. These are the features which ally him to Reid and the Scottish School. These we have found to be immediate or intuitive perception and the veracity of consciousness in

* "Works," Note A, p. 754; "Metaphysics," lec. xxxviii.

its original deliverances in the form of "cognitions" or "beliefs."

In France, the philosophy of Reid exerted considerable influence. It was first used by M. Royer-Collard * as a weapon against sensationalism and materialism. The philosophy of Condillac and the French Ideologists was strongly established there. Collard saw that the sensationalism of Condillac rested upon the same foundation as that which underlay the scepticism of Hume; and, with Reid, he felt that if the premises be accepted the conclusion legitimately followed. The premises of scepticism and sensationalism are the same, the "theory of ideas." The same means which Reid used for the overthrowal of these premises were used by Collard—the theory of immediate perception and the principle of common sense—meaning by common sense a sort of mental instinct.

Another French philosopher on whose thinking Reid's philosophy exerted considerable influence was M. Victor Cousin,† the real father of eclecticism in France. He borrows largely from the Scottish and German schools of philosophy, but acknowledges the principal factor of this eclecticism to be taken from the Scottish philosophy. In the adoption of the inductive method, in basing philosophy upon psychology, in the use of the doctrine of common sense in a modified form, we see the influence of Reid's philosophy upon the thinking of Cousin.

* "Fragmens de Royer-Collard," Jouffroy's trans. of the works of Reid.

† "Philosophie Ecossaise," Paris, 1846.

Th. Jouffroy,* the pupil of Cousin, was also greatly influenced by Reid's philosophy. He translated the works of Reid into French, and it was through his teaching, together with the teaching of Collard and Cousin, that the Scottish philosophy became for a while the prevailing philosophy in France. He, too, is an eclectic, but some of the positions of the Scottish School are prominent factors in his eclecticism. The application of the inductive method to the study of the phenomena of consciousness, and the common-sense attitude toward the problem of substance, indicate the influence of Reid and Stewart upon his thinking. †

In Germany, Reid's influence upon philosophy amounts to very little indeed. Kant regarded his philosophy with more or less contempt. There are some evidences of its influence in the philosophy of Benecke.‡

In America, directly and indirectly (through his disciples) Reid's philosophy has exerted great influence. Dr. Porter says: "The Scottish philosophy has had a wide-spread influence in this country. The works of Reid were not so generally circulated on account of the pre-occupations of the American War for Independence and the organization of the new political union, 1770-1800, but when the attention of thinking men was aroused to the practical consequences of the theological and political philosophy of England and France, the works of Reid were studied for a better system. As soon as Dugald Stewart appeared upon the arena, his

* "Préface à la Traduction des Œuvres de Reid," 1835.

† Cf. McCosh, "The Scottish Philosophy," pp. 302-3.

‡ "Die Neue Psychologie," Berlin, 1845.

lectures were resorted to by a few favored American pupils, and his works were reprinted as fast as they appeared, and some of them became the favored text-books in our leading colleges."* Later, through the works of Hamilton, widely circulated in this country, and the works of prominent American thinkers identified with the Scottish School, the essential principles of Reid's philosophy became widely known, being taught in many colleges. Among the American writers on philosophy, just referred to, Dr. James McCosh and Dr. Noah Porter may be mentioned. McCosh,† though differing from Reid in points of minor importance, accepts with slight alterations the cardinal features of his philosophy.

1. His theory of perception is intuitive or immediate perception. In sense-perception we have an immediate knowledge of extra-mental material objects.‡ These objects are the bodily organism, the various parts of which "as affected" are immediately perceived through the different senses; and extra-bodily material objects in correlation to the body, perceived specially through the muscular sense.

"We may notice here that sense-perception gives us (1) Externality. We perceive all material objects as out of, and independent of, the perceiving mind. This is associated with (2) Extension. We perceive things as extended by all the senses, not only as Locke thought by sight and touch, but by smell, taste and hearing; by

* "Ueberweg's History of Philosophy," Appendix I, vol. ii, pp. 451-2.

† "Psychology," New York, 1886; "Realistic Philosophy," New York, 1887, 2 vols., etc.

‡ "Psychology," pp. 20-69.

all these we know our affected organism as in a certain direction and so in space; by taste and smell we know the palate and nostrils as affected, and by hearing, our ear as affected. (3) We perceive body exercising energy. We do so especially by the muscular sense; we find body resisting locomotive energy. Perhaps we have some vague sense of energy by all the senses: the objects perceived seem to affect us. But the sense of power is specially given by our energy and the resistance to our energy."* These three cognitions Dr. McCosh calls primitive or intuitive cognitions.

2. His doctrine of "First and Fundamental Truths" evinces the influence of Reid. Demonstration, he says, cannot go on forever. We cannot prove all things by mediate evidence. We can show, however, that we are justified in making certain fundamental assumptions. Of these assumptions, which he calls fundamental truths, the tests are: self-evidence, necessity, and universality.†

Dr. Porter's writings‡ evince the influence of German speculative thought, as well as that of Reid and his School. However, the influence of the Scottish thinkers is predominant. As in Dr. McCosh's philosophy, this may be seen in his theory of perception and primary truths.

1. His theory of perception is intuitive perception. The object is known immediately. The object thus known

* "Psychology," p. 68.

† "Realistic Philosophy," vol. i, pp. 33-43. Cf. also "Intuitions of the Mind."

‡ "The Human Intellect," New York, 1875; "The Elements of Intellectual Science," New York, 1884.

is "the sensorium in some form of excited action." The eye, ear, nostril, hand, etc., "with the nerves attached as capable of the sentient function when acting in a living organism, are known by the collective term, the sensorium, or sensory." This sensorium is known immediately not only as a non-ego, but also as extended.* Extra-organic bodies are not known immediately. Our knowledge of them is "indirect or acquired."† On this latter point he differs from Reid who holds to an immediate perception of extra-organic objects.

2. We have an intuitive knowledge of first principles. The criteria of such principles are: universality, necessity and logical independence and originality.‡

However, notwithstanding the wide influence exerted by the philosophy of Reid in Great Britain, France and America, his historical significance is not great. Cousin regarded him as the modern Socrates. This estimate of his historical position is true in one sense. Being the first philosopher to attempt to save philosophy from the scepticism of Hume, he occupies the same position in modern philosophy which Socrates holds in Greek philosophy in his opposition to the scepticism of the Sophists. But in his influence upon the subsequent development of philosophic thought, Reid cannot be compared with Socrates. To Kant must be awarded the honor of such a comparison. It was his great work which determined the main course of philosophy subsequent to Hume, just as the philosophizing of Socrates determined the

* "Elements of Intellectual Science," p. 106.
† Ibid., p. 155.
‡ Ibid., pp. 416-45.

course of Greek philosophy, subsequent to the Sophists. Indeed, as in the philosophy of Socrates we find the best standpoint from which to survey the development of ancient philosophy from Thales to the Christian era, so in the philosophy of Kant we find the best standpoint from which to view the development of modern philosophy from Des Cartes to Von Hartmann.

E. HERSHEY SNEATH.

AN INQUIRY INTO THE HUMAN MIND ON THE PRINCIPLES OF COMMON SENSE,

BY THOMAS REID, D. D.

DEDICATION.

TO THE RIGHT HONOURABLE JAMES, EARL OF FINDLATER AND SEAFIELD, CHANCELLOR OF THE UNIVERSITY OF OLD ABERDEEN.

My Lord,—Though I apprehend that there are things, new and of some importance, in the following Inquiry, it is not without timidity that I have consented to the publication of it. The subject has been canvassed by men of very great penetration and genius: for who does not acknowledge Des Cartes, Malebranche, Locke, Berkeley, and Hume, to be such? A view of the human understanding, so different from that which they have exhibited, will, no doubt, be condemned by many, without examination, as proceeding from temerity and vanity.

But I hope the candid and discerning Few, who are capable of attending to the operations of their own minds, will weigh deliberately what is here advanced, before they pass sentence upon it. To such I appeal, as the only competent judges. If they disapprove, I am probably in the wrong, and shall be ready to change my opinion upon conviction. If they approve, the Many will at last yield to their authority, as they always do.

However contrary my notions are to those of the writers I have mentioned, their speculations have been of great use to me, and seem even to point out the road which I have taken: and your Lordship knows, that the merit of useful discoveries is sometimes not more justly due to those that have hit upon them, than to others that have ripened them, and brought them to the birth.

I acknowledge, my Lord, that I never thought of calling in question the principles commonly received with regard to the human understanding, until the "Treatise of Human Nature" was published in the year 1739. The ingenious author of that treatise upon the principles of Locke—who was no sceptic—hath built a system of scepticism, which leaves no ground to believe any one thing rather than its contrary. His reasoning appeared to me to be just; there was, therefore, a necessity to call in question the principles upon which it was founded, or to admit the conclusion.*

But can any ingenuous mind admit this sceptical system without reluctance? I truly could not, my Lord; for I am persuaded, that absolute scepticism is not more destructive of the faith of a Christian than of the science of a philosopher, and of the prudence of a man of common understanding. I am persuaded, that the unjust *live by faith* as well as the *just;* that, if all belief could be laid aside, piety, patriotism, friendship, parental affection, and private virtue, would appear as ridiculous as knight-errantry; and that the pursuits of pleasure, of ambition, and of avarice, must be grounded upon belief as well as those that are honourable or virtuous.

* "This doctrine of ideas" (says Dr. Reid, in a subsequent work), "I once believed so firmly, as to embrace the whole of Berkeley's system in consequence of it; till, finding other consequences to follow from it, which gave me more uneasiness than the want of a material world, it came into my mind, more than forty years ago, to put the question, What evidence have I for this doctrine, that all the objects of my knowledge are ideas in my own mind?"—*Essays on the Intellectual Powers, Ess. II. ch. x. p. 162.*

In like manner, Kant informs us, that it was by Hume's sceptical inferences, in regard to the causal nexus, that he also "was first roused from his dogmatic slumber." See the "Prolegomena," p. 13. —H.

The day-labourer toils at his work, in the belief that he shall receive his wages at night; and, if he had not this belief, he would not toil. We may venture to say, that even the author of this sceptical system wrote it in the belief that it should be read and regarded. I hope he wrote it in the belief also that it would be useful to mankind; and, perhaps, it may prove so at last. For I conceive the sceptical writers to be a set of men whose business it is to pick holes in the fabric of knowledge wherever it is weak and faulty; and, when these places are properly repaired, the whole building becomes more firm and solid than it was formerly.

For my own satisfaction, I entered into a serious examination of the principles upon which this sceptical system is built; and was not a little surprised to find, that it leans with its whole weight upon a hypothesis, which is ancient indeed, and hath been very generally received by philosophers, but of which I could find no solid proof. The hypothesis I mean is, That nothing is perceived but what is in the mind which perceives it: That we do not really perceive things that are external, but only certain images and pictures of them imprinted upon the mind, which are called *impressions and ideas.*

If this be true, supposing certain impressions and ideas to exist in my mind, I cannot, from their existence, infer the existence of anything else: my impressions and ideas are the only existences of which I can have any knowledge or conception; and they are such fleeting and transitory beings, that they can have no existence at all, any longer than I am conscious of them. So that, upon this hypothesis, the whole universe about me, bodies and spirits, sun, moon, stars, and earth, friends and relations, all things without exception, which I imagined to have a permanent existence, whether I thought of them or not, vanish at once;

"And, like the baseless fabric of a vision,
Leave not a track behind."

I thought it unreasonable, my Lord, upon the authority of philosophers, to admit a hypothesis which, in my opinion, overturns all philosophy, all religion and virtue, and all common sense—and, finding that all the systems concerning the human understanding which I was acquainted with, were built upon this hypothesis, I resolved to inquire into this subject anew, without regard to any hypothesis.

What I now humbly present to your Lordship, is the fruit of this inquiry, so far only as it regards the five senses: in which I claim no other merit than that of having given great attention to the operations of my own mind, and of having expressed, with all the perspicuity I was able, what I conceive every man, who gives the same attention, will feel and perceive. The productions of imagination require a genius which soars above the common rank; but the treasures of knowledge are commonly buried deep, and may be reached by those drudges who can dig with labour and patience, though they have not wings to fly. The experiments that were to be made in this investigation suited me, as they required no other expense but that of time and attention, which I could bestow. The leisure of an academical life, disengaged from the pursuits of interest and ambition; the duty of my profession, which obliged me to give prelections on these subjects to the youth; and an early inclination to speculations of this kind, have enabled me, as I flatter myself, to give a more minute attention to the subject of this inquiry, than has been given before.

My thoughts upon this subject were, a good many years ago, put together in another form, for the use of my pupils, and afterwards were submitted to the judgment of a private philosophical society,* of which I have the honour to be a member. A great part of this Inquiry was honoured even by your Lordship's perusal. And the en-

* Aberdeen Philosophical Society founded by Reid and Dr. John Gregory.—S.

couragement which you, my. Lord, and others, whose friendship is my boast, and whose judgment I reverence, were pleased to give me, counterbalanced my timidity and diffidence, and determined me to offer it to the public.

If it appears to your Lordship to justify the common sense and reason of mankind, against the sceptical subtilties which, in this age, have endeavoured to put them out of countenance—if it appears to throw any new light upon one of the noblest parts of the divine workmanship—your Lordship's respect for the arts and sciences, and your attention to everything which tends to the improvement of them, as well as to everything else that contributes to the felicity of your country, leave me no room to doubt of your favourable acceptance of this essay, as the fruit of my industry in a profession wherein I was accountable to your Lordship; and as a testimony of the great esteem and respect wherewith I have the honour to be,

My Lord, your Lordship's most obliged and most devoted Servant,

THO. REID.

AN

INQUIRY INTO THE HUMAN MIND.

CHAPTER I.

INTRODUCTION.

Section I.

THE IMPORTANCE OF THE SUBJECT, AND THE MEANS OF PROSECUTING IT.

THE fabric of the human mind is curious and wonderful, as well as that of the human body. The faculties of the one are with no less wisdom adapted to their several ends than the organs of the other. Nay, it is reasonable to think, that, as the mind is a nobler work and of a higher order than the body, even more of the wisdom and skill of the divine Architect hath been employed in its structure. It is, therefore, a subject highly worthy of inquiry on its own account, but still more worthy on account of the extensive influence which the knowledge of it hath over every other branch of science.

In the arts and sciences which have least connection with the mind, its faculties are the engines which we must employ; and the better we understand their nature and use, their defects and disorders, the more skilfully we shall apply them, and with the greater success. But in the noblest arts, the mind is also the subject upon which we operate. The painter, the poet, the actor, the orator, the moralist, and the statesman, attempt to operate upon the mind in different ways, and for different ends; and they succeed according as they touch properly the strings of the human frame. Nor can their several arts ever stand on a solid foundation, or rise to the dignity of science, until they are built on the principles of the human constitution.

Wise men now agree, or ought to agree, in this, that there is but one way to the knowledge of nature's works —the way of observation and experiment. By our constitution, we have a strong propensity to trace particular facts and observations to general rules, and to apply such general rules to account for other effects, or to direct us in the production of them. This procedure of the understanding is familiar to every human creature in the common affairs of life, and it is the only one by which any real discovery in philosophy can be made.

The man who first discovered that cold freezes water, and that heat turns it into vapour, proceeded on the same general principles, and in the same method by which Newton discovered the law of gravitation and the properties of light. His *regulæ philosophandi* are maxims of common sense, and are practised every day in common life; and he who philosophizes by other rules, either concerning the material system or concerning the mind, mistakes his aim.

Conjectures and theories are the creatures of men, and will always be found very unlike the creatures of God. If we would know the works of God, we must consult themselves with attention and humility, without daring to add anything of ours to what they declare. A just interpretation of nature is the only sound and orthodox philosophy: whatever we add of our own, is apocryphal, and of no authority.

All our curious theories of the formation of the earth, of the generation of animals, of the origin of natural and moral evil, so far as they go beyond a just induction from facts, are vanity and folly, no less than the Vortices of Des Cartes, or the Archæus of Paracelsus. Perhaps the philosophy of the mind hath been no less adulterated by theories, than that of the material system. The theory of Ideas is indeed very ancient, and hath been very universally received; but, as neither of these titles can give it authenticity, they ought not to screen it from a free and candid examination; especially in this age, when it hath produced a system of scepticism that seems to triumph over all science, and even over the dictates of common sense.

All that we know of the body, is owing to anatomical dissection and observation, and it must be by an anatomy of the mind that we can discover its powers and principles.

Section II.

THE IMPEDIMENTS TO OUR KNOWLEDGE OF THE MIND.

But it must be acknowledged, that this kind of anatomy is much more difficult than the other; and, therefore, it needs not seem strange that mankind have made less progress in it. To attend accurately to the operations of our minds, and make them an object of thought, is no easy matter even to the contemplative, and to the bulk of mankind is next to impossible.

An anatomist who hath happy opportunities, may have access to examine with his own eyes, and with equal accuracy, bodies of all different ages, sexes, and conditions; so that what is defective, obscure or preternatural in one, may be discerned clearly and in its most perfect state in another. But the anatomist of the mind cannot have the same advantage. It is his own mind only that he can examine with any degree of accuracy and distinctness. This is the only subject he can look into. He may, from outward signs, collect the operations of other minds; but these signs are for the most part ambiguous, and must be interpreted by what he perceives within himself.

So that, if a philosopher could delineate to us, distinctly and methodically, all the operations of the thinking principle within him, which no man was ever able to do, this would be only the anatomy of one particular subject; which would be both deficient and erroneous, if applied to human nature in general. For a little reflection may satisfy us, that the difference of minds is greater than that of any other beings which we consider as of the same species.

Of the various powers and faculties we possess, there are some which nature seems both to have planted and reared, so as to have left nothing to human industry. Such are the powers which we have in common with the brutes, and which are necessary to the preservation of the individual, or the continuance of the kind. There are other powers, of which nature hath only planted the seeds in our minds, but hath left the rearing of them to human culture. It is by the proper culture of these that we are capable of all those improvements in intellectuals, in taste, and in morals, which exalt and dignify human nature; while, on the other hand, the neglect or perversion of them makes its degeneracy and corruption.

The two-legged animal that eats of nature's dainties, what his taste or appetite craves, and satisfies his thirst at the crystal fountain, who propagates his kind as occasion and lust prompt, repels injuries, and takes alternate labour and repose, is, like a tree in the forest, purely of nature's growth. But this same savage hath within him the seeds of the logician, the man of taste and breeding, the orator, the statesman, the man of virtue, and the saint; which seeds, though planted in his mind by nature, yet, through want of culture and exercise, must lie for ever buried, and be hardly perceivable by himself or by others.

The lowest degree of social life will bring to light some of those principles which lay hid in the savage state;

and, according to his training, and company, and manner of life, some of them, either by their native vigor, or by the force of culture, will thrive and grow up to great perfection, others will be strangely perverted from their natural form, and others checked, or perhaps quite eradicated.

This makes human nature so various and multiform in the individuals that partake of it, that, in point of morals and intellectual endowments, it fills up all that gap which we conceive to be between brutes and devils below, and the celestial orders above; and such a prodigious diversity of minds must make it extremely difficult to discover the common principles of the species.

The language of philosophers, with regard to the original faculties of the mind, is so adapted to the prevailing system, that it cannot fit any other; like a coat that fits the man for whom it was made, and shews him to advantage, which yet will sit very awkward upon one of a different make, although perhaps as handsome and as well proportioned. It is hardly possible to make any innovation in our philosophy concerning the mind and its operations, without using new words and phrases, or giving a different meaning to those that are received—a liberty which, even when necessary, creates prejudice and misconstruction, and which must wait the sanction of time to authorize it; for innovations in language, like those in religion and government, are always suspected and disliked by the many, till use hath made them familiar, and prescription hath given them a title.

If the original perceptions and notions of the mind were to make their appearance single and unmixed, as we first received them from the hand of nature, one accustomed to reflection would have less difficulty in tracing them; but before we are capable of reflection, they are so mixed, compounded, and decompounded, by habits, associations, and abstractions, that it is hard to know what they were originally. The mind may, in this respect, be compared to an apothecary or a chemist, whose materials indeed are furnished by nature; but, for the purposes of his art, he mixes, compounds, dissolves, evaporates, and sublimes them, till they put on a quite different appearance; so that it is very difficult to know what they were at first, and much more to bring them back to their original and natural form. And this work of the mind is not carried on by deliberate acts of mature reason, which we might recollect, but by means of instincts, habits, associations, and other principles, which operate before we come to the use of reason; so that it is extremely difficult for the mind to return upon its own footsteps, and trace back those operations which have employed it since it first began to think and to act.

Could we obtain a distinct and full history of all that hath past in the mind of a child, from the beginning of life and sensation, till it grows up to the use of reason—how its infant faculties began to work, and how they brought forth and ripened all the various notions, opinions and sentiments which we find in ourselves when we come to be capable of reflection—this would be a treasure of natural history, which would probably give more light into the human faculties, than all the systems of philosophers about them since the beginning of the world. But it is in vain to wish for what nature has not put within the reach of our power. Reflection, the only instrument by which we can discern the powers of the mind, comes too late to observe the progress of nature, in raising them from their infancy to perfection.

It must therefore require great caution, and great application of mind, for a man that is grown up in all the prejudices of education, fashion, and philosophy, to unravel his notions and opinions, till he find out the simple and original principles of his constitution, of which no account can be given but the will of our Maker. This may be truly called an *analysis* of the human faculties; and, till this is performed, it is in vain we expect any just *system* of the mind—that is, an enumeration of the original powers and laws of our constitution, and an explication from them of the various phænomena of human nature.

Success in an inquiry of this kind, it is not in human power to command ; but, perhaps, it is possible, by caution and humility, to avoid error and delusion. The labyrinth may be too intricate, and the thread too fine, to be traced through all its windings; but, if we stop where we can trace it no farther, and secure the ground we have gained, there is no harm done; a quicker eye may in time trace it farther.

It is genius, and not the want of it, that adulterates philosophy, and fills it with error and false theory. A creative imagination disdains the mean offices of digging for a foundation, of removing rubbish, and carrying materials; leaving these servile employments to the drudges in science, it plans a design, and raises a fabric. Invention supplies materials where they are wanting, and fancy adds colouring and every befitting ornament. The work pleases the eye, and wants nothing but solidity and a good foundation. It seems even to vie with the works of nature, till some succeeding architect blows it into rubbish, and builds as goodly a fabric of his own in its place. Happily for the present age, the castle-builders employ themselves more in romance than in philosophy. That is undoubtedly their province, and in those regions the offspring of fancy is legitimate, but in philosophy it is all spurious.

Section III.

THE PRESENT STATE OF THIS PART OF PHILOSOPHY—OF DES CARTES, MALEBRANCHE, AND LOCKE.

That our philosophy concerning the mind and its faculties is but in a very low state, may be reasonably conjectured even by those who never have narrowly examined it. Are there any principles, with regard to the mind, settled with that perspicuity and evidence which attends the principles of mechanics, astronomy and optics? These are really sciences built upon laws of nature which universally obtain. What is discovered in them is no longer matter of dispute: future ages may add to it; but, till the course of nature be changed, what is already established can never be overturned. But when we turn our attention inward, and consider the phænomena of human thoughts, opinions, and perceptions, and endeavour to trace them to the general laws and the first principles of our constitution, we are immediately involved in darkness and perplexity; and, if common sense, or the principles of education, happen not to be stubborn, it is odds but we end in absolute scepticism.

Des Cartes, finding nothing established in this part of philosophy, in order to lay the foundation of it deep, resolved not to believe his own existence till he should be able to give a good reason for it. He was, perhaps, the first that took up such a resolution; but, if he could indeed have effected his purpose, and really become diffident of his existence, his case would have been deplorable, and without any remedy from reason or philosophy. A man that disbelieves his own existence, is surely as unfit to be reasoned with as a man that believes he is made of glass. There may be disorders in the human frame that may produce such extravagancies, but they will never be cured by reasoning. Des Cartes, indeed, would make us believe that he got out of this delirium by this logical argument, *Cogito, ergo sum;* but it is evident he was in his senses all the time, and never seriously doubted of his existence; for he takes it for granted in this argument, and proves nothing at all. I am thinking, says he—therefore, I am. And is it not as good reasoning to say, I am sleeping—therefore, I am? or, I am doing nothing—therefore, I am? If a body moves, it must exist, no doubt; but, if it is at rest it must exist likewise.*

Perhaps Des Cartes meant not to assume his own existence in this enthymeme, but the existence of thought; and to infer from that the existence of a mind, or subject of thought. But why did he not prove the existence of his thought? Consciousness, it may be said, vouches that. But who is voucher for consciousness? Can any man prove that his consciousness may not deceive him? No man can; nor can we give a better reason for trusting to it, than that every man, while his mind is sound, is determined, by the constitution of his nature, to give implicit belief to it, and to laugh at or pity the man who doubts its testimony. And is not every man, in his wits, as much determined to take his existence upon trust as his consciousness?

The other proposition assumed in this argument, That thought cannot be without a mind or subject, is liable to the same objection: not that it wants evidence but that its evidence is no clearer, nor more immediate, than that of the proposition to be proved by it. And, taking all these propositions together—I think; I am conscious; Everything that thinks, exists; I exist—would not every sober man form the same opinion of the man who seriously doubted any one of them? And if he was his friend, would he not hope for his cure from physic and good regimen, rather than from metaphysic and logic?

But supposing it proved, that my thought and my consciousness must have a subject, and consequently that I exist, how do I know that all that train and succession of thoughts which I remember belong to one subject, and that the I of this moment is the very individual I of yesterday and of times past?

* The nature of the Cartesian Doubt and its solution is here misapprehended.—H. See note, I. P., Essay II, ch. 8.

Des Cartes did not think proper to start this doubt; but Locke has done it; and, in order to resolve it, gravely determines that personal identity consists in consciousness—that is, if you are conscious that you did such a thing a twelvemonth ago, this consciousness makes you to be the very person that did it. Now consciousness of what is past can signify nothing else but the remembrance that I did it; so that Locke's principle must be, That identity consists in remembrance; and, consequently, a man must lose his personal identity with regard to everything he forgets.

Nor are these the only instances whereby our philosophy concerning the mind appears to be very fruitful in creating doubts, but very unhappy in resolving them.

Des Cartes, Malebranche, and Locke, have all employed their genius and skill to prove the existence of a material world: and with very bad success. Poor untaught mortals believe undoubtedly that there is a sun, moon, and stars; an earth, which we inhabit; country, friends, and relations, which we enjoy; land, houses, and movables, which we possess. But philosophers, pitying the credulity of the vulgar, resolve to have no faith but what is founded upon reason.* They apply to philosophy to furnish them with reasons for the belief of those things which all mankind have believed, without being able to give any reason for it. And surely one would expect, that, in matters of such importance, the proof would not be difficult: but it is the most difficult thing in the world. For these three great men, with the best good will, have not been able, from all the treasures of philosophy, to draw one argument that is fit to convince a man that can reason, of the existence of any one thing without him. Admired Philosophy!

* Reason is here employed, by Reid, not as a synonyme for Common Sense, (νοῦς, locus principiorum) and as he himself more correctly employs it in his later works, but as equivalent to Reasoning, (διάνοια, discursus mentalis.) See Note A.—H.

daughter of light! parent of wisdom and knowledge! if thou art she, surely thou hast not yet arisen upon the human mind, nor blessed us with more of thy rays than are sufficient to shed a darkness visible upon the human faculties, and to disturb that repose and security which happier mortals enjoy, who never approached thine altar, nor felt thine influence! But if, indeed, thou hast not power to dispel those clouds and phantoms which thou hast discovered or created, withdraw this penurious and malignant ray; I despise Philosophy, and renounce its guidance—let my soul dwell with Common Sense.*

Section IV.

APOLOGY FOR THOSE PHILOSOPHERS.

But, instead of despising the dawn of light, we ought rather to hope for its increase: instead of blaming the philosophers I have mentioned for the defects and blemishes of their system we ought rather to honour their memories, as the first discoverers of a region in philosophy formerly unknown; and however lame and imperfect the system may be, they have opened the way to future discoveries, and are justly entitled to a great share in the merit of them. They have removed an infinite deal of dust and rubbish, collected in the ages of scholastic sophistry, which had obstructed the way. They have put us in the right road—that of experience and accurate reflection. They have taught us to avoid the snares of ambiguous and ill-defined words, and have spoken and thought upon this subject with a distinctness and perspicuity formerly unknown. They have made many openings that may lead to the discovery of truths which they did not reach, or to the detection of errors in which they were involuntarily entangled.

* Mr. Stewart very justly censures the vagueness and ambiguity of this passage. *Elem.* vol ii., ch. i., § 3, p. 92, 8vo editions.—H.

It may be observed, that the defects and blemishes in the received philosophy concerning the mind, which have most exposed it to the contempt and ridicule of sensible men, have chiefly been owing to this—that the votaries of this Philosophy, from a natural prejudice in her favour, have endeavoured to extend her jurisdiction beyond its just limits, and to call to her bar the dictates of Common Sense. But these decline this jurisdiction ; they disdain the trial of reasoning, and disown its authority; they neither claim its aid, nor dread its attacks.

In this unequal contest betwixt Common Sense and Philosophy, the latter will always come off both with dishonour and loss; nor can she ever thrive till this rivalship is dropt, these encroachments given up, and a cordial friendship restored: for, in reality, Common Sense holds nothing of Philosophy, nor needs her aid. But, on the other hand, Philosophy (if I may be permitted to change the metaphor) has no other root but the principles of Common Sense ; it grows out of them, and draws its nourishment from them. Severed from this root, its honours wither, its sap is dried up, it dies and rots.

The philosophers of the last age, whom I have mentioned, did not attend to the preserving this union and subordination so carefully as the honour and interest of philosophy required: but those of the present have waged open war with Common Sense, and hope to make a complete conquest of it by the subtilties of Philosophy—an attempt no less audacious and vain than that of the giants to dethrone almighty Jove.

Section V.

OF BISHOP BERKELEY—THE "TREATISE OF HUMAN NATURE"—AND OF SCEPTICISM.

The present age, I apprehend, has not produced two more acute or more practised in this part of philosophy, than the Bishop of Cloyne, and the author of the "Treatise of Human Nature." The first was no friend to scepticism, but had that warm concern for religious and moral principles which became his order: yet the result of his inquiry was a serious conviction that there is no such thing as a material world—nothing in nature but spirits and ideas; and that the belief of material substances, and of abstract ideas, are the chief causes of all our errors in philosophy, and of all infidelity and heresy in religion. His arguments are founded upon the principles which were formerly laid down by Des Cartes, Malebranche, and Locke, and which have been very generally received.

And the opinion of the ablest judges seems to be, that they neither have been, nor can be confuted; and that he hath proved by unanswerable arguments what no man in his senses can believe.

The second proceeds upon the same principles, but carries them to their full length; and, as the Bishop undid the whole material world, this author, upon the same grounds, undoes the world of spirits, and leaves nothing in nature but ideas and impressions, without any subject on which they may be impressed.

It seems to be a peculiar strain of humour in this author, to set out in his introduction by promising, with a grave face, no less than a complete system of the sciences, upon a foundation entirely new—to wit, that of human nature—when the intention of the whole work is to shew, that there is neither human nature nor science in the world. It may perhaps be unreasonable to complain of this conduct in an author who neither believes his own existence nor that of his reader; and therefore could not mean to disappoint him, or to laugh at his credulity. Yet I cannot imagine that the author of the "Treatise of Human Nature" is so sceptical as to plead this apology. He believed, against his principles, that he should be read, and that he should retain his personal identity, till he reaped the honour and reputation justly due to his metaphysical *acumen*. Indeed, he ingeniously acknowledges, that it was only in solitude and retirement that he could yield any assent to his own philosophy; society, like daylight, dispelled the darkness and fogs of scepticism, and made him yield to the dominion of common sense. Nor did I ever hear him charged with doing anything, even in solitude, that argued such a degree of scepticism as his principles maintain. Surely if his friends apprehended this, they would have the charity never to leave him alone.

Pyrrho the Elean, the father of this philosophy, seems to have carried it to greater perfection than any of his successors: for, if we may believe Antigonus the Carystian, quoted by Diogenes Laertius, his life corresponded to his doctrine. And, therefore, if a cart run against him, or a dog attacked him, or if he came upon a precipice, he would not stir a foot to avoid the danger, giving no credit to his senses. But his attendants, who, happily for him, were not so great sceptics, took care to keep him out of harm's way; so that he lived till he was ninety years of age. Nor is it to be doubted but this author's friends would have been equally careful to keep him from harm, if ever his principles had taken too strong a hold of him.

It is probable the "Treatise of Human Nature" was not written in company; yet it contains manifest indications that the author every now and then relapsed into the faith of the vulgar, and could hardly, for half a dozen pages, keep up the sceptical character.

In like manner, the great Pyrrho himself forgot his principles on some occasions; and is said once to have been in such a passion with his cook, who probably had not roasted his dinner to his mind, that with the spit in his hand, and the meat upon it, he pursued him even into the market-place.

It is a bold philosophy that rejects, without ceremony,

principles which irresistibly govern the belief and the conduct of all mankind in the common concerns of life; and to which the philosopher himself must yield, after he imagines he hath confuted them. Such principles are older, and of more authority, than Philosophy: she rests upon them as her basis, not they upon her. If she could overturn them, she must be buried in their ruins; but all the engines of philosophical subtilty are too weak for this purpose; and the attempt is no less ridiculous than if a mechanic should contrive an *axis in peritrochio* to remove the earth out of its place; or if a mathematician should pretend to demonstrate that things equal to the same thing are not equal to one another.

Zeno endeavoured to demonstrate the impossibility of motion; Hobbes, that there was no difference between right and wrong; and this author, that no credit is to be given to our senses, to our memory, or even to demonstration. Such philosophy is justly ridiculous, even to those who cannot detect the fallacy of it. It can have no other tendency, than to shew the acuteness of the sophist, at the expense of disgracing reason and human nature, and making mankind Yahoos.

Section VI.

OF THE "TREATISE OF HUMAN NATURE."

There are other prejudices against this system of human nature, which, even upon a general view, may make one diffident of it.

Des Cartes, Hobbes, and this author, have each of them given us a system of human nature; an undertaking too vast for any one man, how great soever his genius and abilities may be. There must surely be reason to apprehend, that many parts of human nature never came under their observation; and that others have been stretched and distorted, to fill up blanks, and complete the system. Christopher Columbus, or Sebastian Cabot, might almost as reasonably have undertaken to give us a complete map of America.

There is a certain character and style in Nature's works, which is never attained in the most perfect imitation of them. This seems to be wanting in the systems of human nature I have mentioned, and particularly in the last. One may see a puppet make variety of motions and gesticulations, which strike much at first view; but when it is accurately observed, and taken to pieces, our admiration ceases: we comprehend the whole art of the maker. How unlike is it to that which it represents! What a poor piece of work compared with the body of a man, whose structure the more we know, the more wonders we discover in it, and the more sensible we are of our ignorance! Is the mechanism of the mind so easily comprehended, when that of the body is so difficult? Yet, by this system, three laws of association, joined to a few original feelings, explain the whole mechanism of sense, imagination, memory, belief, and of all the actions, and passions of the mind. Is this the man that Nature made? I suspect it is not so easy to look behind the scenes in Nature's work. This is a puppet, surely, contrived by too bold an apprentice of Nature, to mimic her work. It shews tolerably by candle-light; but, brought into clear day, and taken to pieces, it will appear to be a man made with mortar and a trowel. The more we know of other parts of nature, the more we like and approve them. The little I know of the planetary system, of the earth, which we inhabit; of minerals, vegetables, and animals; of my own body; and of the laws which obtain in these parts of nature—opens to my mind grand and beautiful scenes, and contributes equally to my happiness and power. But, when I look within, and consider the mind itself, which makes me capable of all these prospects and enjoyments—if it is, indeed, what the "Treatise of Human Nature" makes it—I find

I have been only in an enchanted castle, imposed upon by spectres and apparitions. I blush inwardly to think how I have been deluded ; I am ashamed of my frame, and can hardly forbear expostulating with my destiny. Is this thy pastime, O Nature, to put such tricks upon a silly creature, and then to take off the mask, and shew him how he hath been befooled? If this is the philosophy of human nature, my soul, enter thou not into her secrets ! It is surely the forbidden tree of knowledge ; I no sooner taste of it, than I perceive myself naked, and stript of all things—yea, even of my very self. I see myself, and the whole frame of nature, shrink into fleeting ideas, which, like Epicurus's atoms, dance about in emptiness.

Section VII.

THE SYSTEM OF ALL THESE AUTHORS IS THE SAME, AND LEADS TO SCEPTICISM.

But what if these profound disquisitions into the first principles of human nature, do naturally and necessarily plunge a man into this abyss of scepticism? May we not reasonably judge so from what hath happened? Des Cartes no sooner began to dig in this mine, than scepticism was ready to break in upon him. He did what he could to shut it out. Malebranche and Locke, who dug deeper, found the difficulty of keeping out this enemy still to increase; but they laboured honestly in the design. Then Berkeley, who carried on the work, despairing of securing all, bethought himself of an expedient:—By giving up the material world, which he thought might be spared without loss, and even with advantage, he hoped, by an impregnable partition, to secure the world of spirits. But alas ! the "Treatise of Human Nature" wantonly sapped the foundation of this partition, and drowned all in one universal deluge.

These facts, which are undeniable, do, indeed, give

reason to apprehend that Des Cartes' system of the human understanding, which I shall beg leave to call *the ideal system*, and which, with some improvements made by later writers, is now generally received, hath some original defect; that this scepticism is inlaid in it, and reared along with it: and, therefore, that we must lay it open to the foundation, and examine the materials, before we can expect to raise any solid and useful fabric of knowledge on this subject.

Section VIII.

WE OUGHT NOT TO DESPAIR OF A BETTER.

But is this to be despaired of, because Des Cartes and his followers have failed? By no means. This pusillanimity would be injurious to ourselves and injurious to truth. Useful discoveries are sometimes indeed the effect of superior genius, but more frequently they are the birth of time and of accidents. A traveller of good judgment may mistake his way, and be unawares led into a wrong track; and while the road is fair before him, he may go on without suspicion and be followed by others; but, when it ends in a coal-pit, it requires no great judgment to know that he hath gone wrong, nor perhaps to find out what misled him.

In the meantime, the unprosperous state of this part of philosophy hath produced an effect, somewhat discouraging indeed to any attempt of this nature, but an effect which might be expected, and which time only and better success can remedy. Sensible men, who never will be sceptics in matters of common life, are apt to treat with sovereign contempt everything that hath been said, or is to be said, upon this subject. It is metaphysic, say they: who minds it? Let scholastic sophisters entangle themselves in their own cobwebs; I am resolved to take my own existence, and the existence of other things, upon trust; and to believe that snow is cold, and honey sweet, whatever they may say to the contrary. He must either be a fool, or want to make a fool of me, that would reason me out of my reason and senses.

I confess I know not what a sceptic can answer to this, nor by what good argument he can plead even for a hearing; for either his reasoning is sophistry, and so deserves contempt; or there is no truth in human faculties—and then why should we reason?

If, therefore, a man find himself intangled in these metaphysical toils, and can find no other way to escape, let him bravely cut the knot which he cannot loose, curse metaphysic, and dissuade every man from meddling with it; for, if I have been led into bogs and quagmires by following an *ignis fatuus*, what can I do better than to warn others to beware of it? If philosophy contradicts herself, befools her votaries, and deprives them of every object worthy to be pursued or enjoyed, let her be sent back to the infernal regions from which she must have had her original.

But is it absolutely certain that this fair lady is of the party? Is it not possible she may have been misrepresented? Have not men of genius in former ages often made their own dreams to pass for her oracles? Ought she then to be condemned without any further hearing? This would be unreasonable. I have found her in all other matters an agreeable companion, a faithful counsellor, a friend to common sense, and to the happiness of mankind. This justly entitles her to my correspondence and confidence, till I find infallible proofs of her infidelity.

CHAPTER II.

OF SMELLING.

Section I.

THE ORDER OF PROCEEDING—OF THE MEDIUM AND ORGAN OF SMELL.

IT is so difficult to unravel the operations of the human understanding, and to reduce them to their first principles, that we cannot expect to succeed in the attempt, but by beginning with the simplest, and proceeding by very cautious steps to the more complex. The five external senses may, for this reason, claim to be first considered in an analysis of the human faculties. And the same reason ought to determine us to make a choice even among the senses, and to give the precedence, not to the noblest or most useful, but to the simplest, and that whose objects are least in danger of being mistaken for other things.

In this view, an analysis of our sensations may be carried on, perhaps with most ease and distinctness, by taking them in this order: Smelling, Tasting, Hearing, Touch, and, last of all, Seeing.

Natural philosophy informs us, that all animal and vegetable bodies, and probably all or most other bodies, while exposed to the air, are continually sending forth effluvia of vast subtilty, not only in their state of life and growth, but in the states of fermentation and putrefaction. These volatile particles do probably repel each other, and so scatter themselves in the air, until they meet with other bodies to which they have some chemical affinity, and with which they unite, and form new concretes. All the smell of plants, and of other bodies, is caused by these volatile parts, and is smelled wherever they are scattered in the air: and the acuteness of smell in some animals, shews us, that these effluvia spread far, and must be inconceivably subtile.

Whether, as some chemists conceive, every species of bodies hath a *spiritus rector*, a kind of soul, which causes the smell and all the specific virtues of that body, and which, being extremely volatile, flies about in the air in quest of a proper receptacle, I do not inquire. This, like most other theories, is perhaps rather the product of imagination than of just induction. But that all bodies are smelled by means of effluvia which they emit, and which are drawn into the nostrils along with the air, there is no reason to doubt. So that there is manifest appearance of design in placing the organ of smell in the inside of that canal, through which the air is continually passing in inspiration and expiration.

Anatomy informs us, that the *membrana pituitaria*, and the olfactory nerves, which are distributed to the villous parts of this membrane, are the organs destined by the wisdom of nature to this sense; so that when a body emits no effluvia, or when they do not enter into the nose, or when the pituitary membrane or olfactory nerves are rendered unfit to perform their office, it cannot be smelled.

Yet, notwithstanding this, it is evident that neither the organ of smell, nor the medium, nor any motions we can conceive excited in the membrane above mentioned, or in the nerve or animal spirits, do in the least resemble the sensation of smelling; nor could that sensation of itself ever have led us to think of nerves, animal spirits, or effluvia.

Section II.

THE SENSATION CONSIDERED ABSTRACTLY.

Having premised these things with regard to the medium and organ of this sense, let us now attend carefully to what the mind is conscious of when we smell a rose or a lily; and, since our language affords no other name for this sensation, we shall call it a *smell* or *odour*, carefully excluding from the meaning of those names everything but the sensation itself, at least till we have examined it.

Suppose a person who never had this sense before, to receive it all at once, and to smell a rose—can he perceive any similitude or agreement between the smell and the rose? or indeed between it and any other object whatsoever? Certainly he cannot. He finds himself affected in a new way, he knows not why or from what cause. Like a man that feels some pain or pleasure, formerly unknown to him, he is conscious that he is not the cause of it himself; but cannot, from the nature of the thing, determine whether it is caused by body or spirit, by something near, or by something at a distance. It has no similitude to anything else, so as to admit of a comparison; and, therefore, he can conclude nothing from it, unless, perhaps, that there must be some unknown cause of it.

It is evidently ridiculous to ascribe to it figure, colour, extension, or any other quality of bodies. He cannot give it a place, any more than he can give a place to melancholy or joy; nor can he conceive it to have any existence, but when it is smelled. So that it appears to be a simple and original affection or feeling of the mind, altogether inexplicable and unaccountable. It is, indeed, impossible that it can be in any body: it is a sensation, and a sensation can only be in a sentient thing.

The various odours have each their different degrees of strength or weakness. Most of them are agreeable or disagreeable; and frequently those that are agreeable when weak, are disagreeable when stronger. When we compare different smells together, we can perceive very few resemblances or contrarieties, or, indeed, relations of any kind between them. They are all so simple in themselves, and so different from each other, that it is hardly possible to divide them into *genera* and *species*. Most of the names we give them are particular; as the smell of a *rose*, of a *jessamine*, and the like. Yet there are some general names—as *sweet*, *stinking*, *musty*, *putrid*, *cadaverous*, *aromatic*. Some of them seem to refresh and animate the mind, others to deaden and depress it.

Section III.

SENSATION AND REMEMBRANCE, NATURAL PRINCIPLES OF BELIEF.

So far we have considered this sensation abstractly. Let us next compare it with other things to which it bears some relation. And first I shall compare this sensation with the remembrance, and the imagination of it.

I can think of the smell of a rose when I do not smell it; and it is possible that when I think of it, there is neither rose nor smell anywhere existing. But when I smell it, I am necessarily determined to believe that the sensation really exists. This is common to all sensations, that, as they cannot exist but in being perceived, so they cannot be perceived but they must exist. I could as easily doubt of my own existence, as of the existence of my sensations. Even those profound philosophers who have endeavoured to disprove their own existence, have yet left their sensations to stand upon their own bottom, stript of a subject, rather than call in question the reality of their existence.

Here, then, a sensation, a smell, for instance, may be presented to the mind three different ways: it may be smelled, it may be remembered, it may be imagined or thought of. In the first case, it is necessarily accompanied with a belief of its present existence; in the second, it is necessarily accompanied with a belief of its past existence; and in the last, it is not accompanied with belief at all,* but is what the logicians call *a simple apprehension.*

Why sensation should compel our belief of the present existence of the thing, memory a belief of its past existence, and imagination no belief at all, I believe no philosopher can give a shadow of reason, but that such is the nature of these operations: they are all simple and original, and therefore inexplicable acts of the mind.

Suppose that once, and only once, I smelled a tuberose in a certain room, where it grew in a pot, and gave a very grateful perfume. Next day I relate what I saw and smelled. When I attend as carefully as I can to what passes in my mind in this case, it appears evident that the very thing I saw yesterday, and the fragrance I smelled, are now the immediate objects of my mind, when I remember it. Further, I can imagine this pot and flower transported to the room where I now sit, and yielding the same perfume. Here likewise it appears, that the individual thing which I saw and smelled, is the object of my imagination.

Philosophers indeed tell me, that the immediate object of my memory and imagination in this case, is not the past sensation, but an idea of it, an image, phantasm, or species,† of the odour I smelled: that this idea now exists in my mind, or in my sensorium; and the mind, contemplating this present idea, finds it a representation of what is past, or of what may exist; and accordingly calls it memory, or imagination. This is the doctrine of the ideal philosophy; which we shall not

* This is not strictly correct. The *imagination* of an object is necessarily accompanied with a belief of the existence of the mental representation. Reid uses the term existence for *objective existence* only; and takes no account of the possibility of a *subjective existence.*—H.

† It will be observed, that Reid understands by *Idea*, *Image*, *Phantasm*, *Species*, *&c.*, always a *tertium quid* numerically different both from the Object existing and from the Subject knowing. He had formed no conception of a doctrine in which a representative ob-

now examine, that we may not interrupt the thread of the present investigation. Upon the strictest attention, memory appears to me to have things that are past, and not present ideas, for its object. We shall afterwards examine this system of ideas, and endeavour to make it appear, that no solid proof has ever been advanced of the existence of ideas; that they are a mere fiction and hypothesis, contrived to solve the phænomena of the human understanding; that they do not at all answer this end; and that this hypothesis of ideas or images of things in the mind, or in the sensorium, is the parent of those many paradoxes so shocking to common sense, and of that scepticism which disgrace our philosophy of the mind, and have brought upon it the ridicule and contempt of sensible men.

In the meantime, I beg leave to think, with the vulgar, that, when I remember the smell of the tuberose, that very sensation which I had yesterday, and which has now no more any existence, is the immediate object of my memory; and when I imagine it present, the sensation itself, and not any idea of it, is the object of my imagination. But, though the object of my sensation, memory, and imagination, be in this case the same, yet these acts or operations of the mind are as different, and as easily distinguishable, as smell, taste, and sound. I am conscious of a difference in kind between sensation and memory, and between both and imagination. I find this also, that the sensation compels my belief of the present existence of the smell, and memory my belief of its past existence. There is a smell, is the immediate testimony of sense; there was a smell, is the immediate testimony of memory. If you ask me, why I believe that the smell exists, I can give no other reason, nor

ject is allowed, but only as a modification of the mind itself. On the evil consequences of this error, both on his own philosophy and on his criticism of other opinions,—H.

shall ever be able to give any other, than that I smell it. If you ask, why I believe that it existed yesterday, I can give no other reason but that I remember it.

Sensation and memory, therefore, are simple, original, and perfectly distinct operations of the mind, and both of them are original principles of belief. Imagination is distinct from both, but is no principle of belief. Sensation implies the present existence of its object, memory its past existence, but imagination views its object naked, and without any belief of its existence or non-existence, and is therefore what the schools call *Simple Apprehension.* *

Section IV.

JUDGMENT AND BELIEF IN SOME CASES PRECEDE SIMPLE APPREHENSION.

But here, again, the ideal system comes in our way: it teaches us that the first operation of the mind about its ideas, is simple apprehension—that is, the bare conception of a thing without any belief about it: and that, after we have got simple apprehensions, by comparing them together, we perceive agreements or disagreements between them; and that this perception of the agreement or disagreement of ideas, is all that we call belief, judgment, or knowledge. Now, this appears to me to be all fiction, without any foundation in nature; for it is acknowledged by all, that sensation must go before memory and imagination; and hence it necessarily follows, that apprehension, accompanied with belief and knowledge, must go before simple apprehension, at least in the matters we are now speaking of. So that here, in-

* *Simple Apprehension*, in the language of the Schools, has no reference to any exclusion of belief. It was merely given to the conception of simple, in contrast to the cognition of complex, terms. —H.

stead of saying that the belief or knowledge is got by putting together and comparing the simple apprehensions, we ought rather to say that the simple apprehension is performed by resolving and analysing a natural and original judgment. And it is with the operations of the mind, in this case, as with natural bodies, which are, indeed, compounded of simple principles or elements. Nature does not exhibit these elements separate, to be compounded by us; she exhibits them mixed and compounded in concrete bodies, and it is only by art and chemical analysis that they can be separated.

Section V.

TWO THEORIES OF THE NATURE OF BELIEF REFUTED—CONCLUSIONS FROM WHAT HATH BEEN SAID.

But what is this belief or knowledge which accompanies sensation and memory? Every man knows what it is, but no man can define it. Does any man pretend to define sensation, or to define consciousness? It is happy, indeed, that no man does. And if no philosopher had endeavoured to define and explain belief, some paradoxes in philosophy, more incredible than ever were brought forth by the most abject superstition or the most frantic enthusiasm, had never seen the light. Of this kind surely is that modern discovery of the ideal philosophy, that sensation, memory, belief, and imagination, when they have the same object, are only different degrees of strength and vivacity in the idea.* Suppose the idea to be that of a future state after death: one man believes it firmly—this means no more than that he hath a strong and lively idea of it; another neither believes nor disbelieves—that is, he has a weak and faint idea. Suppose, now, a third person believes firmly that there is no

* He refers to Hume.—H.

such thing, I am at a loss to know whether his idea be faint or lively: if it is faint, then there may be a firm belief where the idea is faint; if the idea is lively, then the belief of a future state and the belief of no future state must be one and the same. The same arguments that are used to prove that belief implies only a stronger idea of the object than simple apprehension, might as well be used to prove that love implies only a stronger idea of the object than indifference. And then what shall we say of hatred, which must upon this hypothesis be a degree of love, or a degree of indifference? If it should be said, that in love there is something more than an idea—to wit, an affection of the mind—may it not be said with equal reason, that in belief there is something more than an idea—to wit, an assent or persuasion of the mind?

But perhaps it may be thought as ridiculous to argue against this strange opinion, as to maintain it. Indeed, if a man should maintain that a circle, a square, and a triangle differ only in magnitude, and not in figure, I believe he would find nobody disposed either to believe him or to argue against him; and yet I do not think it less shocking to common sense, to maintain that sensation, memory, and imagination differ only in degree, and not in kind. I know it is said, that, in a delirium, or in dreaming, men are apt to mistake one for the other. But does it follow from this, that men who are neither dreaming nor in a delirium cannot distinguish them? But how does a man know that he is not in a delirium? I cannot tell: neither can I tell how a man knows that he exists. But, if any man seriously doubts whether he is in a delirium, I think it highly probable that he is, and that it is time to seek for a cure, which I am persuaded he will not find in the whole system of logic.

I mentioned before Locke's notion of belief or knowledge; he holds that it consists in a perception of the agreement or disagreement of ideas; and this he values himself upon as a very important discovery.

We shall have occasion afterwards to examine more particularly this grand principle of Locke's philosophy, and to shew that it is one of the main pillars of modern scepticism, although he had no intention to make that use of it. At present let us only consider how it agrees with the instances of belief now under consideration; and whether it gives any light to them. I believe that the sensation I have exists; and that the sensation I remember does not now exist, but did exist yesterday. Here, according to Locke's system, I compare the idea of a sensation with the ideas of past and present existence: at one time I perceive that this idea agrees with that of present existence, but disagrees with that of past existence; but, at another time, it agrees with the idea of past existence, and disagrees with that of present existence. Truly these ideas seem to be very capricious in their agreements and disagreements. Besides, I cannot, for my heart, conceive what is meant by either. I say a sensation exists, and I think I understand clearly what I mean. But you want to make the thing clearer, and for that end tell me, that there is an agreement between the idea of that sensation and the idea of existence. To speak freely, this conveys to me no light, but darkness; I can conceive no otherwise of it, than as an odd and obscure circumlocution. I conclude, then, that the belief which accompanies sensation and memory, is a simple act of the mind, which cannot be defined. It is, in this respect, like seeing and hearing, which can never be so defined as to be understood by those who have not these faculties; and to such as have them, no definition can make these operations more clear than they are already. In like manner, every man that has any belief—and he must be a curiosity that has none—knows perfectly what belief is, but can never define or explain it. I conclude, also, that sensation, memory, and imagination, even where they have the same object, are operations of a quite different nature, and perfectly distinguishable by those who are sound and sober. A man that is in danger of confounding them, is indeed to be pitied; but whatever relief he may find from another art, he can find none from logic or metaphysic. I conclude further, that it is no less a part of the human constitution, to believe the present existence of our sensations, and to believe the past existence of what we remember, than it is to believe that twice two make four. The evidence of sense, the evidence of memory, and the evidence of the necessary relations of things, are all distinct and original kinds of evidence, equally grounded on our constitution: none of them depends upon, or can be resolved into another. To reason against any of these kinds of evidence, is absurd; nay, to reason for them is absurd. They are first principles; and such fall not within the province of reason,* but of common sense.

Section VI.

APOLOGY FOR METAPHYSICAL ABSURDITIES—SENSATION WITHOUT A SENTIENT, A CONSEQUENCE OF THE THEORY OF IDEAS—CONSEQUENCES OF THIS STRANGE OPINION.

Having considered the relation which the sensation of smelling bears to the remembrance and imagination of it, I proceed to consider what relation it bears to a mind or sentient principle. It is certain, no man can conceive or believe smelling to exist of itself, without a mind, or something that has the power of smelling, of which it is called a sensation, an operation, or feeling. Yet, if any man should demand a proof, that sensation cannot be without a mind or sentient being, I confess

* See note, p. 79.—H.

that I can give none; and that to pretend to prove it, seems to me almost as absurd as to deny it.

This might have been said without any apology before the "Treatise of Human Nature" appeared in the world. For till that time, no man, as far as I know, ever thought either of calling in question that principle, or of giving a reason for his belief of it. Whether thinking beings were of an ethereal or igneous nature, whether material or immaterial, was variously disputed; but that thinking is an operation of some kind of being or other, was always taken for granted, as a principle that could not possibly admit of doubt.

However, since the author above mentioned, who is undoubtedly one of the most acute metaphysicians that this or any age hath produced, hath treated it as a vulgar prejudice, and maintained that the mind is only a succession of ideas and impressions without any subject; his opinion, however contrary to the common apprehensions of mankind, deserves respect. I beg therefore, once for all, that no offence may be taken at charging this or other metaphysical notions with absurdity, or with being contrary to the common sense of mankind. No disparagement is meant to the understandings of the authors or maintainers of such opinions. Indeed, they commonly proceed, not from defect of understanding, but from an excess of refinement the reasoning that leads to them often gives new light to the subject, and shews real genius and deep penetration in the author; and the premises do more than atone for the conclusion.

If there are certain principles, as I think there are, which the constitution of our nature leads us to believe, and which we are under a necessity to take for granted in the common concerns of life, without being able to give a reason for them—these are what we call the principles of common sense; and what is manifestly contrary to them, is what we call absurd.

Indeed, if it is true, and to be received as a principle of philosophy, that sensation and thought may be without a thinking being, it must be acknowledged to be the most wonderful discovery that this or any other age hath produced. The received doctrine of ideas is the principle from which it is deduced, and of which indeed it seems to be a just and natural consequence. And it is probable, that it would not have been so late a discovery, but that it is so shocking and repugnant to the common apprehensions of mankind, that it required an uncommon degree of philosophical intrepidity to usher it into the world. It is a fundamental principle of the ideal system, that every object of thought must be an impression or an idea—that is, a faint copy of some preceding impression. This is a principle so commonly received, that the author above mentioned, although his whole system is built upon it, never offers the least proof of it. It is upon this principle, as a fixed point, that he erects his metaphysical engines, to overturn heaven and earth, body and spirit. And, indeed, in my apprehension, it is altogether sufficient for the purpose. For, if impressions and ideas are the only objects of thought, then heaven and earth, and body and spirit, and everything you please, must signify only impressions and ideas, or they must be words without any meaning. It seems, therefore, that this notion, however strange, is closely connected with the received doctrine of ideas, and we must either admit the conclusion, or call in question the premises.

Ideas seem to have something in their nature unfriendly to other existences. They were first introduced into philosophy, in the humble character of images or representatives of things : and in this character they seemed not only to be inoffensive, but to serve admirably well for explaining the operations of the human understanding. But, since men began to reason clearly and distinctly about them, they have by degrees supplanted their constituents, and undermined the existence of everything but themselves. First, they discarded all secondary qualities of bodies; and it was found out by their means, that fire is not hot, nor snow cold, nor honey sweet; and, in a word, that heat and cold, sound, colour, taste, and smell, are nothing but ideas or impressions. Bishop Berkeley advanced them a step higher, and found out, by just reasoning from the same principles, that extension, solidity, space, figure, and body, are ideas, and that there is nothing in nature but ideas and spirits. But the triumph of ideas was completed by the "Treatise of Human Nature," which discards spirits also, and leaves ideas and impressions as the sole existences in the universe. What if, at last, having nothing else to contend with, they should fall foul of one another, and leave no existence in nature at all? This would surely bring philosophy into danger; for what should we have left to talk or to dispute about?

However, hitherto these philosophers acknowledge the existence of impressions and ideas; they acknowledge certain laws of attraction, or rules of precedence, according to which, ideas and impressions range themselves in various forms, and succeed one another: but that they should belong to a mind, as its proper goods and chattels, this they have found to be a vulgar error. These ideas are as free and independent as the birds of the air, or as Epicurus's atoms when they pursued their journey in the vast inane. Shall we conceive them like the films of things in the Epicurean system?

> Principio hoc dico, rerum simulacra vagari,
> Multa modis multis, in cunctas undique parteis
> Tenuia, quæ facile inter se junguntur in auris,
> Obvia cum veniunt.—LUCR.

Or do they rather resemble Aristotle's intelligible species, after they are shot forth from the object, and before they have yet struck upon the passive intellect? But why should we seek to compare them with anything, since there is nothing in nature but themselves? They make the whole furniture of the universe; starting into existence, or out of it, without any cause; combining into parcels, which the vulgar call *minds*; and succeeding one another by fixed laws, without time, place, or author of those laws.

Yet, after all, these self-existent and independent ideas look pitifully naked and destitute, when left thus alone in the universe, and seem, upon the whole, to be in a worse condition than they were before. Des Cartes, Malebranche, and Locke, as they made much use of ideas, treated them handsomely, and provided them in decent accommodation; lodging them either in the pineal gland, or in the pure intellect, or even in the divine mind. They moreover clothed them with a commission, and made them representatives of things, which gave them some dignity and character. But the "Treatise of Human Nature," though no less indebted to them, seems to have made but a bad return, by bestowing upon them this independent existence: since thereby they are turned out of house and home, and set adrift in the world, without friend or connection, without a rag to cover their nakedness; and who knows but the whole system of ideas may perish by the indiscreet zeal of their friends to exalt them?

However this may be, it is certainly a most amazing discovery that thought and ideas may be without any thinking being—a discovery big with consequences which cannot easily be traced by those deluded mortals who think and reason in the common track. We were always apt to imagine, that thought supposed a thinker, and love a lover, and treason a traitor: but this, it seems, was all a mistake; and it is found out, that there may be treason without a traitor, and love without a lover, laws without a legislator, and punishment without a sufferer, succession without time, and motion without anything moved, or space in which it may move: or if, in these cases, ideas are the lover, the sufferer, the traitor, it were to be wished that the author of this discovery had farther condescended to acquaint us whether ideas can converse together, and be under obligations of duty or gratitude to each other; whether they can make promises and enter into leagues and covenants, and fulfil or break them, and be punished for the breach. If one set of ideas makes a covenant, another breaks it, and a third is punished for it, there is reason to think that justice is no natural virtue in this system.

It seemed very natural to think, that the "Treatise of Human Nature" required an author, and a very ingenious one too; but now we learn that it is only a set of ideas which came together and arranged themselves by certain associations and attractions.

After all, this curious system appears not to be fitted to the present state of human nature. How far it may suit some choice spirits, who are refined from the dregs of common sense, I cannot say. It is acknowledged, I think, that even these can enter into this system only in their most speculative hours, when they soar so high in pursuit of those self-existent ideas as to lose sight of all other things. But when they condescend to mingle again with the human race, and to converse with a friend, a companion, or a fellow-citizen, the ideal system vanishes; common sense, like an irresistible torrent, carries them along; and, in spite of all their reasoning and philosophy, they believe their own existence, and the existence of other things.

Indeed, it is happy they do so; for, if they should carry their closet belief into the world, the rest of mankind would consider them as diseased, and send them to an infirmary. Therefore, as Plato required certain previous qualifications of those who entered his school, I think it would be prudent for the doctors of this ideal philosophy to do the same, and to refuse admittance to every man who is so weak as to imagine that he ought to have the same belief in solitude and in company, or that his principles ought to have any influence upon his practice ; for this philosophy is like a hobby-horse, which a man in bad health may ride in his closet, without hurting his reputation; but, if he should take him abroad with him to church, or to the exchange, or to the play-house, his heir would immediately call a jury, and seize his estate.

Section VII.

THE CONCEPTION AND BELIEF OF A SENTIENT BEING OR MIND IS SUGGESTED BY OUR CONSTITUTION—THE NOTION OF RELATIONS NOT ALWAYS GOT BY COMPARING THE RELATED IDEAS.

Leaving this philosophy, therefore, to those who have occasion for it, and can use it discreetly as a chamber exercise, we may still inquire how the rest of mankind, and even the adepts themselves, except in some solitary moments, have got so strong and irresistible a belief, that thought must have a subject, and be the act of some thinking being; how every man believes himself to be something distinct from his ideas and impressions—something which continues the same identical self when all his ideas and impressions are changed. It is impossible to trace the origin of this opinion in history; for all languages have it interwoven in their original construction. All nations have always believed it. The constitution of all laws and governments, as well as the common transactions of life, suppose it.

It is no less impossible for any man to recollect when he himself came by this notion; for, as far back as we can remember, we were already in possession of it, and as fully persuaded of our own existence, and the existence of other things, as that one and one make two. It seems, therefore, that this opinion preceded all reasoning, and experience, and instruction; and this is the more probable, because we could not get it by any of these means. It appears, then, to be an undeniable fact, that, from thought or sensation, all mankind, constantly and invariably, from the first dawning of reflection, do infer a power or faculty of thinking and a permanent being or mind to which that faculty belongs; and that we as invariably ascribe all the various kinds of sensation and thought we are conscious of, to one individual mind or self.

But by what rules of logic we make these inferences, it is impossible to shew; nay, it is impossible to shew how our sensations and thoughts can give us the very notion and conception either of a mind or of a faculty. The faculty of smelling is something very different from the actual sensation of smelling; for the faculty may remain when we have no sensation. And the mind is no less different from the faculty; for it continues the same individual being when that faculty is lost. Yet this sensation suggests to us both a faculty and a mind; and not only suggests the notion of them, but creates a belief of their existence; although it is impossible to discover, by reason, any tie or connection between one and the other.

What shall we say, then? Either those inferences which we draw from our sensations—namely, the existence of a mind, and of powers or faculties belonging to it—are prejudices of philosophy or education, mere fictions of the mind, which a wise man should throw off as he does the belief of fairies; or they are judgments of nature—judgments not got by comparing ideas, and perceiving agreements and disagreements, but immediately inspired by our constitution.

If this last is the case, as I apprehend it is, it will be impossible to shake off those opinions, and we must yield to them at last, though we struggle hard to get rid of them. And if we could, by a determined obstinacy, shake off the principles of our nature, this is not to act the philosopher, but the fool or the madman. It is incumbent upon those who think that these are not natural principles, to shew, in the first place, how we can otherwise get the notion of a mind and its faculties; and then to shew how we come to deceive ourselves into the opinion that sensation cannot be without a sentient being.

It is the received doctrine of philosophers, that our notions of relations can only be got by comparing the related ideas: but, in the present case, there seems to be an instance to the contrary. It is not by having first the notions of mind and sensation, and then comparing them together, that we perceive the one to have the relation of a subject or substratum, and the other that of an act or operation: on the contrary, one of the related things—to wit, sensation—suggests to us both the correlate and the relation.

I beg leave to make use of the word *suggestion*, because I know not one more proper, to express a power of the mind, which seems entirely to have escaped the notice of philosophers, and to which we owe many of our simple notions which are neither impressions nor ideas, as well as many original principles of belief. I shall endeavor to illustrate, by an example, what I understand by this word. We all know, that a certain kind of sound suggests immediately to the mind, a coach passing in the street; and not only produces the imagination, but the belief, that a coach is passing. Yet there is here no comparing of ideas, no perception of agreements or disagreements, to produce this belief: nor is there the least similitude between the sound we hear and the coach we imagine and believe to be passing.*

* "The word *suggest*" (says Mr. Stewart, in reference to the preceding passage) "is much used by Berkeley, in this appropriate and technical sense, not only in his 'Theory of Vision,' but in his 'Prin-

It is true that this suggestion is not natural and original; it is the result of experience and habit. But I think it appears, from what hath been said, that there are natural suggestions: particularly, that sensation suggests the notion of present existence, and the belief that what we perceive or feel does now exist; that memory suggests the notion of past existence, and the belief that what we remember did exist in time past; and that our sensations and thoughts do also suggest the notion of a mind, and the belief of its existence, and of its relation to our

ciples of Human Knowledge,' and in his 'Minute Philosopher.' It expresses, indeed, the cardinal principle on which his 'Theory of Vision' hinges, and is now so incorporated with some of our best metaphysical speculations, that one cannot easily conceive how the use of it was so long dispensed with. Locke uses the word *excite* for the same purpose; but it seems to imply an hypothesis concerning the *mechanism* of the mind, and by no means expresses the fact in question with the same force and precision.

"It is remarkable, that Dr. Reid should have thought it incumbent on him to apologise for introducing into philosophy a word so familiar to every person conversant with Berkeley's works. 'I beg leave to make use of the word *suggestion*, because,' &c. . . . .

"So far Dr. Reid's use of the word coincides exactly with that of Berkeley; but the former will be found to annex to it a meaning more extensive than the latter, by employing it to comprehend, not only those *intimations* which are the result of experience and habit; but another class of *intimations*, (quite overlooked by Berkeley,) those which result from the original frame of the human mind."—*Dissertation on the History of Metaphysical and Ethical Science.* P. 167. Second edition.

Mr. Stewart might have adduced, perhaps, a higher and, certainly, a more proximate authority, in favour, not merely of the term in general, but of Reid's restricted employment of it, as an intimation of what he and others have designated the Common Sense of mankind. The following sentence of Tertullian contains a singular anticipation, both of the philosophy and of the philosophical phraseology of our author. Speaking of the universal belief of the soul's immortality:—"Natura pleraque *suggeruntur*, quasi de *publico sensu* quo animam Deus ditare dignatus est."—DE ANIMA, c. 2.

Some strictures on Reid's employment of the term *suggestion* may be seen in the "Versuche" of Tetens, I., p. 508, sqq.—H.

thoughts. By a like natural principle it is, that a beginning of existence, or any change in nature, suggests to us the notion of a cause, and compels our belief of its existence. And, in like manner, as shall be shewn when we come to the sense of touch, certain sensations of touch, by the constitution of our nature, suggest to us extension, solidity, and motion, which are nowise like to sensations, although they have been hitherto confounded with them.

Section VIII.

THERE IS A QUALITY OR VIRTUE IN BODIES, WHICH WE CALL THEIR SMELL—HOW THIS IS CONNECTED IN THE IMAGINATION WITH THE SENSATION.

We have considered smell as signifying a sensation, feeling, or impression upon the mind; and in this sense, it can only be in a mind, or sentient being: but it is evident that mankind gives the name of *smell* much more frequently to something which they conceive to be external, and to be a quality of body: they understand something by it which does not at all infer a mind; and have not the least difficulty in conceiving the air perfumed with aromatic odours in the deserts of Arabia, or in some uninhabited island, where the human foot never trod. Every sensible day-labourer hath as clear a notion of this, and as full a conviction of the possibility of it, as he hath of his own existence; and can no more doubt of the one than of the other.

Suppose that such a man meets with a modern philosopher, and wants to be informed what smell in plants is. The philosopher tells him, that there is no smell in plants, nor in anything but in the mind; that it is impossible there can be smell but in a mind; and that all this hath been demonstrated by modern philosophy. The plain man will, no doubt, be apt to think him merry: but, if he finds that he is serious, his next conclusion will be that he is mad; or that philosophy, like magic, puts men into a new world, and gives them different faculties from common men. And thus philosophy and common sense are set at variance. But who is to blame for it? In my opinion the philosopher is to blame. For if he means by smell, what the rest of mankind most commonly mean, he is certainly mad. But if he puts a different meaning upon the word, without observing it himself, or giving warning to others, he abuses language and disgraces philosophy, without doing any service to truth: as if a man should exchange the meaning of the words *daughter* and *cow*, and then endeavour to prove to his plain neighbour, that his cow is his daughter, and his daughter his cow.

I believe there is not much more wisdom in many of those paradoxes of the ideal philosophy, which to plain sensible men appear to be palpable absurdities, but with the adepts pass for profound discoveries. I resolve, for my own part, always to pay a great regard to the dictates of common sense, and not to depart from them without absolute necessity: and, therefore, I am apt to think that there is really something in the rose or lily, which is by the vulgar called *smell*, and which continues to exist when it is not smelled: and shall proceed to inquire what this is; how we come by the notion of it; and what relation this quality or virtue of smell hath to the sensation which we have been obliged to call by the same name, for want of another.

Let us therefore suppose, as before, a person beginning to exercise the sense of smelling; a little experience will discover to him that the nose is the organ of this sense, and that the air, or something in the air, is a medium of it. And finding, by farther experience, that, when a rose is near, he has a certain sensation, when it is removed, the sensation is gone, he finds a connection in nature betwixt the rose and this sensation. The rose is considered as a cause, occasion, or antecedent of the sensation; the sensation as an effect or consequence of the presence of the rose; they are associated in the mind, and constantly found conjoined in the imagination.

But here it deserves our notice, that, although the sensation may seem more closely related to the mind its subject, or to the nose its organ, yet neither of these connections operate so powerfully upon the imagination as its connection with the rose its concomitant. The reason of this seems to be, that its connection with the mind is more general, and noway distinguisheth it from other smells, or even from tastes, sounds, and other kinds of sensations. The relation it hath to the organ is likewise general, and doth not distinguish it from other smells; but the connection it hath with the rose is special and constant; by which means they become almost inseparable in the imagination, in like manner as thunder and lightning, freezing and cold.

Section IX.

THAT THERE IS A PRINCIPLE IN HUMAN NATURE, FROM WHICH THE NOTION OF THIS, AS WELL AS ALL OTHER NATURAL VIRTUES OR CAUSES, IS DERIVED.

In order to illustrate further how we come to conceive a quality or virtue in the rose which we call *smell*, and what this smell is, it is proper to observe, that the mind begins very early to thirst after principles which may direct it in the exertion of its powers. The smell of a rose is a certain affection or feeling of the mind; and, as it is not constant, but comes and goes, we want to know when and where we may expect it; and are uneasy till we find something which, being present, brings this feeling along with it, and, being removed, removes it. This, when found, we call the cause of it; not in a strict and philosophical sense, as if the feeling were really effected or produced by that cause, but in a popular sense; for the mind is satisfied if there is a constant conjunction between them; and such causes are in reality nothing else but laws of nature. Having found the smell thus constantly conjoined with the rose, the mind is at rest, without inquiring whether this conjunction is owing to a real efficiency or not; that being a philosophical inquiry, which does not concern human life. But every discovery of such a constant conjunction is of real importance in life, and makes a strong impression upon the mind.

So ardently do we desire to find everything that happens within our observation thus connected with something else as its cause or occasion, that we are apt to fancy connections upon the slightest grounds; and this weakness is most remarkable in the ignorant, who know least of the real connections established in nature. A man meets with an unlucky accident on a certain day of the year, and, knowing no other cause of his misfortune, he is apt to conceive something unlucky in that day of the calendar; and, if he finds the same connection hold a second time, is strongly confirmed in his superstition. I remember, many years ago, a white ox was brought into this country, of so enormous a size that people came many miles to see him. There happened, some months after, an uncommon fatality among women in child-bearing. Two such uncommon events, following one another, gave a suspicion of their connection, and occasioned a common opinion among the country-people that the white ox was the cause of this fatality.

However silly and ridiculous this opinion was, it sprung from the same root in human nature on which all natural philosophy grows—namely, an eager desire to find out connections in things, and a natural, original, and unaccountable propensity to believe that the connections which we have observed in time past will continue in time to come. Omens, portents, good and bad luck, palmistry, astrology, all the numerous arts of divination and of interpreting dreams, false hypotheses and systems, and true principles in the philosophy of nature, are all built upon the same foundation in the human constitution, and are distinguished only according as we conclude rashly from too few instances, or cautiously from a sufficient induction.

As it is experience only that discovers these connections between natural causes and their effects; without inquiring further, we attribute to the cause some vague and indistinct notion of power or virtue to produce the effect. And, in many cases, the purposes of life do not make it necessary to give distinct names to the cause and the effect. Whence it happens, that, being closely connected in the imagination, although very unlike to each other, one name serves for both; and, in common discourse, is most frequently applied to that which, of the two, is most the object of our attention. This occasions an ambiguity in many words, which, having the same causes in all languages, is common to all, and is apt to be overlooked even by philosophers. Some instances will serve both to illustrate and confirm what we have said.

Magnetism signifies both the tendency of the iron towards the magnet, and the power of the magnet to produce that tendency; and, if it was asked, whether it is a quality of the iron or of the magnet, one would perhaps be puzzled at first; but a little attention would discover, that we conceive a power or virtue in the magnet as the cause, and a motion in the iron as the effect; and, although these are things quite unlike, they are so united in the imagination, that we give the common name of *magnetism* to both. The same thing may be said of *gravitation*, which sometimes signifies the tendency of bodies towards the earth, sometimes the attractive power of the earth, which we conceive as the cause of that tendency. We may observe the same ambiguity in some of Sir Isaac Newton's definitions; and that even in words of his own making. In three of his definitions, he explains very distinctly what he understands by the *absolute* quantity, what by the *accelerative* quantity, and what by the *motive* quantity, of a centripetal force. In the first of these three definitions, centripetal force is put for the cause, which we conceive to be some power or virtue in the centre or central body; in the two last, the same word is put for the effect of this cause, in producing velocity, or in producing motion towards that centre.

Heat signifies a sensation, and *cold* a contrary one; but *heat* likewise signifies a quality or state of bodies, which hath no contrary, but different degrees. When a man feels the same water hot to one hand and cold to the other, this gives him occasion to distinguish between the feeling and the heat of the body; and, although he knows that the sensations are contrary, he does not imagine that the body can have contrary qualities at the same time. And when he finds a different taste in the same body in sickness and in health, he is easily convinced, that the quality in the body called *taste* is the same as before, although the sensations he has from it are perhaps opposite.

The vulgar are commonly charged by philosophers, with the absurdity of imagining the smell in the rose to be something like to the sensation of smelling; but I think unjustly; for they neither give the same epithets to both, nor do they reason in the same manner from them. What is smell in the rose? It is a quality or virtue of the rose, or of something proceeding from it, which we perceive by the sense of smelling; and this is all we know of the matter. But what is smelling? It is an act of the mind, but is never imagined to be a quality of the mind. Again, the sensation of smelling is conceived to infer necessarily a mind or sentient being; but smell in the rose infers no such thing. We say, this body smells sweet, that stinks; but we do not say, this mind smells sweet and that stinks. Therefore, smell in the rose, and the sensation which it causes, are not conceived, even by the vulgar, to be things of the same kind, although they have the same name.

From what hath been said, we may learn that the smell of a rose signifies two things: *First*, a sensation, which can have no existence but when it is perceived, and can only be in a sentient being or mind; *Secondly*, it signifies some power, quality, or virtue, in the rose, or in effluvia proceeding from it, which hath a permanent existence, independent of the mind, and which, by the constitution of nature, produces the sensation in us. By the original constitution of our nature, we are both led to believe that there is a permanent cause of the sensation, and prompted to seek after it; and experience determines us to place it in the rose. The names of all smells, tastes, sounds, as well as heat and cold, have a like ambiguity in all languages; but it deserves our attention, that these names are but rarely, in common language, used to signify the sensations; for the most part, they signify the external qualities which are indicated by the sensations—the cause of which phænomenon I take to be this. Our sensations have very different degrees of strength. Some of them are so quick and lively as to give us a great deal either of pleasure or of uneasiness. When this is the case, we are compelled to attend to the sensation itself, and to make it an object of thought and discourse; we give it a name, which signifies nothing but the sensation; and in this case we readily acknowledge, that the thing meant by that name is in the mind only, and not in anything external. Such are the various kinds of pain, sickness, and the sensations of hunger and other appetites. But, where the sensation is not so interesting as to require to be made an object of thought, our constitution leads us to consider it as a sign of something external, which hath a constant conjunction with it; and, having found what it indicates, we give a name to that: the sensation, having no proper name, falls in as an accessory to the thing signified by it, and is confounded under the same name. So that the name may, indeed, be applied to the sensation, but most properly and commonly is applied to the thing indicated by that sensation. The sensations of smell, taste, sound, and colour, are of infinitely more importance as signs or indications, than they are upon their own account; like the words of a language, wherein we do not attend to the sound but to the sense.

Section X.

WHETHER IN SENSATION THE MIND IS ACTIVE OR PASSIVE?

There is one inquiry remains, Whether, in smelling, and in other sensations, the mind is active or passive? This possibly may seem to be a question about words, or, at least, of very small importance; however, if it leads us to attend more accurately to the operations of our minds than we are accustomed to do, it is, upon that very account, not altogether unprofitable. I think the opinion of modern philosophers is, that in sensation the mind is altogether passive.* And this undoubtedly is so far true, that we cannot raise any sensation in our minds by willing it; and, on the other hand, it seems hardly possible to avoid having the sensation when the object is presented. Yet it seems likewise to be true, that, in proportion as the attention is more or less turned to a sensation or diverted from it, that sensation is more or less perceived and remembered. Every one knows that very intense pain may be diverted by a surprise, or by anything that entirely occupies the mind. When we are engaged in earnest conversation, the clock may strike by us without being heard; at least, we remember not, the next moment, that we did hear it. The noise and tumult of a great trading city is not heard by them who have lived in it all their days; but it stuns those strangers who have lived in the peaceful retirement of the

* This is far too absolutely stated.—H.

country. Whether, therefore, there can be any sensation where the mind is purely passive, I will not say; but I think we are conscious of having given some attention to every sensation which we remember, though ever so recent.

No doubt, where the impulse is strong and uncommon, it is as difficult to withhold attention as it is to forbear crying out in racking pain, or starting in a sudden fright. But how far both might be attained by strong resolution and practice, is not easy to determine. So that, although the Peripatetics had no good reason to suppose an active and a passive intellect, since attention may be well enough accounted an act of the will, yet I think they came nearer to the truth, in holding the mind to be in sensation partly passive and partly active, than the moderns in affirming it to be purely passive. Sensation, imagination, memory and judgment, have, by the vulgar in all ages, been considered as acts of the mind. The manner in which they are expressed in all languages, shews this. When the mind is much employed in them, we say it is very active; whereas, if they were impressions only, as the ideal philosophy would lead us to conceive, we ought, in such a case, rather to say, that the mind is very passive; for, I suppose, no man would attribute great activity to the paper I write upon, because it receives variety of characters.

The relation which the sensation of smell bears to the memory and imagination of it, and to a mind or subject, is common to all our sensations, and, indeed, to all the operations of the mind: the relation it bears to the will is common to it with all the powers of understanding: and the relation it bears to that quality or virtue of bodies which it indicates, is common to it with the sensations of taste, hearing, colour, heat, and cold—so that what hath been said of this sense, may easily be applied to several of our senses, and to other operations of the mind; and this, I hope, will apologize for our insisting so long upon it.

CHAPTER III.

OF TASTING.

A GREAT part of what hath been said of the sense of smelling, is so easily applied to those of tasting and hearing, that we shall leave the application entirely to the reader's judgment, and save ourselves the trouble of a tedious repetition.

It is probable that everything that affects the taste is, in some degree, soluble in the *saliva*. It is not conceivable how any thing should enter readily, and of its own accord, as it were, into the pores of the tongue, palate, and *fauces*, unless it had some chemical affinity to that liquor with which these pores are always replete. It is, therefore, an admirable contrivance of nature, that the organs of taste should always be moist with a liquor which is so universal a menstruum, and which deserves to be examined more than it hath been hitherto, both in that capacity, and as a medical unguent. Nature teaches dogs, and other animals, to use it in this last way; and its subserviency both to taste and digestion shews its efficacy in the former.

It is with manifest design and propriety, that the organ of this sense guards the entrance of the alimentary canal, as that of smell the entrance of the canal for respiration. And from these organs being placed in such manner that everything that enters into the stomach must undergo the scrutiny of both senses, it is plain that they were intended by nature to distinguish wholesome food from that which is noxious. The brutes have no other means of choosing their food; nor would mankind, in the savage state. And it is very probable that the smell and taste, noway vitiated by luxury or bad habits, would rarely, if ever, lead us to a wrong choice of food among the productions of nature; although the artificial compositions of a refined and luxurious cookery, or of chemistry and pharmacy, may often impose upon both, and produce things agreeable to the taste and smell, which are noxious to health. And it is probable that both smell and taste are vitiated, and rendered less fit to perform their natural offices, by the unnatural kind of life men commonly lead in society.

These senses are likewise of great use to distinguish bodies that cannot be distinguished by our other senses, and to discern the changes which the same body undergoes, which, in many cases, are sooner perceived by taste and smell than by any other means. How many things are there in the market, the eating-house, and the tavern, as well as in the apothecary and chemist's shops, which are known to be what they are given out to be, and are perceived to be good or bad in their kind, only by taste or smell? And how far our judgment of things, by means of our senses, might be improved by accurate attention to the small differences of taste and smell, and other sensible qualities, is not easy to determine. Sir Isaac Newton, by a noble effort of his great genius, attempted, from the colour of opaque bodies, to discover the magnitude of the minute pellucid parts of which they are compounded: and who knows what new lights natural philosophy may yet receive from other secondary qualities duly examined?

Some tastes and smells stimulate the nerves and raise the spirits: but such an artificial elevation of the spirits is, by the laws of nature, followed by a depression, which can only be relieved by time, or by the repeated use of the like *stimulus*. By the use of such things we create an appetite for them, which very much resembles, and hath all the force of a natural one. It is in this manner that men acquire an appetite for snuff, tobacco, strong liquors, laudanum, and the like.

Nature, indeed, seems studiously to have set bounds to the pleasures and pains we have by these two senses, and to have confined them within very narrow limits, that we might not place any part of our happiness in them; there being hardly any smell or taste so disagreeable that use will not make it tolerable, and at last perhaps agreeable, nor any so agreeable as not to lose its relish by constant use. Neither is there any pleasure or pain of these senses which is not introduced or followed by some degree of its contrary, which nearly balances it; so that we may here apply the beautiful allegory of the divine Socrates—that, although pleasure and pain are contrary in their nature, and their faces look different ways, yet Jupiter hath tied them so together that he that lays hold of the one draws the other along with it.

As there is a great variety of smells, seemingly simple and uncompounded, not only altogether unlike, but some of them contrary to others, and as the same thing may be said of tastes, it would seem that one taste is not less different from another than it is from a smell: and therefore it may be a question, how all smells come to be considered as one *genus*, and all tastes as another? What is the generical distinction? Is it only that the nose is the organ of the one and the palate of the other? or, abstracting from the organ, is there not in the sensations themselves something common to smells, and something else common to tastes, whereby the one is distinguished from the other? It seems most probable that the latter is the case; and that, under the appearance of the greatest simplicity, there is still in these sensations something of composition.

If one considers the matter abstractly, it would seem that a number of sensations, or, indeed, of any other individual things, which are perfectly simple and uncompounded, are incapable of being reduced into *genera* and *species;* because individuals which belong to a species must have something peculiar to each, by which they are distinguished, and something common to the whole species. And the same may be said of *species* which belong to one *genus*. And, whether this does not imply some kind of composition, we shall leave to metaphysicians to determine.

The sensations both of smell and taste do undoubtedly admit of an immense variety of modifications, which no language can express. If a man was to examine five hundred different wines, he would hardly find two of them that had precisely the same taste. The same thing holds in cheese, and in many other things. Yet, of five hundred different tastes in cheese or wine, we can hardly describe twenty, so as to give a distinct notion of them to one who had not tasted them.

Dr. Nehemiah Grew, a most judicious and laborious naturalist, in a discourse read before the Royal Society, *anno* 1675, hath endeavoured to shew that there are at least sixteen different simple tastes, which he enumerates. How many compounded ones may be made out of all the various combinations of two, three, four, or more of these simple ones, they who are acquainted with the theory of combinations will easily perceive. All these have various degrees of intenseness and weakness. Many of them have other varieties; in some the taste is more quickly perceived upon the application of the sapid body, in others more slowly—in some the sensation is more permanent, in others more transient—in some it seems to undulate or return after certain intervals, in others it is constant; the various parts of the organ—as the lips, the tip of the tongue, the root of the tongue, the *fauces*, the *uvula*, and the throat—are some of them chiefly affected by one sapid body, and others by another. All these, and other varieties of tastes, that accurate writer illustrates by a number of examples. Nor is it to be doubted, but smells, if examined with the same accuracy, would appear to have as great variety.

CHAPTER IV.

OF HEARING.

Section I.

VARIETY OF SOUNDS—THEIR PLACE AND DISTANCE LEARNED BY CUSTOM, WITHOUT REASONING.

Sounds have probably no less variety of modifications, than either tastes or odours. For, first, sounds differ in tone. The ear is capable of perceiving four or five hundred variations of tone in sound, and probably as many different degrees of strength; by combining these, we have above twenty thousand simple sounds that differ either in tone or strength, supposing every tone to be perfect. But it is to be observed, that to make a perfect tone, a great many undulations of elastic air are required, which must all be of equal duration and extent, and follow one another with perfect regularity; and each undulation must be made up of the advance and recoil of innumerable particles of elastic air, whose motions are all uniform in direction, force, and time. Hence we may easily conceive a prodigious variety in the same tone, arising from irregularities of it, occasioned by the constitution, figure, situation, or manner of striking the sonorous body; from the constitution of the elastic medium, or its being disturbed by other motions; and from the constitution of the ear itself, upon which the impression is made.

A flute, a violin, a hautboy, and a French horn, may all sound the same tone and be easily distinguishable. Nay, if twenty human voices sound the same note, and with equal strength, there will still be some difference.

The same voice, while it retains its proper distinctions, may yet be varied many ways, by sickness or health, youth or age, leanness or fatness, good or bad humour. The same words spoken by foreigners and natives—nay, by persons of different provinces of the same nation—may be distinguished.

Such an immense variety of sensations of smell, taste, and sound, surely was not given us in vain. They are signs by which we know and distinguish things without us; and it was fit that the variety of the signs should, in some degree, correspond with the variety of the things signified by them.

It seems to be by custom that we learn to distinguish both the place of things, and their nature, by means of their sound. That such a noise is in the street, such another in the room above me; that this is a knock at my door, that a person walking up stairs—is probably learnt by experience. I remember, that once lying abed, and having been put into a fright, I heard my own heart beat; but I took it to be one knocking at the door, and arose and opened the door oftener than once, before I discovered that the sound was in my own breast. It is probable, that, previous to all experience, we should as little know whether a sound came from the right or left, from above or below, from a great or a small distance, as we should know whether it was the sound of a drum, or a bell, or a cart. Nature is frugal in her operations, and will not be at the expense of a particular instinct, to give us that knowledge which experience will soon produce, by means of a general principle of human nature.

For a little experience, by the constitution of human nature, ties together, not only in our imagination, but in our belief, those things which were in their nature unconnected. When I hear a certain sound, I conclude immediately, without reasoning, that a coach passes by. There are no premises from which this conclusion is inferred by any rules of logic. It is the effect of a principle of our nature, common to us with the brutes.

Although it is by hearing that we are capable of the perceptions of harmony and melody, and of all the charms of music, yet it would seem that these require a higher faculty, which we call *a musical ear*. This seems to be in very different degrees, in those who have the bare faculty of hearing equally perfect; and, therefore, ought not to be classed with the external senses, but in a higher order.

Section II.

OF NATURAL LANGUAGE.

One of the noblest purposes of sound undoubtedly is language, without which mankind would hardly be able to attain any degree of improvement above the brutes. Language is commonly considered as purely an invention of men, who by nature are no less mute than the brutes; but, having a superior degree of invention and reason, have been able to contrive artificial signs of their thoughts and purposes, and to establish them by common consent. But the origin of language deserves to be more carefully inquired into, not only as this inquiry may be of importance for the improvement of language, but as it is related to the present subject, and tends to lay open some of the first principles of human nature. I shall, therefore, offer some thoughts upon this subject.

By language I understand all those signs which mankind use in order to communicate to others their thoughts and intentions, their purposes and desires. And such signs may be conceived to be of two kinds: First, such as have no meaning but what is affixed to them by compact or agreement among those who use them—these are artificial signs; Secondly, such as, previous to all compact or agreement, have a meaning which every man understands by the principles of his nature. Language, so far as it consists of artificial signs, may be called *artificial;* so far as it consists of natural signs, I call it *natural.*

Having premised these definitions, I think it is demonstrable, that, if mankind had not a natural language they could never have invented an artificial one by their reason and ingenuity. For all artificial language supposes some compact or agreement to affix a certain meaning to certain signs; therefore, there must be compacts or agreements before the use of artificial signs; but there can be no compact or agreement without signs, nor without language; and, therefore, there must be a natural language before any artificial language can be invented: which was to be demonstrated.

Had language in general been a human invention, as much as writing or printing, we should find whole nations as mute as the brutes. Indeed, even the brutes have some natural signs by which they express their own thoughts, affections, and desires, and understand those of others. A chick, as soon as hatched, understands the different sounds whereby its dam calls it to food, or gives the alarm of danger. A dog or a horse understands, by nature, when the human voice caresses, and when it threatens him. But brutes, as far as we know, have no notion of contracts or covenants, or of moral obligation to perform them. If nature had given them these notions, she would probably have given them natural signs to express them. And where nature has denied these notions, it is as impossible to acquire them by art, as it is for a blind man to acquire the notion of colours. Some brutes are sensible of honour or disgrace; they have resentment and gratitude; but none of them, as far as we know, can make a promise or plight their faith, having no such notions from their constitution. And if mankind had not these notions by nature, and natural signs to express them by, with all their wit and ingenuity they could never have invented language.

The elements of this natural language of mankind, or the signs that are naturally expressive of our thoughts, may, I think, be reduced to these three kinds: modulations of the voice, gestures, and features. By means of these, two savages who have no common artificial language, can converse together, can communicate their thoughts in some tolerable manner; can ask and refuse, affirm and deny, threaten and supplicate; can traffic, enter into covenants, and plight their faith. This might be confirmed by historical facts of undoubted credit, if it were necessary.

Mankind having thus a common language by nature, though a scanty one, adapted only to the necessities of nature, there is no great ingenuity required in improving it by the addition of artificial signs, to supply the deficiency of the natural. These artificial signs must multiply with the arts of life, and the improvements of knowledge. The articulations of the voice seem to be, of all signs, the most proper for artificial language; and as mankind have universally used them for that purpose, we may reasonably judge that nature intended them for it. But nature probably does not intend that we should lay aside the use of the natural signs; it is enough that we supply their defects by artificial ones. A man that rides always in a chariot, by degrees loses the use of his legs; and one who uses artificial signs only, loses both the knowledge and use of the natural. Dumb people retain much more of the natural language than others, because necessity obliges them to use it. And for the same reason, savages have much more of it than civilized nations. It is by natural signs chiefly that we give force and energy to language; and the less language has of them, it is the less expressive and persuasive. Thus, writing is less expressive than reading, and reading less expressive than speaking without book; speaking without the proper and natural modulations, force, and variations of the voice, is a frigid and dead language, compared with that which is attended with them; it is still more expressive when we add the language of the eyes and features; and is then only in its perfect and natural state, and attended with its proper energy, when to all these we superadd the force of action.

Where speech is natural, it will be an exercise, not of the voice and lungs only, but of all the muscles of the body; like that of dumb people and savages, whose language, as it has more of nature, is more expressive, and is more easily learned.

Is it not pity that the refinements of a civilized life, instead of supplying the defects of natural language, should root it out and plant in its stead dull and lifeless articulations of unmeaning sounds, or the scrawling of insignificant characters? The perfection of language is commonly thought to be, to express human thoughts and sentiments distinctly by these dull signs; but if this is the perfection of artificial language, it is surely the corruption of the natural.

Artificial signs signify, but they do not express; they speak to the understanding, as algebraical characters may do, but the passions, the affections, and the will, hear them not; these continue dormant and inactive, till we speak to them in the language of nature, to which they are all attention and obedience.

It were easy to show, that the fine arts of the musician, the painter, the actor, and the orator, so far as they are expressive—although the knowledge of them requires in us a delicate taste, a nice judgment, and much study and practice—yet they are nothing else but the language of nature, which we brought into the world with us, but have unlearned by disuse, and so find the greatest difficulty in recovering it.

Abolish the use of articulate sounds and writing among mankind for a century, and every man would be a painter, an actor, and an orator. We mean not to affirm that such an expedient is practicable; or, if it were, that the advantage would counterbalance the loss; but that, as men are led by nature and necessity to converse together, they will use every mean in their power to make themselves understood; and where they cannot do this by artificial signs, they will do it, as far as possible, by natural ones: and he that understands perfectly the use of natural signs, must be the best judge in all the expressive arts.

CHAPTER V.

OF TOUCH.

Section I.

OF HEAT AND COLD.

THE senses which we have hitherto considered, are very simple and uniform, each of them exhibiting only one kind of sensation, and thereby indicating only one quality of bodies. By the ear we perceive sounds, and nothing else; by the palate, tastes; and by the nose, odours. These qualities are all likewise of one order, being all secondary qualities; whereas, by touch we perceive not one quality only, but many, and those of very different kinds. The chief of them are heat and cold, hardness and softness, roughness and smoothness, figure, solidity, motion, and extension. We shall consider these in order.

As to heat and cold, it will easily be allowed that they are secondary qualities, of the same order with smell, taste, and sound. And, therefore, what hath been already said of smell, is easily applicable to them; that is, that the words *heat* and *cold* have each of them two significations; they sometimes signify certain sensations of the mind, which can have no existence when they are not felt, nor can exist anywhere but in a mind or sentient-being; but more frequently they signify a quality in bodies, which, by the laws of nature, occasions the sensations of heat and cold in us—a quality which, though connected by custom so closely with the sensation, that we cannot, without difficulty, separate them, yet hath not the least resemblance to it, and may continue to exist when there is no sensation at all.

The sensations of heat and cold are perfectly known; for they neither are, nor can be, anything else than what we feel them to be; but the qualities in bodies which we call *heat* and *cold* are unknown. They are only conceived by us, as unknown causes or occasions of the sensations to which we give the same names. But, though common sense says nothing of the nature of these qualities, it plainly dictates the existence of them; and to deny that there can be heat and cold when they are not felt, is an absurdity too gross to merit confutation. For what could be more absurd, than to say, that the thermometer cannot rise or fall, unless some person be present, or that the coast of Guinea would be as cold as Nova Zembla, if it had no inhabitants?

It is the business of philosophers to investigate, by proper experiments and induction, what heat and cold are in bodies. And whether they make heat a particular element diffused through nature, and accumulated in the heated body, or whether they make it a certain vibration of the parts of the heated body; whether they determine that heat and cold are contrary qualities, as the sensations undoubtedly are contrary, or that heat only is a quality, and cold its privation: these questions are within the province of philosophy; for common sense says nothing on the one side or the other.

But, whatever be the nature of that quality in bodies which we call *heat*, we certainly know this, that it cannot in the least resemble the sensation of heat. It is no less absurd to suppose a likeness between the sensation and the quality, than it would be to suppose that the pain of the gout resembles a square or a triangle. The simplest man that hath common sense, does not imagine the sensation of heat, or anything that resembles that sensation, to be in the fire. He only imagines that there is something in the fire which makes him and other sentient beings feel heat. Yet, as the name of *heat*, in common language, more frequently and more properly signifies this unknown something in the fire, than the sensation occasioned by it, he justly laughs at the philosopher who denies that there is any heat in the fire, and thinks that he speaks contrary to common sense.

Section II.

OF HARDNESS AND SOFTNESS.

Let us next consider hardness and softness; by which words we always understand real properties or qualities of bodies of which we have a distinct conception.

When the parts of a body adhere so firmly that it cannot easily be made to change its figure, we call it *hard;* when its parts are easily displaced, we call it *soft.* This is the notion which all mankind have of hardness and softness; they are neither sensations, nor like any sensation; they were real qualities before they were perceived by touch, and continue to be so when they are not perceived; for if any man will affirm that diamonds were not hard till they were handled, who would reason with him?

There is, no doubt, a sensation by which we perceive a body to be hard or soft. This sensation of hardness may easily be had, by pressing one's hand against the table, and attending to the feeling that ensues, setting aside, as much as possible, all thought of the table and its qualities, or of any external thing. But it is one thing to have the sensation, and another to attend to it, and make it a distinct object of reflection. The first is very easy; the last, in most cases, extremely difficult.

We are so accustomed to use the sensation as a sign, and to pass immediately to the hardness signified, that, as far as appears, it was never made an object of thought, either by the vulgar or by philosophers; nor has it a name in any language. There is no sensation more distinct, or more frequent; yet it is never attended to, but passes through the mind instantaneously, and serves only to introduce that quality in bodies, which, by a law of our constitution, it suggests.

There are, indeed, some cases, wherein it is no difficult matter to attend to the sensation occasioned by the hardness of a body; for instance, when it is so violent as to occasion considerable pain: then nature calls upon us to attend to it, and then we acknowledge that it is a mere sensation, and can only be in a sentient being. If a man runs his head with violence against a pillar, I appeal to him whether the pain he feels resembles the hardness of the stone, or if he can conceive anything like what he feels to be in an inanimate piece of matter.

The attention of the mind is here entirely turned towards the painful feeling; and, to speak in the common language of mankind, he feels nothing in the stone, but feels a violent pain in his head. It is quite otherwise when he leans his head gently against the pillar; for then he will tell you that he feels nothing in his head, but feels hardness in the stone. Hath he not a sensation in this case as well as in the other? Undoubtedly he hath; but it is a sensation which nature intended only as a sign of something in the stone; and, accordingly, he instantly fixes his attention upon the thing signified; and cannot, without great difficulty, attend so much to the sensation as to be persuaded that there is any such thing distinct from the hardness it signifies.

But, however difficult it may be to attend to this fugitive sensation, to stop its rapid progress, and to disjoin it from the external quality of hardness, in whose shadow it is apt immediately to hide itself; this is what a philosopher by pains and practice must attain, otherwise it will be impossible for him to reason justly upon this subject, or even to understand what is here advanced. For the last appeal, in subjects of this nature, must be to what a man feels and perceives in his own mind.

It is indeed strange that a sensation which we have every time we feel a body hard, and which, consequently, we can command as often and continue as long as we please, a sensation as distinct and determinate as any other, should yet be so much unknown as never to have been made an object of thought and reflection, nor to have been honoured with a name in any language: that philosophers, as well as the vulgar, should have entirely overlooked it, or confounded it with that quality of bodies which we call *hardness*, to which it hath not the least similitude. May we not hence conclude, that the knowledge of the human faculties is but in its infancy?—that we have not yet learned to attend to those operations of the mind, of which we are conscious every hour of our lives?—that there are habits of inattention acquired very early, which are as hard to be overcome as other habits? For I think it is probable, that the novelty of this sensation will procure some attention to it in children at first; but, being in nowise interesting in itself, as soon as it becomes familiar, it is overlooked, and the attention turned solely to that which it signifies. Thus, when one is learning a language, he attends to the sounds; but when he is master of it, he attends only to the sense of what he would express. If this is the case, we must become as little children again, if we will be philosophers; we must overcome this habit of inattention which has been gathering strength ever since we began to think—a habit, the usefulness of which, in common life, atones for the difficulty it creates to the philosopher in discovering the first principles of the human mind.

The firm cohesion of the parts of a body, is no more like that sensation by which I perceive it to be hard, than the vibration of a sonorous body is like the sound I hear: nor can I possibly perceive, by my reason, any connection between the one and the other. No man can give a reason, why the vibration of a body might not have given the sensation of smelling, and the effluvia of bodies affected our hearing, if it had so pleased our Maker. In like manner, no man can give a reason why the sensations of smell, or taste, or sound, might not have indicated hardness, as well as that sensation which, by our constitution, does indicate it. Indeed, no man can conceive any sensation to resemble any known quality of bodies. Nor can any man show, by any good argument, that all our sensations might not have been as they are, though no body, nor quality of body, had ever existed.

Here, then, is a phænomenon of human nature, which comes to be resolved. Hardness of bodies is a thing that we conceive as distinctly, and believe as firmly, as anything in nature. We have no way of coming at this conception and belief, but by means of a certain sensation of touch, to which hardness hath not the least similitude; nor can we, by any rules of reasoning, infer the one from the other. The question is, How we come by this conception and belief?

First, as to the conception: Shall we call it an idea of sensation, or of reflection? The last will not be affirmed; and as little can the first, unless we will call that an idea of sensation which hath no resemblance to any sensation. So that the origin of this idea of hardness, one of the most common and most distinct we have, is not to be found in all our systems of the mind: not even in those which have so copiously endeavoured to deduce all our notions from sensation and reflection.

But, secondly, supposing we have got the conception of hardness, how come we by the belief of it? Is it self-evident, from comparing the ideas, that such a sensation could not be felt, unless such a quality of bodies existed? No. Can it be proved by probable or certain arguments? No; it cannot. Have we got this belief, then, by tradition, by education, or by experience? No; it is not got in any of these ways. Shall we then throw off this belief as having no foundation in reason? Alas! it is not in our power; it triumphs over reason, and laughs at all the arguments of a philosopher. Even the author of the "Treatise of Human Nature," though he saw no reason for this belief, but many against it, could hardly conquer it in his speculative and solitary moments; at other times, he fairly yielded to it, and confesses that he found himself under a necessity to do so.

What shall we say, then, of this conception, and this belief, which are so unaccountable and untractable? I see nothing left, but to conclude, that, by an original principle of our constitution, a certain sensation of touch both suggests to the mind the conception of hardness, and creates the belief of it: or, in other words, that this sensation is a natural sign of hardness. And this I shall endeavour more fully to explain.

Section III.

OF NATURAL SIGNS.

As in artificial signs there is often neither similitude between the sign and thing signified, nor any connection that arises necessarily from the nature of the things, so it is also in natural signs. The word *gold* has no similitude to the substance signified by it; nor is it in its own nature more fit to signify this than any other substance; yet, by habit and custom, it suggests this and no other. In like manner, a sensation of touch suggests hardness, although it hath neither similitude to hardness, nor, as far as we can perceive, any necessary connection with it. The difference betwixt these two signs lies only in this—that, in the first, the suggestion is the effect of habit and custom; in the second, it is not the effect of habit, but of the original constitution of our minds.

It appears evident from what hath been said on the

subject of language, that there are natural signs as well as artificial; and particularly, that the thoughts, purposes, and dispositions of the mind, have their natural signs in the features of the face, the modulation of the voice, and the motion and attitude of the body: that, without a natural knowledge of the connection between these signs and the things signified by them, language could never have been invented and established among men: and, that the fine arts are all founded upon this connection, which we may call *the natural language of mankind.* It is now proper to observe, that there are different orders of natural signs, and to point out the different classes into which they may be distinguished, that we may more distinctly conceive the relation between our sensations and the things they suggest, and what we mean by calling sensations signs of external things.

The first class of natural signs comprehends those whose connection with the thing signified is established by nature, but discovered only by experience. The whole of genuine philosophy consists in discovering such connections, and reducing them to general rules. The great Lord Verulam had a perfect comprehension of this, when he called it *an interpretation of nature.* No man ever more distinctly understood or happily expressed the nature and foundation of the philosophic art. What is all we know of mechanics, astronomy, and optics, but connections established by nature, and discovered by experience or observation, and consequences deduced from them? All the knowledge we have in agriculture, gardening, chemistry, and medicine, is built upon the same foundation. And if ever our philosophy concerning the human mind is carried so far as to deserve the name of science, which ought never to be despaired of, it must be by observing facts, reducing them to general rules, and drawing just conclusions from them. What we commonly call natural *causes* might, with more propriety, be called natural *signs*, and what we call *effects*, the things signified. The causes have no proper efficiency or causality, as far as we know: and all we can certainly affirm is, that nature hath established a constant conjunction between them and the things called their effects; and hath given to mankind a disposition to observe those connections, to confide in their continuance, and to make use of them for the improvement of our knowledge, and increase of our power.

A second class is that wherein the connection between the sign and thing signified, is not only established by nature, but discovered to us by a natural principle, without reasoning or experience. Of this kind are the natural signs of human thoughts, purposes, and desires, which have been already mentioned as the natural language of mankind. An infant may be put into a fright by an angry countenance, and soothed again by smiles and blandishments. A child that has a good musical ear, may be put to sleep or to dance, may be made merry or sorrowful, by the modulation of musical sounds. The principles of all the fine arts, and of what we call *a fine taste*, may be resolved into connections of this kind. A fine taste may be improved by reasoning and experience; but if the first principles of it were not planted in our minds by nature, it could never be acquired. Nay, we have already made it appear, that a great part of this knowledge which we have by nature, is lost by the disuse of natural signs, and the substitution of artificial in their place.

A third class of natural signs comprehends those which, though we never before had any notion or conception of the thing signified, do suggest it, or conjure it up, as it were, by a natural kind of magic, and at once give us a conception and create a belief of it. I shewed formerly, that our sensations suggest to us a sentient being or mind to which they belong—a being which hath a permanent existence, although the sensations are transient and of short duration—a being which is still the same, while its sensations and other operations are varied ten thousand ways—a being which hath the same relation to all that infinite variety of thoughts, purposes, actions, affections, enjoyments, and sufferings, which we are conscious of, or can remember. The conception of a mind is neither an idea of sensation nor of reflection; for it is neither like any of our sensations, nor like anything we are conscious of. The first conception of it, as well as the belief of it, and of the common relation it bears to all that we are conscious of, or remember, is suggested to every thinking being, we do not know how.

The notion of hardness in bodies, as well as the belief of it, are got in a similar manner; being, by an original principle of our nature, annexed to that sensation which we have when we feel a hard body. And so naturally and necessarily does the sensation convey the notion and belief of hardness, that hitherto they have been confounded by the most acute inquirers into the principles of human nature, although they appear, upon accurate reflection, not only to be different things, but as unlike as pain is to the point of a sword.

It may be observed, that, as the first class of natural signs I have mentioned is the foundation of true philosophy, and the second the foundation of the fine arts, or of taste—so the last is the foundation of common sense—a part of human nature which hath never been explained.

I take it for granted, that the notion of hardness, and the belief of it, is first got by means of that particular sensation which, as far back as we can remember, does invariably suggest it; and that, if we had never had such a feeling, we should never have had any notion of hardness. I think it is evident, that we cannot, by reasoning from our sensations, collect the existence of bodies at all, far less any of their qualities. This hath been proved by unanswerable arguments by the Bishop of Cloyne, and by the author of the "Treatise of Human Nature." It appears as evident that this connection between our sensations and the conception and belief of external existences cannot be produced by habit, experience, education, or any principle of human nature that hath been admitted by philosophers. At the same time, it is a fact that such sensations are invariably connected with the conception and belief of external existences. Hence, by all rules of just reasoning, we must conclude that this connection is the effect of our constitution, and ought to be considered as an original principle of human nature, till we find some more general principle into which it may be resolved.*

Section IV.

OF HARDNESS, AND OTHER PRIMARY QUALITIES.

Further, I observe that hardness is a quality, of which we have as clear and distinct a conception as of anything whatsoever. The cohesion of the parts of a body with more or less force, is perfectly understood, though its cause is not; we know what it is, as well as how it affects the touch. It is, therefore, a quality of a quite different order from those secondary qualities we have already taken notice of, whereof we know no more naturally than that they are adapted to raise certain sensations in us. If hardness were a quality of the same kind, it would be a proper inquiry for philosophers, what hardness in bodies is? and we should have had various hypotheses about it, as well as about colour and heat.

* This whole doctrine of *natural signs*, on which his philosophy is in a great measure established, was borrowed by Reid, in principle, and even in expression, from Berkeley. Compare "Minute Philosopher," Dial. IV., §§ 7, 11, 12; "New Theory of Vision," §§ 144, 147; "Theory of Vision Vindicated," §§ 38-43.—H.

But it is evident that any such hypothesis would be ridiculous. If any man should say, that hardness in bodies is a certain vibration of their parts, or that it is certain effluvia emitted by them which affect our touch in the manner we feel—such hypotheses would shock common sense; because we all know that, if the parts of a body adhere strongly, it is hard, although it should neither emit effluvia nor vibrate. Yet, at the same time, no man can say, but that effluvia or the vibration of the parts of a body, might have affected our touch, in the same manner that hardness now does, if it had so pleased the Author of our nature; and, if either of these hypotheses is applied to explain a secondary quality—such as smell, or taste, or sound, or colour, or heat—there appears no manifest absurdity in the supposition.

The distinction betwixt primary and secondary qualities hath had several revolutions. Democritus and Epicurus, and their followers, maintained it. Aristotle and the Peripatetics abolished it. Des Cartes, Malebranche, and Locke, revived it, and were thought to have put it in a very clear light. But Bishop Berkeley again discarded this distinction, by such proofs as must be convincing to those that hold the received doctrine of ideas.* Yet, after all, there appears to be a real foundation for it in the principles of our nature.

What hath been said of hardness, is so easily applicable not only to its opposite, softness, but likewise to roughness and smoothness, to figure and motion, that we may be excused from making the application, which would only be a repetition of what hath been said. All these, by means of certain corresponding sensations of touch, are presented to the mind as real external qualities; the conception and the belief of them are invariably

* On this distinction of *Primary* and *Secondary* Qualities, see "Essays on the Intellectual Powers," Essay II., chap. 17, and Note D, at the end of the volume.—H.

connected with the corresponding sensations, by an original principle of human nature. Their sensations have no name in any language; they have not only been overlooked by the vulgar, but by philosophers; or, if they have been at all taken notice of, they have been confounded with the external qualities which they suggest.

Section V.

OF EXTENSION.

It is further to be observed, that hardness and softness, roughness and smoothness, figure and motion, do all suppose extension, and cannot be conceived without it; yet, I think it must, on the other hand, be allowed that, if we had never felt any thing hard or soft, rough or smooth, figured or moved, we should never have had a conception of extension;* so that, as there is good ground to believe that the notion of extension could not be prior to that of other primary qualities, so it is certain that it could not be posterior to the notion of any of them, being necessarily implied in them all.†

Extension, therefore, seems to be a quality *suggested* to us, by the very same sensations which suggest the other qualities above mentioned. When I grasp a ball in my hand, I perceive it at once hard, figured, and ex-

* According to Reid, Extension (Space) is a notion *a posteriori*, the result of experience. According to Kant, it is *a priori*; experience only affording the occasions required by the mind to exert the acts, of which the intuition of space is a condition. To the former it is thus a *contingent*: to the latter, a *necessary* mental possession.—H.

† In this paragraph, to say nothing of others in the "Inquiry," Reid evidently excludes *sight* as a sense, through which the notion of *extension* or space, enters into the mind. In his later work, the "Essays on the Intellectual Powers," he, however, expressly allows that function to *sight and touch*, and to those senses alone. See Essay II., chap. 19, p. 262, quarto edition.—H.

tended. The feeling is very simple, and hath not the least resemblance to any quality of body. Yet it suggests to us three primary qualities perfectly distinct from one another, as well as from the sensation which indicates them. When I move my hand along the table, the feeling is so simple that I find it difficult to distinguish it into things of different natures ; yet, it immediately suggests hardness, smoothness, extension, and motion—things of very different natures, and all of them as distinctly understood as the feeling which suggests them.

We are commonly told by philosophers, that we get the idea of extension by feeling along the extremities of a body, as if there was no manner of difficulty in the matter. I have sought, with great pains, I confess, to find out how this idea can be got by feeling ; but I have sought in vain. Yet it is one of the clearest and most distinct notions we have ; nor is there anything whatsoever about which the human understanding can carry on so many long and demonstrative trains of reasoning.

The notion of extension is so familiar to us from infancy, and so constantly obtruded by everything we see and feel, that we are apt to think it obvious how it comes into the mind ; but upon a narrower examination we shall find it utterly inexplicable. It is true we have feelings of touch, which every moment present extension to the mind ; but how they come to do so, is the question ; for those feelings do no more resemble extension, than they resemble justice or courage—nor can the existence of extended things be inferred from those feelings by any rules of reasoning; so that the feelings we have by touch, can neither explain how we get the notion, nor how we come by the belief of extended things.

What hath imposed upon philosophers in this matter is, that the feelings of touch, which suggest primary qualities, have no names, nor are they ever reflected upon. They pass through the mind instantaneously, and serve only to introduce the notion and belief of external things, which, by our constitution, are connected with them. They are natural signs, and the mind immediately passes to the thing signified, without making the least reflection upon the sign, or observing that there was any such thing. Hence it hath always been taken for granted, that the ideas of extension, figure, and motion, are ideas of sensation, which enter into the mind by the sense of touch, in the same manner as the sensations of sound and smell do by the ear and nose. The sensations of touch are so connected, by our constitution, with the notions of extension, figure, and motion, that philosophers have mistaken the one for the other, and never have been able to discern that they were not only distinct things, but altogether unlike. However, if we will reason distinctly upon this subject, we ought to give names to those feelings of touch; we must accustom ourselves to attend to them, and to reflect upon them, that we may be able to disjoin them from, and to compare them with, the qualities signified or suggested by them.

The habit of doing this is not to be attained without pains and practice; and till a man hath acquired this habit, it will be impossible for him to think distinctly, or to judge right, upon this subject.

Let a man press his hand against the table—*he feels it hard.* But what is the meaning of this?—The meaning undoubtedly is, that he hath a certain feeling of touch, from which he concludes, without any reasoning, or comparing ideas, that there is something external really existing, whose parts stick so firmly together, that they cannot be displaced without considerable force.

There is here a feeling, and a conclusion drawn from it, or some way suggested by it. In order to compare these, we must view them separately, and then consider by what tie they are connected, and wherein they resemble one another. The hardness of the table is the conclusion, the feeling is the medium by which we are led to that conclusion. Let a man attend distinctly to this medium, and to the conclusion, and he will perceive them to be as unlike as any two things in nature. The one is a sensation of the mind, which can have no existence but in a sentient being; nor can it exist one moment longer than it is felt; the other is in the table, and we conclude, without any difficulty, that it was in the table before it was felt, and continues after the feeling is over. The one implies no kind of extension, nor parts, nor cohesion; the other implies all these. Both, indeed, admit of degrees, and the feeling, beyond a certain degree, is a species of pain; but adamantine hardness does not imply the least pain.

And as the feeling hath no similitude to hardness, so neither can our reason perceive the least tie or connection between them; nor will the logician ever be able to shew a reason why we should conclude hardness from this feeling, rather than softness, or any other quality whatsoever. But, in reality, all mankind are led by their constitution to conclude hardness from this feeling.

The sensation of heat, and the sensation we have by pressing a hard body, are equally feelings; nor can we, by reasoning, draw any conclusion from the one but what may be drawn from the other; but, by our constitution, we conclude from the first an obscure or occult quality, of which we have only this relative conception, that it is something adapted to raise in us the sensation of heat; from the second, we conclude a quality of which we have a clear and distinct conception—to wit, the hardness of the body.

Section VI.

OF EXTENSION.

To put this matter in another light, it may be proper to try, whether from sensation alone we can collect any notion of extension, figure, motion, and space. I take it for granted, that a blind man hath the same notions of extension, figure, and motion, as a man that sees; that Dr. Saunderson had the same notion of a cone, a cylinder, and a sphere, and of the motions and distances of the heavenly bodies, as Sir Isaac Newton.

As sight, therefore, is not necessary for our acquiring those notions, we shall leave it out altogether in our inquiry into the first origin of them; and shall suppose a blind man, by some strange distemper, to have lost all the experience, and habits, and notions he had got by touch; not to have the least conception of the existence, figure, dimensions, or extension, either of his own body, or of any other; but to have all his knowledge of external things to acquire anew, by means of sensation, and the power of reason, which we suppose to remain entire.

We shall, first, suppose his body fixed immovably in one place, and that he can only have the feelings of touch, by the application of other bodies to it. Suppose him first to be pricked with a pin—this will, no doubt, give a smart sensation: he feels pain; but what can he infer from it? Nothing, surely, with regard to the existence or figure of a pin. He can infer nothing from this species of pain, which he may not as well infer from the gout or sciatica. Common sense may lead him to think that this pain has a cause; but whether this cause is body or spirit, extended or unextended, figured or not figured, he cannot possibly, from any principles he is supposed to have, form the least conjecture. Having had formerly no notion of body or of extension, the prick of a pin can give him none.

Suppose, next, a body not pointed, but blunt, is applied to his body with a force gradually increased until it bruises him. What has he got by this, but another sensation or train of sensations, from which he is able to conclude as little as from the former? A scirrhous tumour in any inward part of the body, by pressing upon the adjacent parts, may give the same kind of sensation as the pressure of an external body, without conveying any notion but that of pain, which, surely, hath no resemblance to extension.

Suppose, thirdly, that the body applied to him touches a larger or a lesser part of his body. Can this give him any notion of its extension or dimensions? To me it seems impossible that it should, unless he had some previous notion of the dimensions and figure of his own body, to serve him as a measure. When my two hands touch the extremities of a body, if I know them to be a foot asunder, I easily collect that the body is a foot long; and, if I know them to be five feet asunder, that it is five feet long; but, if I know not what the distance of my hands is, I cannot know the length of the object they grasp; and, if I have no previous notion of hands at all, or of distance between them, I can never get that notion by their being touched.

Suppose, again, that a body is drawn along his hands or face, while they are at rest. Can this give him any notion of space or motion? It no doubt gives a new feeling; but how it should convey a notion of space or motion to one who had none before, I cannot conceive. The blood moves along the arteries and veins, and this motion, when violent, is felt: but I imagine no man, by this feeling, could get the conception of space or motion, if he had it not before. Such a motion may give a certain succession of feelings, as the colic may do; but no feelings, nor any combination of feelings, can ever resemble space or motion

Let us next suppose, that he makes some instinctive effort to move his head or his hand; but that no motion follows, either on account of external resistance, or of palsy. Can this effort convey the notion of space and motion to one who never had it before? Surely it cannot.

Last of all, let us suppose that he moves a limb by

instinct, without having had any previous notion of space or motion. He has here a new sensation, which accompanies the flexure of joints, and the swelling of muscles. But how this sensation can convey into his mind the idea of space and motion, is still altogether mysterious and unintelligible. The motions of the heart and lungs are all performed by the contraction of muscles, yet give no conception of space or motion. An embryo in the womb has many such motions, and probably the feelings that accompany them, without any idea of space or motion.

Upon the whole, it appears that our philosophers have imposed upon themselves and upon us, in pretending to deduce from sensation the first origin of our notions of external existences, of space, motion, and extension,* and all the primary qualities of body—that is, the qualities whereof we have the most clear and distinct conception. These qualities do not at all tally with any system of the human faculties that hath been advanced. They have no resemblance to any sensation, or to any operation of our minds; and, therefore, they cannot be ideas either of sensation or of reflection. The very conception of them is irreconcilable to the principles of all our philosophic systems of the understanding. The belief of them is no less so.

* That the notion of Space is a necessary condition of thought, and that, as *such*, it is impossible to derive it from experience, has been cogently demonstrated by Kant. But that we may not, through sense, have empirically an immediate perception of something *extended*, I have yet seen no valid reason to doubt. The *a priori* Conception does not exclude the *a posteriori* Perception; and this latter cannot be rejected without belying the evidence of consciousness, which assures us that we are immediately cognizant, not only of a *Self* but of a *Not Self*, not only of *mind* but of *matter:* and matter cannot be immediately known—that is known as existing —except as something extended. In this, however, I venture a step beyond Reid and Stewart, no less than beyond Kant; though I am convinced that the philosophy of the two former tended to this conclusion, which is, in fact, that of the common sense of mankind.—H.

Section VII.

OF THE EXISTENCE OF A MATERIAL WORLD.

It is beyond our power to say when, or in what order, we came by our notions of these qualities. When we trace the operations of our minds as far back as memory and reflection can carry us, we find them already in possession of our imagination and belief, and quite familiar to the mind: but how they came first into its acquaintance, or what has given them so strong a hold of our belief, and what regard they deserve, are, no doubt, very important questions in the philosophy of human nature.

Shall we, with the Bishop of Cloyne, serve them with a *quo warranto*, and have them tried at the bar of philosophy, upon the statute of the ideal system? Indeed, in this trial they seem to have come off very pitifully; for, although they had very able counsel, learned in the law—viz., Des Cartes, Malebranche, and Locke, who said everything they could for their clients—the Bishop of Cloyne, believing them to be aiders and abetters of heresy and schism, prosecuted them with great vigour, fully answered all that had been pleaded in their defence, and silenced their ablest advocates, who seem, for half a century past, to decline the argument, and to trust to the favour of the jury rather than to the strength of their pleadings.

Thus, the wisdom of *philosophy* is set in opposition to the *common sense* of mankind. The first pretends to demonstrate, *a priori*, that there can be no such thing as a material world; that sun, moon, stars, and earth, vegetable and animal bodies, are, and can be nothing else, but sensations in the mind, or images of those sensations in the memory and imagination; that, like pain and joy, they can have no existence when they are not thought of. The last can conceive no otherwise of this opinion, than as a kind of metaphysical lunacy, and concludes that too much learning is apt to make men mad; and that the man who seriously entertains this belief, though in other respects he may be a very good man, as a man may be who believes that he is made of glass; yet, surely he hath a soft place in his understanding, and hath been hurt by much thinking.

This opposition betwixt philosophy and common sense, is apt to have a very unhappy influence upon the philosopher himself. He sees human nature in an odd, unamiable, and mortifying light. He considers himself, and the rest of his species, as born under a necessity of believing ten thousand absurdities and contradictions, and endowed with such a pittance of reason as is just sufficient to make this unhappy discovery: and this is all the fruit of his profound speculations. Such notions of human nature tend to slacken every nerve of the soul, to put every noble purpose and sentiment out of countenance, and spread a melancholy gloom over the whole face of things.

If this is wisdom, let me be deluded with the vulgar. I find something within me that recoils against it, and inspires more reverent sentiments of the human kind, and of the universal administration. Common Sense and Reason* have both one author; that Almighty Author in all whose other works we observe a consistency, uniformity, and beauty which charm and delight the understanding: there must, therefore, be some order and consistency in the human faculties, as well as in other parts of his workmanship. A man that thinks reverently of his own kind, and esteems true wisdom and philosophy, will not be fond, nay, will be very suspicious, of such strange and paradoxical opinions. If they are false, they disgrace philosophy; and, if they are true,

* The reader will again notice this and the other instances which follow, of the inaccuracy of Reid's language in his earlier work, constituting, as different, *Reason* and *Common Sense*.—H.

they degrade the human species, and make us justly ashamed of our frame.

To what purpose is it for philosophy to decide against common sense in this or any other matter? The belief of a material world is older, and of more authority, than any principles of philosophy. It declines the tribunal of reason,* and laughs at all the artillery of the logician. It retains its sovereign authority in spite of all the edicts of philosophy, and reason itself must stoop to its orders. Even those philosophers who have disowned the authority of our notions of an external material world, confess that they find themselves under a necessity of submitting to their power.

Methinks, therefore, it were better to make a virtue of necessity; and, since we cannot get rid of the vulgar notion and belief of an external world, to reconcile our reason to it as well as we can; for, if Reason* should stomach and fret ever so much at this yoke, she cannot throw it off; if she will not be the servant of Common Sense, she must be her slave.

In order, therefore, to reconcile Reason to Common Sense* in this matter, I beg leave to offer to the consideration of philosophers these two observations. First, That, in all this debate about the existence of a material world, it hath been taken for granted on both sides, that this same material world, if any such there be, must be the express image of our sensations; that we can have no conception of any material thing which is not like some sensation in our minds; and particularly that the sensations of touch are images of extension, hardness, figure, and motion. Every argument brought against the existence of a material world, either by the Bishop of Cloyne, or by the author of the "Treatise of Human Nature," supposeth this. If this is true, their arguments are conclusive and unanswerable; but, on the other hand, if it is

* See last note.—H.

not true, there is no shadow of argument left. Have those philosophers, then, given any solid proof of this hypothesis, upon which the whole weight of so strange a system rests. No. They have not so much as attempted to do it. But, because ancient and modern philosophers have agreed in this opinion, they have taken it for granted. But let us, as becomes philosophers, lay aside authority; we need not, surely, consult Aristotle or Locke, to know whether pain be like the point of a sword. I have as clear a conception of extension, hardness, and motion, as I have of the point of a sword; and, with some pains and practice, I can form as clear a notion of the other sensations of touch as I have of pain. When I do so, and compare them together, it appears to me clear as daylight, that the former are not of kin to the latter, nor resemble them in any one feature. They are as unlike, yea as certainly and manifestly unlike, as pain is to the point of a sword. It may be true, that those sensations first introduced the material world to our acquaintance; it may be true, that it seldom or never appears without their company; but, for all that, they are as unlike as the passion of anger is to those features of the countenance which attend it.

So that, in the sentence those philosophers have passed against the material world, there is an *error personæ*. Their proof touches not matter, or any of its qualities; but strikes directly against an idol of their own imagination, a material world made of ideas and sensations, which never had nor can have an existence.

Secondly, The very existence of our conceptions of extension, figure and motion, since they are neither ideas of sensation nor reflection, overturns the whole ideal system, by which the material world hath been tried and condemned;* so that there hath been likewise in this sentence an *error juris*.

* It only overturns that Idealism founded on the clumsy hypothesis of ideas being something different, both from the reality they

It is a very fine and a just observation of Locke, that, as no human art can create a single particle of matter, and the whole extent of our power over the material world consists in compounding, combining, and disjoining the matter made to our hands; so, in the world of thought, the materials are all made by nature, and can only be variously combined and disjoined by us. So that it is impossible for reason or prejudice, true or false philosophy, to produce one simple notion or conception, which is not the work of nature, and the result of our constitution. The conception of extension, motion, and the other attributes of matter, cannot be the effect of error or prejudice; it must be the work of nature. And the power or faculty by which we acquire those conceptions, must be something different from any power of the human mind that hath been explained, since it is neither sensation nor reflection.

This I would, therefore, humbly propose, as an *experimentum crucis*, by which the ideal system must stand or fall; and it brings the matter to a short issue: Extension, figure, motion, may, any one or all of them, be taken for the subject of this experiment. Either they are ideas of sensation, or they are not. If any one of them can be shewn to be an idea of sensation, or to have the least resemblance to any sensation, I lay my hand upon my mouth, and give up all pretense to reconcile reason to common sense in this matter, and must suffer the ideal scepticism to triumph. But if, on the other hand, they are not ideas of sensation, nor like to any sensation, then the ideal system is a rope of sand, and all the laboured arguments of the sceptical philosophy against a material world, and against the existence of

represent, and from the mind contemplating their representation, and which, also, derives all such ideas from without. This doctrine may subvert the Idealism of Berkeley, but it even supplies a basis for an Idealism like that of Fichte.—H.

everything but impressions and ideas, proceed upon a false hypothesis.

If our philosophy concerning the mind be so lame with regard to the origin of our notions of the clearest, most simple, and most familiar objects of thought, and the powers from which they are derived, can we expect that it should be more perfect in the account it gives of the origin of our opinions and belief? We have seen already some instances of its imperfection in this respect: and, perhaps, that same nature which hath given us the power to conceive things altogether unlike to any of our sensations, or to any operation of our minds, hath likewise provided for our belief of them, by some part of our constitution hitherto not explained.

Bishop Berkeley hath proved, beyond the possibility of reply, that we cannot by reasoning infer the existence of matter from our sensations; and the author of the "Treatise of Human Nature" hath proved no less clearly, that we cannot by reasoning infer the existence of our own or other minds from our sensations. But are we to admit nothing but what can be proved by reasoning? Then we must be sceptics indeed, and believe nothing at all. The author of the "Treatise of Human Nature" appears to me to be but a half-sceptic. He hath not followed his principles so far as they lead him; but, after having, with unparalleled intrepidity and success, combated vulgar prejudices, when he had but one blow to strike, his courage fails him, he fairly lays down his arms, and yields himself a captive to the most common of all vulgar prejudices—I mean the belief of the existence of his own impressions and ideas.

I beg, therefore, to have the honour of making an addition to the sceptical system, without which I conceive it cannot hang together. I affirm, that the belief of the existence of impressions and ideas, is as little supported by reason, as that of the existence of minds and bodies. No man ever did or could offer any reason for this belief.

Des Cartes took it for granted, that he thought, and had sensations and ideas; so have all his followers done. Even the hero of scepticism hath yielded this point, I crave leave to say, weakly and imprudently. I say so, because I am persuaded that there is no principle of his philosophy that obliged him to make this concession. And what is there in impressions and ideas so formidable, that this all-conquering philosophy, after triumphing over every other existence, should pay homage to them? Besides, the concession is dangerous: for belief is of such a nature, that, if you leave any root, it will spread; and you may more easily pull it up altogether, than say, Hitherto shalt thou go and no further: the existence of impressions and ideas I give up to thee; but see thou pretend to nothing more. A thorough and consistent sceptic will never, therefore, yield this point; and while he holds it, you can never oblige him to yield anything else.

To such a sceptic I have nothing to say; but of the semi-sceptics, I should beg to know, why they believe the existence of their impressions and ideas. The true reason I take to be, because they cannot help it; and the same reason will lead them to believe many other things.

All reasoning must be from first principles; and for first principles no other reason can be given but this, that, by the constitution of our nature, we are under a necessity of assenting to them. Such principles are parts of our constitution, no less than the power of thinking: reason can neither make nor destroy them; nor can it do anything without them: it is like a telescope, which may help a man to see farther, who hath eyes; but, without eyes, a telescope shews nothing at all. A mathematician cannot prove the truth of his axioms, nor can he prove anything, unless he takes them for granted. We cannot prove the existence of our minds, nor even of our thoughts and sensations. A historian, or a witness, can prove nothing, unless it is taken for granted that the memory and senses may be trusted. A natural philosopher can prove nothing, unless it is taken for granted that the course of nature is steady and uniform.

How or when I got such first principles, upon which I build all my reasoning, I know not; for I had them before I can remember: but I am sure they are parts of my constitution, and that I cannot throw them off. That our thoughts and sensations must have a subject, which we call *ourself*, is not therefore an opinion got by reasoning, but a natural principle. That our sensations of touch indicate something external, extended, figured, hard or soft, is not a deduction of reason, but a natural principle. The belief of it, and the very conception of it, are equally parts of our constitution. If we are deceived in it, we are deceived by Him that made us, and there is no remedy.*

I do not mean to affirm, that the sensations of touch do, from the very first, suggest the same notions of body and its qualities which they do when we are grown up. Perhaps Nature is frugal in this, as in her other operations. The passion of love, with all its concomitant

* The philosophers who have most loudly appealed to the veracity of God, and the natural conviction of mankind, in refutation of certain obnoxious conclusions, have too often silently contradicted that veracity and those convictions, when opposed to certain favourite opinions. But it is evident that such authority is either good for all, or good for nothing. Our natural consciousness assures us (and the *fact* of that *assurance* is admitted by philosophers of all opinions) that we have an immediate knowledge of the very things themselves of an external and extended world; and, on the ground of this knowledge alone, is the belief of mankind founded, that such a world really exists. Reid ought, therefore, either to have given up his doctrine of the mere *suggestion* of extension, &c., as subjective notions, on the occasion of sensation, or not to appeal to the Divine veracity, and the common sense of mankind, in favour of conclusions of which that doctrine subverts the foundation. In this inconsistency, Reid has, however, besides Des Cartes, many distinguished copartners.—H.

sentiments and desires, is naturally suggested by the perception of beauty in the other sex; yet the same perception does not suggest the tender passion till a certain period of life. A blow given to an infant, raises grief and lamentation; but when he grows up, it as naturally stirs resentment, and prompts him to resistance. Perhaps a child in the womb, or for some short period of its existence, is merely a sentient being; the faculties by which it perceives an external world, by which it reflects on its own thoughts, and existence, and relation to other things, as well as its reasoning and moral faculties, unfold themselves by degrees; so that it is inspired with the various principles of common sense, as with the passions of love and resentment, when it has occasion for them.

Section VIII.

OF THE SYSTEMS OF PHILOSOPHERS CONCERNING THE SENSES.

All the systems of philosophers about our senses and their objects have split upon this rock, of not distinguishing properly sensations which can have no existence but when they are felt, from the things suggested by them. Aristotle—with as distinguishing a head as ever applied to philosophical disquisitions—confounds these two; and makes every sensation to be the form, without the matter, of the thing perceived by it. As the impression of a seal upon wax has the form of the seal but nothing of the matter of it, so he conceived our sensations to be impressions upon the mind, which bear the image, likeness, or form of the external thing perceived, without the matter of it. Colour, sound, and smell, as well as extension, figure, and hardness, are, according to him, various forms of matter: our sensations are the same forms imprinted on the mind, and perceived in its own intellect. It is evident from this, that Aristotle made no distinction between primary and secondary qualities of bodies, although that distinction was made by Democritus, Epicurus, and others of the ancients.

Des Cartes, Malebranche, and Locke, revived the distinction between primary and secondary qualities; but they made the secondary qualities mere sensations, and the primary ones resemblances of our sensations. They maintained that colour, sound, and heat, are not anything in bodies, but sensations of the mind; at the same time, they acknowledged some particular texture or modification of the body to be the cause or occasion of those sensations; but to this modification they gave no name. Whereas, by the vulgar, the names of colour, heat, and sound, are but rarely applied to the sensations, and most commonly to those unknown causes of them, as hath been already explained. The constitution of our nature leads us rather to attend to the things signified by the sensation than to the sensation itself, and to give a name to the former rather than to the latter. Thus we see, that, with regard to secondary qualities, these philosophers thought with the vulgar, and with common sense. Their paradoxes were only an abuse of words; for when they maintain, as an important modern discovery, that there is no heat in the fire, they mean no more, than that the fire does not feel heat, which every one knew before.

With regard to primary qualities, these philosophers erred more grossly. They indeed believed the existence of those qualities; but they did not at all attend to the sensations that suggest them, which, having no names, have been as little considered as if they had no existence. They were aware that figure, extension, and hardness, are perceived by means of sensations of touch; whence they rashly concluded, that these sensations must be images and resemblances of figure, extension, and hardness.

The received hypothesis of ideas naturally led them to this conclusion: and indeed cannot consist with any other; for, according to that hypothesis, external things must be perceived by means of images of them in the mind; and what can those images of external things in the mind be, but the sensations by which we perceive them?

This, however, was to draw a conclusion from a hypothesis against fact. We need not have recourse to any hypothesis to know what our sensations are, or what they are like. By a proper degree of reflection and attention we may understand them perfectly, and be as certain that they are not like any quality of body, as we can be, that the toothache is not like a triangle. How a sensation should instantly make us conceive and believe the existence of an external thing altogether unlike to it, I do not pretend to know; and when I say that the one suggests the other, I mean not to explain the manner of their connection, but to express a fact, which every one may be conscious of—namely, that, by a law of our nature, such a conception and belief constantly and immediately follow the sensation.

Bishop Berkeley gave new light to this subject, by shewing, that the qualities of an inanimate thing, such as matter is conceived to be, cannot resemble any sensation; that it is impossible to conceive anything like the sensations of our minds, but the sensations of other minds. Every one that attends properly to his sensations must assent to this: yet it had escaped all the philosophers that came before Berkeley; it had escaped even the ingenious Locke, who had so much practised reflection on the operations of his own mind. So difficult it is to attend properly even to our own feelings. They are so accustomed to pass through the mind unobserved and instantly to make way for that which nature intended them to signify, that it is extremely difficult to stop, and survey them; and when we think we have acquired this power, perhaps the mind still fluctuates between the sensation and its associated quality, so that they mix together, and present something to the imagination that is compounded of both. Thus, in a globe or cylinder, whose opposite sides are quite unlike in colour, if you turn it slowly, the colours are perfectly distinguishable and their dissimilitude is manifest; but if it is turned fast, they lose their distinction, and seem to be of one and the same colour.

No succession can be more quick than that of tangible qualities to the sensations with which nature has associated them; but when one has once acquired the art of making them separate and distinct objects of thought, he will then clearly perceive that the maxim of Bishop Berkeley, above-mentioned, is self-evident; and that the features of the face are not more unlike to a passion of the mind which they indicate, than the sensations of touch are to the primary qualities of body.

But let us observe what use the Bishop makes of this important discovery. Why, he concludes, that we can have no conception of an inanimate substance, such as matter is conceived to be, or of any of its qualities; and that there is the strongest ground to believe that there is no existence in nature but minds, sensations, and ideas; if there is any other kind of existence, it must be what we neither have nor can have any conception of. But how does this follow? Why, thus: We can have no conception of anything but what resembles some sensation or idea in our minds; but the sensations and ideas in our minds can resemble nothing but the sensations and ideas in other minds; therefore, the conclusion is evident. This argument, we see, leans upon two propositions. The last of them the ingenious author hath, indeed, made evident to all that understand his reasoning, and can attend to their own sensations: but the first proposition he never attempts to prove; it is taken from the doctrine of ideas, which hath been so universally received by philosophers, that it was thought to need no proof.

We may here again observe, that this acute writer argues from a hypothesis against fact, and against the common sense of mankind. That we can have no conception of anything, unless there is some impression, sensation, or idea, in our minds which resembles it, is indeed an opinion which hath been very generally received among philosophers; but it is neither self-evident, nor hath it been clearly proved; and therefore it hath been more reasonable to call in question this doctrine of philosophers, than to discard the material world, and by that means expose philosophy to the ridicule of all men who will not offer up common sense as a sacrifice to metaphysics.

We ought, however, to do this justice both to the Bishop of Cloyne and to the author of the "Treatise of Human Nature," to acknowledge, that their conclusions are justly drawn from the doctrine of ideas, which has been so universally received. On the other hand, from the character of Bishop Berkeley, and of his predecessors, Des Cartes, Locke, and Malebranche, we may venture to say, that, if they had seen all the consequences of this doctrine, as clearly as the author before mentioned did, they would have suspected it vehemently, and examined it more carefully than they appear to have done.

The theory of ideas, like the Trojan horse, had a specious appearance both of innocence and beauty; but if those philosophers had known that it carried in its belly death and destruction to all science and common sense, they would not have broken down their walls to give it admittance.

That we have clear and distinct conceptions of extension, figure, motion, and other attributes of body, which are neither sensations, nor like any sensation, is a fact of which we may be as certain as that we have sensations. And that all mankind have a fixed belief of an external material world—a belief which is neither got by reasoning nor education, and a belief which we cannot shake off, even when we seem to have strong arguments against it and no shadow of argument for it—is likewise a fact, for which we have all the evidence that the nature of the thing admits. These facts are phænomena of human nature, from which we may justly argue against any hypothesis, however generally received. But to argue from a hypothesis against facts, is contrary to the rules of true philosophy.

CHAPTER VI.

OF SEEING.

Section I.

THE EXCELLENCE AND DIGNITY OF THIS FACULTY.

THE advances made in the knowledge of optics in the last age and in the present, and chiefly the discoveries of Sir Isaac Newton, do honour, not to philosophy only, but to human nature. Such discoveries ought for ever to put to shame the ignoble attempts of our modern sceptics to depreciate the human understanding, and to dispirit men in the search of truth, by representing the human faculties as fit for nothing but to lead us into absurdities and contradictions.

Of the faculties called *the five senses*, sight is without doubt the noblest. The rays of light, which minister to this sense, and of which, without it, we could never have had the least conception, are the most wonderful and astonishing part of the inanimate creation. We must be satisfied of this, if we consider their extreme minuteness; their inconceivable velocity; the regular variety of colours which they exhibit; the invariable laws according to which they are acted upon by other bodies, in their reflections, inflections, and refractions, without the least change of their original properties; and the facility with which they pervade bodies of great density and of the closest texture, without resistance, without crowding or disturbing one another, without giving the least sensible impulse to the lightest bodies.

The structure of the eye, and of all its appurtenances, the admirable contrivances of nature for performing all its various external and internal motions, and the variety in the eyes of different animals, suited to their several natures and ways of life, clearly demonstrate this organ to be a masterpiece of Nature's work. And he must be very ignorant of what hath been discovered about it, or have a very strange cast of understanding, who can seriously doubt whether or not the rays of light and the eye were made for one another, with consummate wisdom, and perfect skill in optics.

If we shall suppose an order of beings, endued with every human faculty but that of sight, how incredible would it appear to such beings, accustomed only to the slow informations of touch, that, by the addition of an organ consisting of a ball and socket of an inch diameter, they might be enabled, in an instant of time, without changing their place to perceive the disposition of a whole army or the order of a battle, the figure of a magnificent palace or all the variety of a landscape! If a man were by feeling to find out the figure of the peak of Teneriffe, or even of St. Peter's Church at Rome, it would be the work of a lifetime.

It would appear still more incredible to such beings as we have supposed, if they were informed of the discoveries which may be made by this little organ in things far beyond the reach of any other sense: that by means of it we can find our way in the pathless ocean; that we can traverse the globe of the earth, determine its figure and dimensions, and delineate every region of it;—yea, that we can measure the planetary orbs, and make discoveries in the sphere of the fixed stars.

Would it not appear still more astonishing to such beings, if they should be farther informed, that, by means of this same organ, we can perceive the tempers and dispositions, the passions and affections, of our fellow-creatures, even when they want most to conceal them? that, when the tongue is taught most artfully to lie and dissemble, the hypocrisy should appear in the countenance to a discerning eye?—and that, by this organ, we can often perceive what is straight and what is crooked in the mind as well as in the body? How many mysterious things must a blind man believe, if he will give credit to the relations of those that see? Surely he needs as strong a faith as is required of a good Christian.

It is not therefore without reason that the faculty of seeing is looked upon, not only as more noble than the other senses, but as having something in it of a nature superior to sensation. The evidence of reason is called *seeing*, not *feeling*, *smelling*, or *tasting*. Yea, we are wont to express the manner of the Divine knowledge by *seeing*, as that kind of knowledge which is most perfect in us.

Section II.

SIGHT DISCOVERS ALMOST NOTHING WHICH THE BLIND MAY NOT COMPREHEND—THE REASON OF THIS.

Notwithstanding what hath been said of the dignity and superior nature of this faculty, it is worthy of our observation, that there is very little of the knowledge acquired by sight, that may not be communicated to a man born blind. One who never saw the light, may be learned and knowing in every science, even in optics; and may make discoveries in every branch of philosophy. He may understand as much as another man, not only of the order, distances, and motions of the heavenly bodies; but of the nature of light, and of the laws of the reflection and refraction of its rays. He may understand distinctly how those laws produce the phænomena of the rainbow, the prism, the camera obscura, and the magic lanthorn, and all the powers of the microscope and telescope. This is a fact sufficiently attested by experience.

In order to perceive the reason of it, we must distinguish the appearance that objects make to the eye, from the things suggested by that appearance; and again, in the visible appearance of objects, we must distinguish the appearance of colour from the appearance of extension, figure, and motion. First, then, as to the visible appearance of the figure, and motion, and extension of bodies, I conceive that a man born blind may have a distinct notion, if not of the very things, at least of something extremely like to them. May not a blind man be made to conceive that a body moving directly from the eye, or directly towards it, may appear to be at rest? and that the same motion may appear quicker or slower, according as it is nearer to the eye or farther off, more direct or more oblique? May he not be made to conceive, that a plain surface, in a certain position, may appear as a straight line, and vary its visible figure, as its position, or the position of the eye, is varied?—that a circle seen obliquely will appear an ellipse; and a square, a rhombus, or an oblong rectangle? Dr. Saunderson understood the projection of the sphere, and the common rules of perspective; and if he did, he must have understood all that I have mentioned. If there were any doubt of Dr. Saunderson's understanding these things, I could mention my having heard him say in conversation, that he found great difficulty in understanding Dr. Halley's demonstration of that proposition, that the angles made by the circles of the sphere, are equal to the angles made by their representatives in the stereographic projection; but, said he, when I laid aside that demonstration, and considered the proposition in my own way, I saw clearly that it must be true. Another gentleman, of undoubted credit and judgment in these matters, who had part in this conversation, remembers it distinctly.

As to the appearance of colour, a blind man must be more at a loss; because he hath no perception that resembles it. Yet he may, by a kind of analogy, in part supply this defect. To those who see, a scarlet colour signifies an unknown quality in bodies, that makes to the eye an appearance which they are well acquainted with and have often observed—to a blind man, it signifies an unknown quality, that makes to the eye an appearance which he is unacquainted with. But he can conceive the eye to be variously affected by different colours, as the nose is by different smells, or the ear by different sounds. Thus he can conceive scarlet to differ from blue, as the sound of a trumpet does from that of a drum; or as the smell of an orange differs from that of an apple. It is impossible to know whether a scarlet colour has the same appearance to me which it hath to another man; and, if the appearance of it to different persons differed as much as colour does from sound, they might never be able to discover this difference. Hence it appears obvious, that a blind man might talk long about colours distinctly and pertinently; and, if you were to examine him in the dark about the nature, composition, and beauty of them, he might be able to answer, so as not to betray his defect.

We have seen how far a blind man may go in the knowledge of the appearances which things make to the eye. As to the things which are suggested by them or inferred from them, although he could never discover them of himself, yet he may understand them perfectly by the information of others. And everything of this kind that enters into our minds by the eye, may enter into his by the ear. Thus, for instance, he could never, if left to the direction of his own faculties, have dreamed of any such thing as light; but he can be informed of everything we know about it. He can conceive, as distinctly as we, the minuteness and velocity of its rays, their various degrees of refrangibility and reflexibility, and all the magical powers and virtues of that wonderful element. He could never of himself have found out, that there are such bodies as the sun, moon, and stars; but he may be informed of all the noble discoveries of astronomers, about their motions, and the laws of nature by which they are regulated. Thus, it appears, that there is very little knowledge got by the eye, which may not be communicated by language to those who have no eyes.

If we should suppose that it were as uncommon for men to see as it is to be born blind, would not the few who had this rare gift appear as prophets and inspired teachers to the many? We conceive inspiration to give a man no new faculty, but to communicate to him, in a new way, and by extraordinary means, what the faculties common to mankind can apprehend, and what he can communicate to others by ordinary means. On the supposition we have made, sight would appear to the blind very similar to this; for the few who had this gift, could communicate the knowledge acquired by it tc those who had it not. They could not, indeed, convey to the blind any distinct notion of the manner in which they acquired this knowledge. A ball and socket would seem, to a blind man, in this case, as improper an instrument for acquiring such a variety and extent of knowledge, as a dream or a vision. The manner in which a man who sees, discerns so many things by means of the eye, is as unintelligible to the blind, as the manner in which a man may be inspired with knowledge by the Almighty, is to us. Ought the blind man, therefore, without examination, to treat all pretences to the gift of seeing as imposture? Might he not, if he were candid and tractable, find reasonable evidence of the reality of this gift in others, and draw great advantages from it to himself?

The distinction we have made between the visible appearances of the objects of sight, and things suggested by them, is necessary to give us a just notion of the intention of nature in giving us eyes. If we attend duly to the operation of our mind in the use of this faculty, we shall perceive that the visible appearance of objects is hardly ever regarded by us. It is not at all made an object of thought or reflection, but serves only as a sign to introduce to the mind something else, which may be distinctly conceived by those who never saw.

Thus, the visible appearance of things in my room varies almost every hour, according as the day is clear or cloudy, as the sun is in the east, or south, or west, and as my eye is in one part of the room or in another; but I never think of these variations, otherwise than as signs of morning, noon, or night, of a clear or cloudy sky. A book or a chair has a different appearance to the eye, in every different distance and position; yet we conceive it to be still the same; and, overlooking the appearance, we immediately conceive the real figure, distance, and position of the body, of which its visible or perspective appearance is a sign and indication.

When I see a man at the distance of ten yards, and afterwards see him at the distance of a hundred yards, his visible appearance, in its length, breadth, and all its linear proportions, is ten times less in the last case than it is in the first; yet I do not conceive him one inch diminished by this diminution of his visible figure. Nay, I do not in the least attend to this diminution, even when I draw from it the conclusion of his being at a greater distance. For such is the subtilty of the mind's operation in this case, that we draw the conclusion, without perceiving that ever the premises entered into the mind. A thousand such instances might be produced, in order to shew that the visible appearances of objects are intended by nature only as signs or indications; and that the mind passes instantly to the things signified, without making the least reflection upon the sign, or even perceiving that there is any such thing. It is in a way somewhat similar, that the sounds of a language, after it is become familiar, are overlooked, and we attend only to the things signified by them.

It is therefore a just and important observation of the Bishop of Cloyne, That the visible appearance of objects is a kind of language used by nature, to inform us of their distance, magnitude, and figure. And this observation hath been very happily applied by that ingenious writer, to the solution of some phænomena in optics, which had before perplexed the greatest masters in that science. The same observation is further improved by the judicious Dr. Smith, in his Optics, for explaining the apparent figure of the heavens, and the apparent distances and magnitudes of objects seen with glasses, or by the naked eye.

Avoiding as much as possible the repetition of what hath been said by these excellent writers, we shall avail ourselves of the distinction between the signs that nature useth in this visual language, and the things signified by them; and in what remains to be said of sight, shall first make some observations upon the signs.

Section III.

OF THE VISIBLE APPEARANCES OF OBJECTS.

In this section we must speak of things which are never made the object of reflection, though almost every moment presented to the mind. Nature intended them only for signs; and in the whole course of life they are put to no other use. The mind has acquired a confirmed and inveterate habit of inattention to them; for they no sooner appear, than quick as lightning the thing signified succeeds, and engrosses all our regard. They have no name in language; and, although we are conscious of them when they pass through the mind, yet their passage is so quick and so familiar, that it is absolutely unheeded; nor do they leave any footsteps of themselves, either in the memory or imagination. That this is the case with regard to the sensations of touch, hath been shewn in the last chapter; and it holds no less with regard to the visible appearances of objects.

I cannot therefore entertain the hope of being intelligible to those readers who have not, by pains and practice, acquired the habit of distinguishing the appearance of objects to the eye, from the judgment which we form by sight of their colour, distance, magnitude, and figure.

The only profession in life wherein it is necessary to make this distinction, is that of painting. The painter hath occasion for an abstraction, with regard to visible objects, somewhat similar to that which we here require: and this indeed is the most difficult part of his art. For it is evident, that, if he could fix in his imagination the visible appearance of objects, without confounding it with the things signified by that appearance, it would be as easy for him to paint from the life, and to give every figure its proper shading and relief, and its perspective proportions, as it is to paint from a copy. Perspective, shading, giving relief, and colouring, are nothing else but copying the appearance which things make to the eye. We may therefore borrow some light on the subject of visible appearance from this art.

Let one look upon any familiar object, such as a book, at different distances and in different positions: is he not able to affirm, upon the testimony of his sight, that it is the same book, the same object, whether seen at the distance of one foot or of ten, whether in one position or another; that the colour is the same, the dimensions the same, and the figure the same, as far as the eye can judge? This surely must be acknowledged. The same individual object is presented to the mind, only placed at different distances and in different positions. Let me ask, in the next place, Whether this object has the same appearance to the eye in these different distances? Infallibly it hath not. For,

First, However certain our judgment may be that the colour is the same, it is as certain that it hath not the same appearance at different distances. There is a certain degradation of the colour, and a certain confusion and indistinctness of the minute parts, which is the natural consequence of the removal of the object to a greater distance. Those that are not painters, or critics in painting, overlook this; and cannot easily be persuaded, that the colour of the same object hath a different appearance at the distance of one foot and of ten, in the shade and in the light. But the masters in painting know how, by the degradation of the colour and the confusion of the minute parts, figures which are upon the same canvas, and at the same distance from the eye, may be made to represent objects which are at the most unequal distances. They know how to make the objects appear to be of the same colour, by making their pictures really of different colours, according to their distances or shades.

Secondly, Every one who is acquainted with the rules of perspective, knows that the appearance of the figure of the book must vary in every different position: yet if you ask a man that has no notion of perspective, whether the figure of it does not appear to his eye to be the same in all its different positions? he can with a good conscience affirm that it does. He hath learned to make allowance for the variety of visible figure arising from the difference of position, and to draw the proper conclusions from it. But he draws these conclusions so readily and habitually, as to lose sight of the premises: and therefore where he hath made the same conclusion, he conceives the visible appearance must have been the same.

Thirdly, Let us consider the apparent magnitude or dimensions of the book. Whether I view it at the distance of one foot or of ten feet, it seems to be about seven inches long, five broad, and one thick. I can judge of these dimensions very nearly by the eye, and I judge them to be the same at both distances. But yet it is certain, that, at the distance of one foot, its visible length and breadth is about ten times as great as at the distance of ten feet; and consequently its surface is about a hundred times as great. This great change of apparent magnitude is altogether overlooked, and every man is apt to imagine, that it appears to the eye of the same size at both distances. Further, when I look at the book, it seems plainly to have three dimensions, of length, breadth, and thickness: but it is certain that the visible appearance hath no more than two, and can be exactly represented upon a canvas which hath only length and breadth.

In the last place, does not every man, by sight, perceive the distance of the book from his eye? Can he not affirm with certainty, that in one case it is not above one foot distant, that in another it is ten? Nevertheless, it appears certain, that distance from the eye is no immediate object of sight. There are certain things in the visible appearance, which are signs of distance from the eye, and from which, as we shall afterwards shew, we learn by experience to judge of that distance within certain limits; but it seems beyond doubt, that a man born blind, and suddenly made to see, could form no judgment at first of the distance of the objects which he saw.

The young man couched by Cheselden thought, at first, that everything he saw touched his eye, and learned only by experience to judge of the distance of visible objects.

I have entered into this long detail, in order to shew that the visible appearance of an object is extremely different from the notion of it which experience teaches us to form by sight; and to enable the reader to attend to the visible appearance of colour, figure, and extension, in visible things, which is no common object of thought, but must be carefully attended to by those who would enter into the philosophy of this sense, or would comprehend what shall be said upon it. To a man newly made to see, the visible appearance of objects would be the same as to us; but he would see nothing at all of their real dimensions, as we do. He could form no conjecture, by means of his sight only, how many inches or feet they were in length, breadth, or thickness. He could perceive little or nothing of their real figure; nor could he discern that this was a cube, that a sphere; that this was a cone, and that a cylinder. His eye could not inform him that this object was near, and that more remote. The habit of a man or of a woman, which appeared to us of one uniform colour, variously folded and shaded, would present to his eye neither fold nor shade, but variety of colour. In a word, his eyes, though ever so perfect, would at first give him almost no information of things without him. They would indeed present the same appearances to him as they do to us, and speak the same language; but to him it is an unknown language; and, therefore, he would attend only to the signs, without knowing the signification of them, whereas to us it is a language perfectly familiar; and, therefore, we take no notice of the signs, but attend only to the thing signified by them.

Section IV.

THAT COLOUR IS A QUALITY OF BODIES, NOT A SENSATION OF THE MIND.

By colour, all men, who have not been tutored by modern philosophy, understand, not a sensation of the mind, which can have no existence when it is not perceived, but a quality or modification of bodies, which continues to be the same whether it is seen or not. The scarlet-rose which is before me, is still a scarlet-rose when I shut my eyes, and was so at midnight when no eye saw it. The colour remains when the appearance ceases; it remains the same when the appearance changes. For when I view this scarlet-rose through a pair of green spectacles, the appearance is changed;

but I do not conceive the colour of the rose changed. To a person in the jaundice, it has still another appearance; but he is easily convinced that the change is in his eye, and not in the colour of the object. Every different degree of light makes it have a different appearance, and total darkness takes away all appearance, but makes not the least change in the colour of the body. We may, by a variety of optical experiments, change the appearance of figure and magnitude in a body, as well as that of colour; we may make one body appear to be ten. But all men believe, that, as a multiplying glass does not really produce ten guineas out of one, nor a microscope turn a guinea into a ten-pound piece, so neither does a coloured glass change the real colour of the object seen through it, when it changes the appearance of that colour.

The common language of mankind shews evidently, that we ought to distinguish between the colour of a body, which is conceived to be a fixed and permanent quality in the body, and the appearance of that colour to the eye, which may be varied a thousand ways, by a variation of the light, of the medium, or of the eye itself. The permanent colour of the body is the cause which, by the mediation of various kinds or degrees of light, and of various transparent bodies interposed, produces all this variety of appearances. When a coloured body is presented, there is a certain apparition to the eye, or to the mind, which we have called *the appearance of colour.* Mr. Locke calls it *an idea;* and, indeed, it may be called so with the greatest propriety. This idea can have no existence but when it is perceived. It is a kind of thought, and can only be the act of a percipient or thinking being. By the constitution of our nature, we are led to conceive this idea as a sign of something external, and are impatient till we learn its meaning. A thousand experiments for this purpose are made every day by children, even before they come to the use of reason. They look at things, they handle them, they put them in various positions, at different distances, and in different lights. The ideas of sight, by these means, come to be associated with, and readily to suggest, things external, and altogether unlike them. In particular, that idea which we have called *the appearance of colour*, suggests the conception and belief of some unknown quality in the body which occasions the idea; and it is to this quality, and not to the idea, that we give the name of *colour.** The various colours, although in their nature equally unknown, are easily distinguished when we think or speak of them, by being associated with the ideas which they excite. In like manner, gravity, magnetism, and electricity, although all unknown qualities, are distinguished by their different effects. As we grow up, the mind acquires a habit of passing so rapidly from the ideas of sight to the external things suggested by them, that the ideas are not in the least attended to, nor have they names given them in common language.

When we think or speak of any particular colour, however simple the notion may seem to be which is presented to the imagination, it is really in some sort compounded. It involves an unknown cause and a known effect. The name of *colour* belongs indeed to the cause only, and not to the effect. But as the cause is unknown, we can form no distinct conception of it but by its relation to the known effect; and, therefore, both go together in the imagination, and are so closely united, that they are mistaken for one simple object of thought.* When I

* It is justly observed by Mr. Stewart, that these passages seem inconsistent with each other. If in the perception of colour, the sensation and the quality "be so closely united as to be mistaken for one simple object of thought," does it not obviously follow, that it is to this compounded notion the name of *colour* must in general be given? On the other hand, when it is said *that the name of colour is never given to the sensation, but to the quality only*, does not this imply, that every time the word is pronounced, the quality is separated from the sensation, even in the imagination of the vulgar?—H.

would conceive those colours of bodies which we call *scarlet* and *blue*—if I conceived them only as unknown qualities, I could perceive no distinction between the one and the other. I must, therefore, for the sake of distinction, join to each of them, in my imagination, some effect or some relation that is peculiar; and the most obvious distinction is, the appearance which one and the other makes to the eye. Hence the appearance is, in the imagination, so closely united with the quality called *a scarlet-colour*, that they are apt to be mistaken for one and the same thing, although they are in reality so different and so unlike, that one is an idea in the mind, and the other is a quality of body.

I conclude, then, that colour is not a sensation, but a secondary quality of bodies, in the sense we have already explained; that it is a certain power or virtue in bodies, that in fair daylight exhibits to the eye an appearance which is very familiar to us, although it hath no name. Colour differs from other secondary qualities in this, that, whereas the name of the quality is sometimes given to the sensation which indicates it, and is occasioned by it, we never, as far as I can judge, give the name of *colour* to the sensation, but to the quality only.* Perhaps the reason of this may be, that the appearances of the same colour are so various and changeable, according to the different modifications of the light, of the medium, and of the eye, that language could not afford names for them. And, indeed, they are so little interesting that they are never attended to, but serve only as signs to introduce the things signified by them. Nor ought it to appear incredible, that appearances so frequent and so familiar should have no names, nor be made objects of thought; since we have before shewn that this is true of many sensations of touch, which are no less frequent nor less familiar.

* See note on p. 175.

Section V.

AN INFERENCE FROM THE PRECEDING.

From what hath been said about colour, we may infer two things. The first is, that one of the most remarkable paradoxes of modern philosophy, which hath been universally esteemed as a great discovery, is, in reality, when examined to the bottom, nothing else but an abuse of words. The paradox I mean is, That colour is not a quality of bodies, but only an idea in the mind. We have shewn, that the word *colour*, as used by the vulgar, cannot signify an idea in the mind, but a permanent quality of body. We have shewn that there is really a permanent quality of body, to which the common use of this word exactly agrees. Can any stronger proof be desired, that this quality is that to which the vulgar give the name of *colour?* If it should be said, that this quality, to which we give the name of *colour*, is unknown to the vulgar, and, therefore, can have no name among them, I answer, it is, indeed, known only by its effects—that is, by its exciting a certain idea in us; but are there not numberless qualities of bodies which are known only by their effects, to which, notwithstanding, we find it necessary to give names? Medicine alone might furnish us with a hundred instances of this kind. Do not the words *astringent*, *narcotic*, *epispastic*, *caustic*, and innumerable others, signify qualities of bodies, which are known only by their effects upon animal bodies? Why, then, should not the vulgar give a name to a quality, whose effects are every moment perceived by their eyes? We have all the reason, therefore, that the nature of the thing admits, to think that the vulgar apply the name of *colour* to that quality of bodies which excites in us what the philosophers call the *idea of colour.* And that there is such a quality in bodies, all philosophers allow, who allow that there is any such thing as body. Philosophers have thought fit to leave that quality of bodies which the vulgar call *colour*, without a name, and to give the name of *colour* to the idea or appearance, to which, as we have shewn, the vulgar give no name, because they never make it an object of thought or reflection. Hence it appears, that when philosophers affirm that colour is not in bodies, but in the mind, and the vulgar affirm that colour is not in the mind, but is a quality of bodies, there is no difference between them about things, but only about the meaning of a word.

The vulgar have undoubted right to give names to things which they are daily conversant about; and philosophers seem justly chargeable with an abuse of language, when they change the meaning of a common word, without giving warning.

If it is a good rule, to think with philosophers and speak with the vulgar, it must be right to speak with the vulgar when we think with them, and not to shock them by philosophical paradoxes, which, when put into common language, express only the common sense of mankind.

If you ask a man that is no philosopher, what colour is, or what makes one body appear white, another scarlet, he cannot tell. He leaves that inquiry to philosophers, and can embrace any hypothesis about it, except that of our modern philosophers, who affirm that colour is not in body, but only in the mind.

Nothing appears more shocking to his apprehension, than that visible objects should have no colour, and that colour should be in that which he conceives to be invisible. Yet this strange paradox is not only universally received, but considered as one of the noblest discoveries of modern philosophy. The ingenious Addison, in the *Spectator*, No. 413, speaks thus of it:—"I have here supposed that my reader is acquainted with that great modern discovery, which is at present universally acknowledged by all the inquirers into natural philosophy—namely, that light and colours, as apprehended by the imagination, are only ideas in the mind, and not qualities that have any existence in matter. As this is a truth which has been proved incontestably by many modern philosophers, and is, indeed, one of the finest speculations in that science, if the English reader would see the notion explained at large, he may find it in the eighth chapter of the second book of Locke's Essay on Human Understanding.'"

Mr. Locke and Mr. Addison are writers who have deserved so well of mankind, that one must feel some uneasiness in differing from them, and would wish to ascribe all the merit that is due to a discovery upon which they put so high a value. And, indeed, it is just to acknowledge that Locke, and other modern philosophers, on the subject of secondary qualities, have the merit of distinguishing more accurately than those that went before them, between the sensation in the mind, and that constitution or quality of bodies which gives occasion to the sensation. They have shewn clearly that these two things are not only distinct, but altogether unlike: that there is no similitude between the effluvia of an odorous body and the sensation of smell, or between the vibrations of a sounding body and the sensation of sound: that there can be no resemblance between the feeling of heat, and the constitution of the heated body which occasions it; or between the appearance which a coloured body makes to the eye, and the texture of the body which causes that appearance.

Nor was the merit small of distinguishing these things accurately; because, however different and unlike in their nature, they have been always so associated in the imagination, as to coalesce, as it were, into one two-faced form, which, from its amphibious nature, could not justly be appropriated either to body or mind; and, until it was properly distinguished into its different constituent parts, it was impossible to assign to either their just shares in it. None of the ancient philosophers had made this distinction.* The followers of Democritus and Epicurus conceived the forms of heat, and sound, and colour, to be in the mind only; but that our senses fallaciously represented them as being in bodies. The Peripatetics imagined that those forms are really in bodies; and that the images of them are conveyed to the mind by our senses.†

The one system made the senses naturally fallacious and deceitful; the other made the qualities of body to resemble the sensations of the mind. Nor was it possible to find a third, without making the distinction we have mentioned; by which, indeed, the errors of both these ancient systems are avoided, and we are not left under the hard necessity of believing, either, on the one hand, that our sensations are like to the qualities of body, or, on the other, that God hath given us one faculty to deceive us, and another to detect the cheat.

We desire, therefore, with pleasure, to do justice to the doctrine of Locke, and other modern philosophers, with regard to colour and other secondary qualities, and to ascribe to it its due merit, while we beg leave to censure the language in which they have expressed their doctrine. When they had explained and established the distinction between the appearance which colour makes to the eye, and the modification of the coloured body which, by the laws of nature, causes that appearance, the question was, whether to give the name of *colour* to

* This is inaccurate. The distinction was known to the ancient philosophers; and Democritus was generally allowed to be its author. This Reid himself elsewhere indeed admits.—(See above, pp. 140, 156, 157).—H.

† These statements concerning both classes of philosophers are vague and incorrect. The latter, in general, only allowed *species* for two senses, Sight and Hearing; few admitted them in Feeling; and some rejected them altogether.—H.

the cause or to the effect? By giving it, as they have done, to the effect, they set philosophy apparently in opposition to common sense, and expose it to the ridicule of the vulgar. But had they given the name of *colour* to the cause, as they ought to have done, they must then have affirmed, with the vulgar, that colour is a quality of bodies; and that there is neither colour nor anything like it in the mind. Their language, as well as their sentiments, would have been perfectly agreeable to the common apprehensions of mankind, and true Philosophy would have joined hands with Common Sense. As Locke was no enemy to common sense, it may be presumed, that, in this instance, as in some others, he was seduced by some received hypothesis; and that this was actually the case, will appear in the following section.

Section VI.

THAT NONE OF OUR SENSATIONS ARE RESEMBLANCES OF ANY OF THE QUALITIES OF BODIES.

A second inference is, that, although colour is really a quality of body, yet it is not represented to the mind by an idea or sensation that resembles it; on the contrary, it is suggested by an idea which does not in the least resemble it. And this inference is applicable, not to colour only, but to all the qualities of body which we have examined.

It deserves to be remarked, that, in the analysis we have hitherto given of the operations of the five senses, and of the qualities of bodies discovered by them, no instance hath occurred, either of any sensation which resembles any quality of body, or of any quality of body whose image or resemblance is conveyed to the mind by means of the senses.

There is no phænomenon in nature more unaccountable than the intercourse that is carried on between the mind and the external world—there is no phænomenon which philosophical spirits have shewn greater avidity to pry into, and to resolve. It is agreed by all, that this intercourse is carried on by means of the senses; and this satisfies the vulgar curiosity, but not the philosophic. Philosophers must have some system, some hypothesis, that shews the manner in which our senses make us acquainted with external things. All the fertility of human invention seems to have produced only one hypothesis for this purpose, which, therefore, hath been universally received; and that is, that the mind, like a mirror, receives the images of things from without, by means of the senses: so that their use must be to convey these images into the mind.*

Whether to these images of external things in the mind, we give the name of *sensible forms*, or *sensible species*, with the Peripatetics, or the name *of ideas of sensation*, with Locke; or whether, with later philosophers, we distinguish *sensations*, which are immediately conveyed by the senses, from *ideas of sensation*, which are faint copies of our sensations retained in the memory and imagination; † these are only differences about words. The hypothesis I have mentioned is common to all these different systems.

The necessary and allowed consequence of this hypothesis is, *that no material thing, nor any quality of material things, can be conceived by us, or made an object of thought, until its image is conveyed to the mind by means of the senses.* We shall examine this hypothesis particularly afterwards, and at this time only observe, that, in consequence

* This is incorrect, especially as it asserts that the *one universal* hypothesis of philosophy was, that "the mind receives the images of things from without," meaning by these images, immediate or representative objects, different from the modifications of the thinking subject itself.—H.

† He refers to Hume; Aristotle, however, and Hobbes, had previously called Imagination a *decaying sense*.—H.

of it, one would naturally expect, that to every quality and attribute of body we know or can conceive, there should be a sensation corresponding, which is the image and resemblance of that quality; and that the sensations which have no similitude or resemblance to body, or to any of its qualities, should give us no conception of a material world, or of anything belonging to it. These things might be expected as the natural consequences of the hypothesis we have mentioned.

Now, we have considered, in this and the preceding chapters, Extension, Figure, Solidity, Motion, Hardness, Roughness, as well as Colour, Heat, and Cold, Sound, Taste, and Smell. We have endeavoured to shew that our nature and constitution lead us to conceive these as qualities of body, as all mankind have always conceived them to be. We have likewise examined with great attention the various sensations we have by means of the five senses, and are not able to find among them all one single image of body, or of any of its qualities. From whence, then, come those images of body and of its qualities into the mind? Let philosophers resolve this question. All I can say is, that they come not by the senses. I am sure that, by proper attention and care, I may know my sensations, and be able to affirm with certainty what they resemble, and what they do not resemble. I have examined them one by one, and compared them with matter and its qualities; and I cannot find one of them that confesses a resembling feature.

A truth so evident as this—that our sensations are not images of matter, or of any of its qualities—ought not to yield to a hypothesis such as that above-mentioned, however ancient, or however universally received by philosophers; nor can there be any amicable union between the two. This will appear by some reflections upon the spirit of the ancient and modern philosophy concerning sensation.

During the reign of the Peripatetic philosophy, our

sensations were not minutely or accurately examined. The attention of philosophers, as well as of the vulgar, was turned to the things signified by them: therefore, in consequence of the common hypothesis, it was taken for granted, that all the sensations we have from external things, are the forms or images of these external things. And thus the truth we have mentioned yielded entirely to the hypothesis, and was altogether suppressed by it.

Des Cartes gave a noble example of turning our attention inward, and scrutinizing our sensations; and this example hath been very worthily followed by modern philosophers, particularly by Malebranche, Locke, Berkeley, and Hume. The effect of this scrutiny hath been, a gradual discovery of the truth above-mentioned—to wit, the dissimilitude between the sensations of our minds, and the qualities or attributes of an insentient inert substance, such as we conceive matter to be. But this valuable and useful discovery, in its different stages, hath still been unhappily united to the ancient hypothesis—and from this inauspicious match of opinions, so unfriendly and discordant in their natures, have arisen those monsters of paradox and scepticism with which the modern philosophy is too justly chargeable.

Locke saw clearly, and proved incontestably, that the sensations we have by taste, smell, and hearing, as well as the sensations of colour, heat, and cold, are not resemblances of anything in bodies; and in this he agrees with Des Cartes and Malebranche. Joining this opinion with the hypothesis, it follows necessarily, that three senses of the five are cut off from giving us any intelligence of the material world, as being altogether inept for that office. Smell, and taste, and sound, as well as colour and heat, can have no more relation to body, than anger or gratitude; nor ought the former to be called qualities of body, whether primary or secondary, any more than the latter. For it was natural and obvious to argue thus from that hypothesis: If heat, and colour, and sound are real qualities of body, the sensations by which we perceive them must be resemblances of those qualities; but these sensations are not resemblances; therefore, those are not real qualities of body.

We see, then, that Locke, having found that the ideas of secondary qualities are no resemblances, was compelled, by a hypothesis common to all philosophers, to deny that they are real qualities of body. It is more difficult to assign a reason why, after this, he should call them *secondary qualities;* for this name, if I mistake not, was of his invention.* Surely he did not mean that they were secondary qualities of the mind; and I do not see with what propriety, or even by what tolerable license, he could call them secondary qualities of body, after finding that they were no qualities of body at all. In this, he seems to have sacrificed to Common Sense, and to have been led by her authority even in opposition to his hypothesis. The same sovereign mistress of our opinions that led this philosopher to call those things secondary qualities of body, which, according to his principles and reasonings, were no qualities of body at all, hath led, not the vulgar of all ages only, but philosophers also, and even the disciples of Locke, to believe them to be real qualities of body—she hath led them to investigate, by experiments, the nature of colour, and sound, and heat, in bodies. Nor hath this investigation been fruitless, as it must have been if there had been no such thing in bodies; on the contrary, it hath produced very noble and useful discoveries, which make a very considerable part of natural philosophy. If, then, natural philosophy be not a dream, there is something in bodies which we call *colour*, and *heat*, and *sound*. And if this

* The terms *First* and *Second*, or *Primary* and *Secondary qualities*, were no more an invention of Locke than the distinction which he applied them to denote. The terms First and Second Qualities, as I have noticed, in the Aristotelian philosophy, marked out, however, a different distribution of qualities than that in question.—H.

be so, the hypothesis from which the contrary is concluded, must be false: for the argument, leading to a false conclusion, recoils against the hypothesis from which it was drawn, and thus directs its force backward. If the qualities of body were known to us only by sensations that resemble them, then colour, and sound, and heat could be no qualities of body; but these are real qualities of body; and, therefore, the qualities of body are not known only by means of sensations that resemble them.

But to proceed. What Locke had proved with regard to the sensations we have by smell, taste, and hearing, Bishop Berkeley proved no less unanswerably with regard to all our other sensations; to wit, that none of them can in the least resemble the qualities of a lifeless and insentient being, such as matter is conceived to be. Mr. Hume hath confirmed this by his authority and reasoning. This opinion surely looks with a very malign aspect upon the old hypothesis; yet that hypothesis hath still been retained, and conjoined with it. And what a brood of monsters hath this produced!

The first-born of this union, and, perhaps, the most harmless, was, that the secondary qualities of body were mere sensations of the mind. To pass by Malebranche's notion of seeing all things in the ideas of the divine mind, as a foreigner, never naturalized in this island; the next was Berkeley's system, That extension, and figure, and hardness, and motion—that land, and sea, and houses, and our own bodies, as well as those of our wives, and children, and friends—are nothing but ideas of the mind: and that there is nothing existing in nature, but minds and ideas.

The progeny that followed, is still more frightful; so that it is surprising, that one could be found who had the courage to act the midwife, to rear it up, and to usher it into the world. No causes nor effects; no substances, material or spiritual; no evidence, even in mathematical demonstration; no liberty nor active power; nothing existing in nature, but impressions and ideas following each other, without time, place, or subject. Surely no age ever produced such a system of opinions, justly deduced with great acuteness, perspicuity, and elegance, from a principle universally received. The hypothesis we have mentioned is the father of them all. The dissimilitude of our sensations and feelings to external things, is the innocent mother of most of them.

As it happens sometimes, in an arithmetical operation, that two errors balance one another, so that the conclusion is little or nothing affected by them; but when one of them is corrected, and the other left, we are led farther from the truth than by both together: so it seems to have happened in the Peripatetic philosophy of sensation, compared with the modern. The Peripatetics adopted two errors; but the last served as a corrective to the first, and rendered it mild and gentle; so that their system had no tendency to scepticism. The moderns have retained the first of those errors, but have gradually detected and corrected the last. The consequence hath been, that the light we have struck out hath created darkness, and scepticism hath advanced hand in hand with knowledge, spreading its melancholy gloom, first over the material world, and at last over the whole face of nature. Such a phænomenon as this, is apt to stagger even the lovers of light and knowledge, while its cause is latent; but, when that is detected, it may give hopes that this darkness shall not be everlasting, but that it shall be succeeded by a more permanent light.

Section VII.

OF VISIBLE FIGURE AND EXTENSION.

Although there is no resemblance, nor, as far as we know, any necessary connection, between that quality in a body which we call its *colour*, and the appearance which that colour makes to the eye, it is quite otherwise with regard to its *figure* and *magnitude.* There is certainly a resemblance, and a necessary connection, between the visible figure and magnitude of a body, and its real figure and magnitude; no man can give a reason why a scarlet colour affects the eye in the manner it does; no man can be sure that it affects his eye in the same manner as it affects the eye of another, and that it has the same appearance to him as it has to another man;—but we can assign a reason why a circle placed obliquely to the eye, should appear in the form of an ellipse. The visible figure, magnitude, and position may, by mathematical reasoning, be deduced from the real; and it may be demonstrated, that every eye that sees distinctly and perfectly, must, in the same situation, see it under this form, and no other. Nay, we may venture to affirm, that a man born blind, if he were instructed in mathematics, would be able to determine the visible figure of a body when its real figure, distance, and position, are given. Dr. Saunderson understood the projection of the sphere, and perspective. Now, I require no more knowledge in a blind man, in order to his being able to determine the visible figure of bodies, than that he can project the outline of a given body, upon the surface of a hollow sphere, whose centre is in the eye. This projection is the visible figure he wants: for it is the same figure with that which is projected upon the *tunica retina* in vision.

A blind man can conceive lines drawn from every point of the object to the centre of the eye, making angles. He can conceive that the length of the object will appear greater or less, in proportion to the angle which it subtends at the eye; and that, in like manner, the breadth, and in general the distance, of any one point of the object from any other point, will appear greater or less, in proportion to the angles which those distances subtend. He can easily be made to conceive, that the visible appearance has no thickness, any more than a projection of the sphere, or a perspective draught. He may be informed, that the eye, until it is aided by experience, does not represent one object as nearer or more remote than another. Indeed, he would probably conjecture this of himself, and be apt to think that the rays of light must make the same impression upon the eye, whether they come from a greater or a less distance.

These are all the principles which we suppose our blind mathematician to have; and these he may certainly acquire by information and reflection. It is no less certain, that, from these principles, having given the real figure and magnitude of a body, and its position and distance with regard to the eye, he can find out its visible figure and magnitude. He can demonstrate in general, from these principles, that the visible figure of all bodies will be the same with that of their projection upon the surface of a hollow sphere, when the eye is placed in the centre. And he can demonstrate that their visible magnitude will be greater or less, according as their projection occupies a greater or less part of the surface of this sphere.

To set this matter in another light, let us distinguish betwixt the *position* of objects with regard to the eye, and their *distance* from it. Objects that lie in the same right line drawn from the centre of the eye, have the same position, however different their distances from the eye may be: but objects which lie in different right lines drawn from the eye's centre, have a different position; and this difference of position is greater or less in proportion to the angle made at the eye by the right lines mentioned. Having thus defined what we mean by the position of objects with regard to the eye, it is evident that, as the real figure of a body consists in the situation of its several parts with regard to one another, so its visible figure consists in the position of its several parts with regard to the eye; and, as he that hath a distinct conception of the situation of the parts of the body with regard to one another, must have a distinct conception of its real figure; so he that conceives distinctly the position of its several parts with regard to the eye, must have a distinct conception of its visible figure. Now, there is nothing, surely, to hinder a blind man from conceiving the position of the several parts of a body with regard to the eye, any more than from conceiving their situation with regard to one another; and, therefore, I conclude, that a blind man may attain a distinct conception of the visible figure of bodies.

Although we think the arguments that have been offered are sufficient to prove that a blind man may conceive the visible extension and figure of bodies; yet, in order to remove some prejudices against this truth, it will be of use to compare the notion which a blind mathematician might form to himself of visible figure, with that which is presented to the eye in vision, and to observe wherein they differ.

First, Visible figure is never presented to the eye but in conjunction with colour: and, although there be no connection between them from the nature of the things, yet, having so invariably kept company together, we are hardly able to disjoin them even in our imagination. What mightily increases this difficulty is, that we have never been accustomed to make visible figure an object of thought. It is only used as a sign, and, having served this purpose, passes away, without leaving a trace behind. The drawer or designer, whose business it is to hunt this fugitive form, and to take a copy of it, finds how difficult his task is, after many years' labour and practice. Happy! if at last he can acquire the art of arresting it in his imagination, until he can delineate it. For then it is evident that he must be able to draw as accurately from the life as from a copy. But how few of the professed masters of designing are ever able to arrive at this degree of perfection! It is no wonder, then, that we should find so great difficulty in conceiving this form apart from its constant associate, when it is so difficult to conceive it at all. But our blind man's notion of visible figure will not be associated with colour, of which he hath no conception, but it will, perhaps, be associated with hardness or smoothness, with which he is acquainted by touch. These different associations are apt to impose upon us, and to make things seem different, which, in reality, are the same.

Secondly, The blind man forms the notion of visible figure to himself, by thought, and by mathematical reasoning from principles; whereas, the man that sees, has it presented to his eye at once, without any labour, without any reasoning, by a kind of inspiration. A man may form to himself the notion of a parabola, or a cycloid, from the mathematical definition of those figures, although he had never seen them drawn or delineated. Another, who knows nothing of the mathematical definition of the figures, may see them delineated on paper, or feel them cut out in wood. Each may have a distinct conception of the figures, one by mathematical reasoning, the other by sense. Now, the blind man forms his notion of visible figure in the same manner as the first of these formed his notion of a parabola or a cycloid, which he never saw.

Thirdly, Visible figure leads the man that sees, directly to the conception of the real figure, of which it is a sign. But the blind man's thoughts move in a contrary direction. For he must first know the real figure, distance, and situation of the body, and from thence he slowly traces out the visible figure by mathematical reasoning. Nor does his nature lead him to conceive this visible figure as a sign; it is a creature of his own reason and imagination.

Section VIII.

SOME QUERIES CONCERNING VISIBLE FIGURE ANSWERED.

It may be asked, What kind of thing is this visible figure? Is it a Sensation, or an Idea? If it is an idea, from what sensation is it copied? These questions may seem trivial or impertinent to one who does not know that there is a tribunal of inquisition erected by certain modern philosophers, before which everything in nature must answer. The articles of inquisition are few indeed, but very dreadful in their consequences. They are only these: Is the prisoner an Impression or an Idea? If an idea, from what impression copied? Now, if it appears that the prisoner is neither an impression, nor an idea copied from some impression, immediately, without being allowed to offer anything in arrest of judgment, he is sentenced to pass out of existence, and to be, in all time to come, an empty unmeaning sound, or the ghost of a departed entity.

Before this dreadful tribunal, cause and effect, time and place, matter and spirit, have been tried and cast: how then shall such a poor flimsy form as visible figure stand before it? It must even plead guilty, and confess that it is neither an impression nor an idea. For, alas! it is notorious, that it is extended in length and breadth; it may be long or short, broad or narrow, triangular, quadrangular, or circular; and, therefore, unless ideas and impressions are extended and figured, it cannot belong to that category.

If it should still be asked, To what category of beings does visible figure then belong? I can only, in answer, give some tokens, by which those who are better acquainted with the categories, may chance to find its place. It is, as we have said, the position of the several parts of a figured body with regard to the eye. The different positions of the several parts of the body with regard to the eye, when put together, make a real figure, which is truly extended in length and breadth, and which represents a figure that is extended in length, breadth, and thickness. In like manner, a projection of the sphere is a real figure, and hath length and breadth, but represents the sphere, which hath three dimensions. A projection of the sphere, or a perspective view of a palace, is a representative in the very same sense as visible figure is; and wherever they have their lodgings in the categories, this will be found to dwell next door to them.

It may farther be asked, Whether there be any sensation proper to visible figure, by which it is suggested in vision?—or by what means it is presented to the mind? This is a question of some importance, in order to our having a distinct notion of the faculty of seeing: and to give all the light to it we can, it is necessary to compare this sense with other senses, and to make some suppositions, by which we may be enabled to distinguish things that are apt to be confounded, although they are totally different.

There are three of our senses which give us intelligence of things at a distance: smell, hearing, and sight. In smelling and in hearing, we have a sensation or impression upon the mind, which, by our constitution, we conceive to be a sign of something external: but the position of this external thing, with regard to the organ of sense, is not presented to the mind along with the sensation. When I hear the sound of a coach, I could not, previous to experience, determine whether the sounding body was above or below, to the right hand or to the left. So that the sensation suggests to me some external object as the cause or occasion of it; but it suggests not the position of that object, whether it lies in this direction or in that. The same thing may be said with regard to smelling. But the case is quite different with regard to seeing. When I see an object, the appearance which the colour of it makes, may be called *the sensation*, which suggests to me some external thing as its cause; but it suggests likewise the individual direction and position of this cause with regard to the eye. I know it is precisely in such a direction, and in no other. At the same time, I am not conscious of anything that can be called *sensation*, but the sensation of colour. The position of the coloured thing is no sensation; but it is by the laws of my constitution presented to the mind along with the colour, without any additional sensation.

Let us suppose that the eye were so constituted that the rays coming from any one point of the object were not, as they are in our eyes, collected in one point of the *retina*, but diffused over the whole: it is evident to those who understand the structure of the eye, that such an eye as we have supposed, would shew the colour of a body as our eyes do, but that it would neither shew figure nor position. The operation of such an eye would be precisely similar to that of hearing and smell; it would give no perception of figure or extension, but merely of colour. Nor is the supposition we have made altogether imaginary: for it is nearly the case of most people who have cataracts, whose crystalline, as Mr. Cheselden observes, does not altogether exclude the rays of light, but diffuses them over the *retina*, so that such persons see things as one does through a glass of broken gelly: they perceive the colour, but nothing of the figure or magnitude of objects.

Again, if we should suppose that smell and sound were conveyed in right lines from the objects, and that every sensation of hearing and smell suggested the precise direction or position of its object; in this case, the operations of hearing and smelling would be similar to that of seeing: we should smell and hear the figure of objects, in the same sense as now we see it; and every smell and sound would be associated with some figure in the imagination, as colour is in our present state.

We have reason to believe, that the rays of light make some impression upon the *retina;* but we are not conscious of this impression; nor have anatomists or philosophers been able to discover the nature and effects of it; whether it produces a vibration in the nerve, or the motion of some subtile fluid contained in the nerve, or something different from either, to which we cannot give a name. Whatever it is, we shall call it the *material impression;* remembering carefully, that it is not an impression upon the mind, but upon the body; and that it is no sensation, nor can resemble sensation, any more than figure or motion can resemble thought. Now, this material impression, made upon a particular point of the *retina,* by the laws of our constitution, suggests two things to the mind—namely, the colour and the position of some external object. No man can give a reason why the same material impression might not have suggested sound, or smell, or either of these, along with the position of the object. That it should suggest colour and position, and nothing else, we can resolve only into our constitution, or the will of our Maker. And since there is no necessary connection between these two things suggested by this material impression, it might, if it had so pleased our Creator, have suggested one of them without the other. Let us suppose, therefore, since it plainly appears to be possible, that our eyes had been so framed as to suggest to us the position of the object, without suggesting colour, or any other quality: What is the consequence of this supposition? It is evidently this, that the person endued with such an eye, would perceive the visible figure of bodies, without having any sensation or impression made upon his mind. The figure he perceives is altogether external; and therefore cannot be called an impression upon the mind, without the grossest abuse of language. If it should be said, that it is impossible to perceive a figure, unless there be some impression of it upon the mind, I beg leave not to admit the impossibility of this without some proof: and I can find none. Neither can I conceive what is meant by an impression of figure upon the mind. I can conceive an impression of figure upon wax, or upon any body that is fit to receive it; but an impression of it upon the mind, is to me quite unintelligible; and, although I form the most distinct conception of the figure, I cannot, upon the strictest examination, find any impression of it upon my mind.

If we suppose, last of all, that the eye hath the power restored of perceiving colour, I apprehend that it will be allowed, that now it perceives figure in the very same manner as before, with this difference only, that colour is always joined with it.

In answer, therefore, to the question proposed, there seems to be no sensation that is appropriated to visible figure, or whose office it is to suggest it. It seems to be suggested immediately by the material impression upon the organ, of which we are not conscious: and why may not a material impression upon the *retina* suggest visible figure, as well as the material impression made upon the hand, when we grasp a ball, suggests real figure? In the one case, one and the same material impression, suggests both colour and visible figure; and in the other case, one and the same material impression suggests hardness, heat, or cold, and real figure, all at the same time.

We shall conclude this section with another question upon this subject. Since the visible figure of bodies is a real and external object to the eye, as their tangible figure is to the touch, it may be asked, Whence arises the difficulty of attending to the first, and the facility of attending to the last? It is certain that the first is more frequently presented to the eye, than the last is to the touch; the first is as distinct and determinate an object as the last, and seems in its own nature as proper for speculation. Yet so little hath it been attended to, that it never had a name in any language, until Bishop Berkeley gave it that which we have used after his example, to distinguish it from the figure which is the object of touch.

The difficulty of attending to the visible figure of bodies, and making it an object of thought, appears so similar to that which we find in attending to our sensations, that both have probably like causes. Nature intended the visible figure as a sign of the tangible figure and situation of bodies, and hath taught us, by a kind of instinct, to put it always to this use. Hence it happens, that the mind passes over it with a rapid motion, to attend to the things signified by it. It is as unnatural to the mind to stop at the visible figure, and attend to it, as it is to a spherical body to stop upon an inclined plane. There is an inward principle, which constantly carries it forward, and which cannot be overcome but by a contrary force.

There are other external things which nature intended for signs; and we find this common to them all, that the mind is disposed to overlook them, and to attend only to the things signified by them. Thus there are certain modifications of the human face, which are natural signs of the present disposition of the mind. Every man understands the meaning of these signs, but not one of a hundred ever attended to the signs themselves, or knows anything about them. Hence you may find many an excellent practical physiognomist who knows nothing of the proportions of a face nor can delineate or describe the expression of any one passion.

An excellent painter or statuary can tell, not only what are the proportions of a good face, but what changes every passion makes in it. This, however, is one of the chief mysteries of his art, to the acquisition of which infinite labour and attention, as well as a happy genius, are required; but when he puts his art in practice, and happily expresses a passion by its proper signs, every one understands the meaning of these signs, without art, and without reflection.

What has been said of painting, might easily be applied to all the fine arts. The difficulty in them all consists in knowing and attending to those natural signs whereof every man understands the meaning.

We pass from the sign to the thing signified, with ease, and by natural impulse; but to go backward from the thing signified to the sign, is a work of labour and difficulty. Visible figure, therefore, being intended by nature to be a sign, we pass on immediately to the thing signified, and cannot easily return to give any attention to the sign.

Nothing shews more clearly our indisposition to attend to visible figure and visible extension than this—that, although mathematical reasoning is no less applicable to them, than to tangible figure and extension, yet they have entirely escaped the notice of mathematicians. While that figure and that extension which are objects of touch, have been tortured ten thousand ways for twenty centuries, and a very noble system of science has been drawn out of them, not a single proposition do we find with regard to the figure and extension which are the immediate objects of sight!

When the geometrician draws a diagram with the most perfect accuracy—when he keeps his eye fixed upon it, while he goes through a long process of reasoning, and demonstrates the relations of the several parts of his figure—he does not consider that the visible figure presented to his eye, is only the representative of a tangible figure, upon which all his attention is fixed; he does not consider that these two figures have really different properties; and that, what he demonstrates to be true of the one, is not true of the other.

This, perhaps, will seem so great a paradox, even to

mathematicians, as to require demonstration before it can be believed. Nor is the demonstration at all difficult, if the reader will have patience to enter but a little into the mathematical consideration of visible figure, which we shall call *the geometry of visibles.*

Section IX.

OF THE GEOMETRY OF VISIBLES.*

In this geometry, the definitions of a point; of a line, whether straight or curve; of an angle, whether acute, or right, or obtuse; and of a circle—are the same as in common geometry. The mathematical reader will easily enter into the whole mystery of this geometry, if he attends duly to these few evident principles.

1. Supposing the eye placed in the centre of a sphere, every great circle of the sphere will have the same appearance to the eye as if it was a straight line; for the curvature of the circle being turned directly toward the eye, is not perceived by it. And, for the same reason, any line which is drawn in the plane of a great circle of the sphere, whether it be in reality straight or curve, will appear straight to the eye.

2. Every visible right line will appear to coincide with some great circle of the sphere; and the circumference of that great circle, even when it is produced until it returns into itself, will appear to be a continuation of the same visible right line, all the parts of it being visibly *in directum.* For the eye, perceiving only the position of objects with regard to itself, and not their distance, will see those points in the same visible place which have the same position with regard to the eye,

* How does this differ from a doctrine of Perspective?—At any rate, the notion is Berkeley's. Compare "New Theory of Vision," §§ 153-159.—H.

how different soever their distances from it may be. Now, since a plane passing through the eye and a given visible right line, will be the plane of some great circle of the sphere, every point of the visible right line will have the same position as some point of the great circle; therefore, they will both have the same visible place, and coincide to the eye ; and the whole circumference of the great circle, continued even until it returns into itself, will appear to be a continuation of the same visible right line.

Hence it follows—

3. That every visible right line, when it is continued *in directum*, as far as it may be continued, will be represented by a great circle of a sphere, in whose centre the eye is placed. It follows—

4. That the visible angle comprehended under two visible right lines, is equal to the spherical angle comprehended under the two great circles, which are the representatives of these visible lines. For, since the visible lines appear to coincide with the great circles, the visible angle comprehended under the former must be equal to the visible angle comprehended under the latter. But the visible angle comprehended under the two great circles, when seen from the centre, is of the same magnitude with the spherical angle which they really comprehend, as mathematicians know ; therefore, the visible angle made by any two visible lines is equal to the spherical angle made by the two great circles of the sphere which are their representatives.

5. Hence it is evident, that every visible right-lined triangle will coincide in all its parts with some spherical triangle. The sides of the one will appear equal to the sides of the other, and the angles of the one to the angles of the other, each to each : and, therefore, the whole of the one triangle will appear equal to the whole of the other. In a word, to the eye they will be one and the same, and have the same mathematical properties. The

properties, therefore, of visible right-lined triangles are not the same with the properties of plain triangles, but are the same with those of spherical triangles.

6. Every lesser circle of the sphere will appear a circle to the eye, placed, as we have supposed all along, in the centre of the sphere; and, on the other hand, every visible circle will appear to coincide with some lesser circle of the sphere.

7. Moreover, the whole surface of the sphere will represent the whole of visible space; for, since every visible point coincides with some point of the surface of the sphere, and has the same visible place, it follows, that all the parts of the spherical surface taken together, will represent all possible visible places—that is, the whole of visible space. And from this it follows, in the last place—

8. That every visible figure will be represented by that part of the surface of the sphere on which it might be projected, the eye being in the centre. And every such visible figure will bear the same *ratio* to the whole of visible space, as the part of the spherical surface which represents it, bears to the whole spherical surface.

The mathematical reader, I hope, will enter into these principles with perfect facility, and will as easily perceive that the following propositions with regard to visible figure and space, which we offer only as a specimen, may be mathematically demonstrated from them, and are not less true nor less evident than the propositions of Euclid, with regard to tangible figures.

Prop. 1. Every right line being produced, will at last return into itself.

2. A right line returning into itself, is the longest possible right line; and all other right lines bear a finite *ratio* to it.

3. A right line returning into itself, divides the whole of visible space into two equal parts, which will both be comprehended under this right line.

4. The whole of visible space bears a finite *ratio* to any part of it.

5. Any two right lines being produced, will meet in two points, and mutually bisect each other.

6. If two lines be parallel—that is, everywhere equally distant from each other—they cannot both be straight.

7. Any right line being given, a point may be found, which is at the same distance from all the points of the given right line.

8. A circle may be parallel to a right line—that is, may be equally distant from it in all its parts.

9. Right-lined triangles that are similar, are also equal.

10. Of every right-lined triangle, the three angles taken together, are greater than two right angles.

11. The angles of a right-lined triangle, may all be right angles, or all obtuse angles.

12. Unequal circles are not as the squares of their diameters, nor are their circumferences in the *ratio* of their diameters.

This small specimen of the geometry of visibles, is intended to lead the reader to a clear and distinct conception of the figure and extension which is presented to the mind by vision; and to demonstrate the truth of what we have affirmed above—namely, that those figures and that extension which are the immediate objects of sight, are not the figures and the extension about which common geometry is employed; that the geometrician, while he looks at his diagram, and demonstrates a proposition, hath a figure presented to his eye, which is only a sign and representative of a tangible figure: that he gives not the least attention to the first, but attends only to the last; and that these two figures have different properties, so that what he demonstrates of the one, is not true of the other.

It deserves, however, to be remarked, that, as a small part of a spherical surface differs not sensibly from a plain surface, so a small part of visible extension differs very little from that extension in length and breadth, which is the object of touch. And it is likewise to be observed, that the human eye is so formed, that an object which is seen distinctly and at one view, can occupy but a small part of visible space; for we never see distinctly what is at a considerable distance from the axis of the eye; and, therefore, when we would see a large object at one view, the eye must be at so great a distance, that the object occupies but a small part of visible space. From these two observations, it follows, that plain figures which are seen at one view, when their planes are not oblique, but direct to the eye, differ little from the visible figures which they present to the eye. The several lines in the tangible figure, have very nearly the same proportion to each other as in the visible; and the angles of the one are very nearly, although not strictly and mathematically, equal to those of the other. Although, therefore, we have found many instances of natural signs which have no similitude to the things signified, this is not the case with regard to visible figure. It hath, in all cases, such a similitude to the thing signified by it, as a plan or profile hath to that which it represents; and, in some cases, the sign and thing signified have to all sense the same figure and the same proportions. If we could find a being endued with sight only, without any other external sense, and capable of reflecting and reasoning upon what he sees, the notions and philosophical speculations of such a being, might assist us in the difficult task of distinguishing the perceptions which we have purely by sight, from those which derive their origin from other senses. Let us suppose such a being, and conceive, as well as we can, what notion he would have of visible objects, and what conclusions he would deduce from them. We must not conceive him disposed by his constitution, as we are, to consider the visible appearance as a sign of something else: it is no sign to him, because there is nothing signified by it; and, therefore, we must suppose him as much disposed to attend to the visible figure and extension of bodies, as we are disposed to attend to their tangible figure and extension.

If various figures were presented to his sense, he might, without doubt, as they grow familiar, compare them together, and perceive wherein they agree, and wherein they differ. He might perceive visible objects to have length and breadth, but could have no notion of a third dimension, any more than we can have of a fourth. All visible objects would appear to be terminated by lines, straight or curve; and objects terminated by the same visible lines, would occupy the same place, and fill the same part of visible space. It would not be possible for him to conceive one object to be behind another, or one to be nearer, another more distant.

To us, who conceive three dimensions, a line may be conceived straight; or it may be conceived incurvated in one dimension, and straight in another; or, lastly, it may be incurvated in two dimensions. Suppose a line to be drawn upwards and downwards, its length makes one dimension, which we shall call *upwards and downwards*; and there are two dimensions remaining, according to which it may be straight or curve. It may be bent to the right or to the left, and, if it has no bending either to right or left, it is straight in this dimension. But supposing it straight in this dimension of right and left, there is still another dimension remaining, in which it may be curve; for it may be bent backwards or forwards. When we conceive a tangible straight line, we exclude curvature in either of these two dimensions: and as what is conceived to be excluded, must be conceived, as well as what is conceived to be included, it follows that all the three dimensions enter into our conception of a straight line. Its length is one dimension, its straightness in two other dimensions is included, or curvature in these two dimensions excluded, in the conception of it.

The being we have supposed, having no conception of more than two dimensions, of which the length of a line is one, cannot possibly conceive it either straight or curve in more than one dimension; so that, in his conception of a right line, curvature to the right hand or left is excluded; but curvature backwards or forwards cannot be excluded, because he neither hath, nor can have any conception of such curvature. Hence we see the reason that a line which is straight to the eye, may return into itself; for its being straight to the eye, implies only straightness in one dimension; and a line which is straight in one dimension may, notwithstanding, be curve in another dimension, and so may return into itself.

To us, who conceive three dimensions, a surface is that which hath length and breadth, excluding thickness; and a surface may be either plain in this third dimension, or it may be incurvated: so that the notion of a third dimension enters into our conception of a surface; for it is only by means of this third dimension that we can distinguish surfaces into plain and curve surfaces; and neither one nor the other can be conceived without conceiving a third dimension.

The being we have supposed, having no conception of a third dimension, his visible figures have length and breadth indeed; but thickness is neither included nor excluded, being a thing of which he has no conception. And, therefore, visible figures, although they have length and breadth, as surfaces have, yet they are neither plain surfaces nor curve surfaces. For a curve surface implies curvature in a third dimension, and a plain surface implies the want of curvature in a third dimension; and such a being can conceive neither of these, because he has no conception of a third dimension. Moreover, although he hath a distinct conception of the inclination of two lines which make an angle, yet he can neither conceive a plain angle nor a spherical angle. Even his notion of a point is somewhat less determined than ours. In the notion of a point, we exclude length, breadth, and thickness; he excludes length and breadth, but cannot either exclude, or include thickness, because he hath no conception of it.

Having thus settled the notions which such a being as we have supposed might form of mathematical points, lines, angles, and figures, it is easy to see, that, by comparing these together, and reasoning about them, he might discover their relations, and form geometrical conclusions built upon self-evident principles. He might likewise, without doubt, have the same notions of numbers as we have, and form a system of arithmetic. It is not material to say in what order he might proceed in such discoveries, or how much time and pains he might employ about them, but what such a being, by reason and ingenuity, without any materials of sensation but those of sight only, might discover.

As it is more difficult to attend to a detail of possibilities than of facts, even of slender authority, I shall beg leave to give an extract from the travels of Johannes Rudolphus Anepigraphus, a Rosicrucian philosopher, who having, by deep study of the occult sciences, acquired the art of transporting himself to various sublunary regions, and of conversing with various orders of intelligences, in the course of his adventures became acquainted with an order of beings exactly such as I have supposed.

How they communicate their sentiments to one another, and by what means he became acquainted with their language, and was initiated into their philosophy; as well as of many other particulars, which might have gratified the curiosity of his readers, and, perhaps, added credibility to his relation, he hath not thought fit to inform us; these being matters proper for adepts only to know.

His account of their philosophy is as follows:—

"The Idomenians," saith he, "are many of them very ingenious, and much given to contemplation. In arithmetic, geometry, metaphysics, and physics, they have most elaborate systems. In the two latter, indeed, they have had many disputes carried on with great subtilty, and are divided into various sects; yet in the two former there hath been no less unanimity than among the human species. Their principles relating to numbers and arithmetic, making allowance for their notation, differ in nothing from ours—but their geometry differs very considerably."

As our author's account of the geometry of the Idomenians agrees in everything with the geometry of visibles, of which we have already given a specimen, we shall pass over it. He goes on thus:—"Colour, extension, and figure, are conceived to be the essential properties of body. A very considerable sect maintains, that colour is the essence of body. If there had been no colour, say they, there had been no perception or sensation. Colour is all that we perceive, or can conceive, that is peculiar to body; extension and figure being modes common to body and to empty space. And if we should suppose a body to be annihilated, colour is the only thing in it that can be annihilated; for its place, and consequently the figure and extension of that place, must remain, and cannot be imagined not to exist. These philosophers hold space to be the place of all bodies, immovable and indestructible, without figure and similar in all its parts, incapable of increase or diminution, yet not unmeasurable; for every the least part of space bears a finite *ratio* to the whole. So that with them the whole extent of space is the common and natural measure of everything that hath length and breadth; and the magnitude of every body and of every figure is expressed by its being such a part of the universe. In like manner, the common and natural measure of length is an infinite right line, which, as hath been before observed, returns into itself, and hath no limits, but bears a finite *ratio* to every other line.

"As to their natural philosophy, it is now acknowledged by the wisest of them to have been for many ages in a very low state. The philosophers observing, that body can differ from another only in colour, figure, or magnitude, it was taken for granted, that all their particular qualities must arise from the various combinations of these their essential attributes; and, therefore, it was looked upon as the end of natural philosophy, to shew how the various combinations of these three qualities in different bodies produced all the phænomena of nature. It were endless to enumerate the various systems that were invented with this view, and the disputes that were carried on for ages; the followers of every system exposing the weak sides of other systems, and palliating those of their own with great art.

"At last, some free and facetious spirits, wearied with eternal disputation, and the labour of patching and propping weak systems, began to complain of the subtilty of nature; of the infinite changes that bodies undergo in figure, colour, and magnitude; and of the difficulty of accounting for these appearances—making this a pretence for giving up all inquiries into the causes of things, as vain and fruitless.

"These wits had ample matter of mirth and ridicule in the systems of philosophers; and, finding it an easier task to pull down than to build or support, and that every sect furnished them with arms and auxiliaries to destroy another, they began to spread mightily, and went on with great success. Thus philosophy gave way to scepticism and irony, and those systems which had been the work of ages, and the admiration of the learned, became the jest of the vulgar: for even the vulgar readily took part in the triumph over a kind of learning which they had long suspected, because it produced nothing but wrangling and altercation. The wits, having now acquired great reputation, and being flushed with success, began to think their triumph incomplete, until every pretence to knowledge was overturned; and accordingly began their attacks upon arithmetic, geometry, and even upon the common notions of untaught Idomenians. So difficult it hath always been," says our author, "for great conquerors to know where to stop.

"In the meantime, natural philosophy began to rise from its ashes, under the direction of a person of great genius, who is looked upon as having had something in him above Idomenian nature. He observed, that the Idomenian faculties were certainly intended for contemplation, and that the works of nature were a nobler subject to exercise them upon, than the follies of systems, or the errors of the learned; and being sensible of the difficulty of finding out the causes of natural things, he proposed, by accurate observation of the phænomena of nature, to find out the rules according to which they happen, without inquiring into the causes of those rules. In this he made considerable progress himself, and planned out much work for his followers, who call themselves *inductive philosophers.* The sceptics look with envy upon this rising sect, as eclipsing their reputation, and threatening to limit their empire; but they are at a loss on what hand to attack it. The vulgar begin to reverence it as producing useful discoveries.

"It is to be observed, that every Idomenian firmly believes, that two or more bodies may exist in the same place. For this they have the testimony of sense, and they can no more doubt of it, than they can doubt whether they have any perception at all. They often see two bodies meet and coincide in the same place, and separate again, without having undergone any change in their sensible qualities by this penetration. When two bodies meet, and occupy the same place, commonly one only appears in that place, and the other disappears.

That which continues to appear is said to overcome, the other to be overcome."

To this quality of bodies they gave a name, which our author tells us hath no word answering to it in any human language. And, therefore, after making a long apology, which I omit, he begs leave to call it *the overcoming quality of bodies.* He assures us, that "the speculations which had been raised about this single quality of bodies, and the hypotheses contrived to account for it, were sufficient to fill many volumes. Nor have there been fewer hypotheses invented by their philosophers, to account for the changes of magnitude and figure; which, in most bodies that move, they perceive to be in a continual fluctuation. The founder of the inductive sect, believing it to be above the reach of Idomenian faculties, to discover the real causes of these phænomena, applied himself to find from observation, by what laws they are connected together; and discovered many mathematical ratios and relations concerning the motions, magnitudes, figures, and overcoming quality of bodies, which constant experience confirms. But the opposers of this sect choose rather to content themselves with feigned causes of these phænomena, than to acknowledge the real laws whereby they are governed, which humble their pride, by being confessedly unaccountable."

Thus far Johannes Rudolphus Anepigraphus. Whether this Anepigraphus be the same who is recorded among the Greek alchemistical writers not yet published, by Borrichius, Fabricius, and others, I do not pretend to determine. The identity of their name, and the similitude of their studies, although no slight arguments, yet are not absolutely conclusive. Nor will I take upon me to judge of the narrative of this learned traveller, by the *external* marks of his credibility; I shall confine myself to those which the critics call *internal.* It would even be of small importance to inquire, whether the Idomenians have a real, or only an ideal existence; since this is disputed among the learned with regard to things with which we are more nearly connected. The important question is, whether the account above given, is a just account of their geometry and philosophy? We have all the faculties which they have, with the addition of others which they have not; we may, therefore, form some judgment of their philosophy and geometry, by separating from all others, the perceptions we have by sight and reasoning upon them. As far as I am able to judge in this way, after a careful examination, their geometry must be such as Anepigraphus hath described. Nor does his account of their philosophy appear to contain any evident marks of imposture; although here, no doubt, proper allowance is to be made for liberties which travellers take, as well as for involuntary mistakes which they are apt to fall into.

Section X.

OF THE PARALLEL MOTION OF THE EYES.

Having explained, as distinctly as we can, visible figure, and shewn its connection with the things signified by it, it will be proper next to consider some phænomena of the eyes, and of vision, which have commonly been referred to custom, to anatomical or to mechanical causes; but which, as I conceive, must be resolved into original powers and principles of the human mind; and, therefore, belong properly to the subject of this inquiry.

The first is the parallel motion of the eyes; by which, when one eye is turned to the right or to the left, upwards or downwards, or straight forwards, the other always goes along with it in the same direction. We see plainly, when both eyes are open, that they are always turned the same way, as if both were acted upon by the same motive force; and if one eye is shut, and the hand laid upon it, while the other turns various ways, we feel the eye that is shut turn at the same time, and that whether we will or not. What makes this phænomenon surprising is, that it is acknowledged, by all anatomists, that the muscles which move the two eyes, and the nerves which serve these muscles, are entirely distinct and unconnected. It would be thought very surprising and unaccountable to see a man, who, from his birth, never moved one arm, without moving the other precisely in the same manner, so as to keep them always parallel—yet it would not be more difficult to find the physical cause of such motion of the arms, than it is to find the cause of the parallel motion of the eyes, which is perfectly similar.

The only cause that hath been assigned of this parallel motion of the eyes, is custom. We find by experience, it is said, when we begin to look at objects, that, in order to have distinct vision, it is necessary to turn both eyes the same way; therefore, we soon acquire the habit of doing it constantly, and by degrees lose the power of doing otherwise.

This account of the matter seems to be insufficient; because habits are not got at once; it takes time to acquire and to confirm them; and if this motion of the eyes were got by habit, we should see children, when they are born, turn their eyes different ways, and move one without the other, as they do their hands or legs. I know some have affirmed that they are apt to do so. But I have never found it true from my own observation, although I have taken pains to make observations of this kind, and have had good opportunities. I have likewise consulted experienced midwives, mothers, and nurses, and found them agree, that they had never observed distortions of this kind in the eyes of children, but when they had reason to suspect convulsions, or some preternatural cause.

It seems, therefore, to be extremely probable, that,

previous to custom, there is something in the constitution, some natural instinct, which directs us to move both eyes always the same way.

We know not how the mind acts upon the body, nor by what power the muscles are contracted and relaxed—but we see that, in some of the voluntary, as well as in some of the involuntary motions, this power is so directed, that many muscles which have no material tie or connection, act in concert, each of them being taught to play its part in exact time and measure. Nor doth a company of expert players in a theatrical performance, or of excellent musicians in a concert, or of good dancers in a country dance, with more regularity and order, conspire and contribute their several parts, to produce one uniform effect, than a number of muscles do, in many of the animal functions, and in many voluntary actions. Yet we see such actions no less skilfully and regularly performed in children, and in those who know not that they have such muscles, than in the most skilful anatomist and physiologist.

Who taught all the muscles that are concerned in sucking, in swallowing our food, in breathing, and in the several natural expulsions, to act their part in such regular order and exact measure? It was not custom surely. It was that same powerful and wise Being who made the fabric of the human body, and fixed the laws by which the mind operates upon every part of it, so that they may answer the purposes intended by them. And when we see, in so many other instances, a system of unconnected muscles conspiring so wonderfully in their several functions, without the aid of habit, it needs not be thought strange, that the muscles of the eyes should, without this aid, conspire to give that direction to the eyes, without which they could not answer their end.

We see a like conspiring action in the muscles which contract the pupils of the two eyes; and in those muscles, whatever they be, by which the conformation of the eyes is varied according to the distance of objects.

It ought, however, to be observed, that, although it appears to be by natural instinct that both eyes are always turned the same way, there is still some latitude left for custom.

What we have said of the parallel motion of the eyes, is not to be understood so strictly as if nature directed us to keep their axes always precisely and mathematically parallel to each other. Indeed, although they are always nearly parallel, they hardly ever are exactly so. When we look at an object, the axes of the eyes meet in that object: and, therefore, make an angle, which is always small, but will be greater or less, according as the object is nearer or more remote. Nature hath very wisely left us the power of varying the parallelism of our eyes a little, so that we can direct them to the same point, whether remote or near. This, no doubt, is learned by custom: and accordingly we see, that it is a long time before children get this habit in perfection.

This power of varying the parallelism of the eyes is naturally no more than is sufficient for the purpose intended by it; but by much practice and straining, it may be increased. Accordingly, we see, that some have acquired the power of distorting their eyes into unnatural directions, as others have acquired the power of distorting their bodies into unnatural postures.

Those who have lost the sight of an eye, commonly lose what they had got by custom, in the direction of their eyes, but retain what they had by nature; that is, although their eyes turn and move always together, yet, when they look upon an object, the blind eye will often have a very small deviation from it; which is not perceived by a slight observer, but may be discerned by one accustomed to make exact observations in these matters.

Section XI.

OF OUR SEEING OBJECTS ERECT BY INVERTED IMAGES.

Another phænomenon which hath perplexed philosophers, is our seeing objects erect, when it is well known that their images or pictures upon the *tunica retina* of the eye are inverted.

The sagacious Kepler first made the noble discovery, that distinct but inverted pictures of visible objects are formed upon the *retina* by the rays of light coming from the object. The same great philosopher demonstrated, from the principles of optics, how these pictures are formed—to wit, That the rays coming from any one point of the object, and falling upon the various parts of the pupil, are, by the *cornea* and crystalline, refracted so as to meet again in one point of the *retina*, and there paint the colour of that point of the object from which they come. As the rays from different points of the object cross each other before they come to the *retina*, the picture they form must be inverted; the upper part of the object being painted upon the lower part of the *retina*, the right side of the object upon the left of the *retina*, and so of the other parts.

This philosopher thought that we see objects erect by means of these inverted pictures, for this reason, that, as the rays from different points of the object cross each other before they fall upon the *retina*, we conclude that the impulse which we feel upon the lower part of the *retina* comes from above, and that the impulse which we feel upon the higher part comes from below.

Des Cartes afterwards gave the same solution of this phænomenon, and illustrated it by the judgment which we form of the position of objects which we feel with our arms crossed, or with two sticks that cross each other.

But we cannot acquiesce in this solution. First, Because it supposes our seeing things erect, to be a deduction of reason, drawn from certain premises: whereas it seems to be an immediate perception. And, secondly, Because the premises from which all mankind are supposed to draw this conclusion, never entered into the minds of the far greater part, but are absolutely unknown to them. We have no feeling or perception of the pictures upon the *retina*, and as little surely of the position of them. In order to see objects erect, according to the principles of Kepler or Des Cartes, we must previously know that the rays of light come from the object to the eye in straight lines; we must know that the rays from different points of the object cross one another before they form the pictures upon the *retina;* and, lastly, we must know that these pictures are really inverted. Now, although all these things are true, and known to philosophers, yet they are absolutely unknown to the far greatest part of mankind: nor is it possible that they who are absolutely ignorant of them, should reason from them, and build conclusions upon them. Since, therefore, visible objects appear erect to the ignorant as well as to the learned, this cannot be a conclusion drawn from premises which never entered into the minds of the ignorant. We have indeed had occasion to observe many instances of conclusions drawn, either by means of original principles, or by habit, from premises which pass through the mind very quickly, and which are never made the objects of reflection; but surely no man will conceive it possible to draw conclusions from premises which never entered into the mind at all.

Bishop Berkeley having justly rejected this solution, gives one founded upon his own principles; wherein he is followed by the judicious Dr. Smith, in his "Optics;" and this we shall next explain and examine.

That ingenious writer conceives the ideas of sight to be altogether unlike those of touch. And, since the notions we have of an object by these different senses have no similitude, we can learn only by experience how one sense will be affected, by what, in a certain manner, affects the other. Figure, position, and even number, in tangible objects, are ideas of touch; and, although there is no similitude between these and the ideas of sight, yet we learn by experience, that a triangle affects the sight in such a manner, and that a square affects it in such another manner—hence we judge that which affects it in the first manner, to be a triangle, and that which affects it in the second, to be a square. In the same way, finding, from experience, that an object in an erect position affects the eye in one manner, and the same object in an inverted position affects it in another, we learn to judge, by the manner in which the eye is affected, whether the object is erect or inverted. In a word, visible ideas, according to this author, are signs of the tangible; and the mind passeth from the sign to the thing signified, not by means of any similitude between the one and the other, nor by any natural principle, but by having found them constantly conjoined in experience, as the sounds of a language are with the things they signify: so that, if the images upon the *retina* had been always erect, they would have shewn the objects erect, in the manner as they do now that they are inverted—nay, if the visible idea which we now have from an inverted object, had been associated from the beginning with the erect position of that object, it would have signified an erect position, as readily as it now signifies an inverted one. And, if the visible appearance of two shillings had been found connected from the beginning with the tangible idea of one shilling, that appearance would as naturally and readily have signified the unity of the object as now it signifies its duplicity.

This opinion is, undoubtedly, very ingenious: and, if it is just, serves to resolve not only the phænomenon now under consideration, but likewise that which we shall next consider—our seeing objects single with two eyes.

It is evident that, in this solution, it is supposed that we do not originally, and previous to acquired habits, see things either erect or inverted, of one figure or another, single or double ; but learn, from experience, to judge of their tangible position, figure, and number, by certain visible signs.

Indeed, it must be acknowledged to be extremely difficult to distinguish the immediate and natural objects of sight, from the conclusions which we have been accustomed from infancy to draw from them. Bishop Berkeley was the first that attempted to distinguish the one from the other, and to trace out the boundary that divides them. And if, in doing so, he hath gone a little to the right hand or to the left, this might be expected in a subject altogether new, and of the greatest subtilty. The nature of vision hath received great light from this distinction ; and many phænomena in optics, which before appeared altogether unaccountable, have been clearly and distinctly resolved by it. It is natural, and almost unavoidable, to one who hath made an important discovery in philosophy, to carry it a little beyond its sphere, and to apply it to the resolution of phænomena which do not fall within its province. Even the great Newton, when he had discovered the universal law of gravitation, and observed how many of the phænomena of nature depend upon this, and other laws of attraction and repulsion, could not help expressing his conjecture, that all the phænomena of the material world depend upon attracting and repelling forces in the particles of matter. And I suspect that the ingenious Bishop of Cloyne, having found so many phænomena of vision reducible to the constant association of the ideas of sight and touch, carried this principle a little beyond its just limits.

In order to judge as well as we can whether it is so, let us suppose such a blind man as Dr. Saunderson, having all the knowledge and abilities which a blind man may have, suddenly made to see perfectly. Let us suppose him kept from all opportunities of associating his ideas of sight with those of touch, until the former become a little familiar; and the first surprise, occasioned by objects so new, being abated, he has time to canvass them, and to compare them, in his mind, with the notions which he formerly had by touch; and, in particular, to compare, in his mind, that visible extension which his eyes present, with the extension in length and breadth with which he was before acquainted.

We have endeavoured to prove, that a blind man may form a notion of the visible extension and figure of bodies, from the relation which it bears to their tangible extension and figure. Much more, when this visible extension and figure are presented to his eye, will he be able to compare them with tangible extension and figure, and to perceive that the one has length and breadth as well as the other; that the one may be bounded by lines, either straight or curve, as well as the other. And, therefore, he will perceive that there may be visible as well as tangible circles, triangles, quadrilateral and multilateral figures. And, although the visible figure is coloured, and the tangible is not, they may, notwithstanding, have the same figure; as two objects of touch may have the same figure, although one is hot and the other cold.

We have demonstrated, that the properties of visible figure differ from those of the plain figures which they represent; but it was observed, at the same time, that when the object is so small as to be seen distinctly at one view, and is placed directly before the eye, the difference between the visible and the tangible figure is too small to be perceived by the senses Thus, it is true, that, of every visible triangle, the three angles are greater than two right angles; whereas, in a plain triangle, the three angles are equal to two right angles; but when the visible triangle is small, its three angles will be so nearly equal to two right angles, that the sense cannot discern the difference. In like manner, the circumferences of unequal visible circles are not, but those of plain circles are, in the *ratio* of their diameters; yet, in small visible circles, the circumferences are very nearly in the *ratio* of their diameters; and the diameter bears the same *ratio* to the circumference as in a plain circle, very nearly.

Hence it appears, that small visible figures (and such only can be seen distinctly at one view) have not only a resemblance to the plain tangible figures which have the same name, but are to all senses the same: so that if Dr. Saunderson had been made to see, and had attentively viewed the figures of the first book of Euclid, he might, by thought and consideration, without touching them, have found out that they were the very figures he was before so well acquainted with by touch.

When plain figures are seen obliquely, their visible figure differs more from the tangible; and the representation which is made to the eye, of solid figures, is still more imperfect; because visible extension hath not three, but two dimensions only. Yet, as it cannot be said that an exact picture of a man hath no resemblance of the man, or that a perspective view of a house hath no resemblance of the house, so it cannot be said, with any propriety, that the visible figure of a man or of a house hath no resemblance of the objects which they represent.

Bishop Berkeley therefore proceeds upon a capital mistake, in supposing that there is no resemblance betwixt the extension, figure, and position which we see, and that which we perceive by touch.

We may further observe, that Bishop Berkeley's system, with regard to material things, must have made him see this question, of the erect appearance of objects, in a very different light from that in which it appears to those who do not adopt his system.

In his theory of vision, he seems indeed to allow, that

there is an external material world: but he believed that this external world is tangible only, and not visible; and that the visible world, the proper object of sight, is not external, but in the mind. If this is supposed, he that affirms that he sees things erect and not inverted, affirms that there is a top and a bottom, a right and a left in the mind. Now, I confess I am not so well acquainted with the topography of the mind, as to be able to affix a meaning to these words when applied to it.

We shall therefore allow, that, if visible objects were not external, but existed only in the mind, they could have no figure, or position, or extension; and that it would be absurd to affirm, that they are seen either erect or inverted, or that there is any resemblance between them and the objects of touch. But when we propose the question, why objects are seen erect and not inverted, we take it for granted, that we are not in Bishop Berkeley's ideal world, but in that world which men who yield to the dictates of common sense, believe themselves to inhabit. We take it for granted, that the objects both of sight and touch, are external, and have a certain figure, and a certain position with regard to one another, and with regard to our bodies, whether we perceive it or not.

When I hold my walking-cane upright in my hand, and look at it, I take it for granted that I see and handle the same individual object. When I say that I feel it erect, my meaning is, that I feel the head directed from the horizon, and the point directed towards it; and when I say that I see it erect, I mean that I see it with the head directed from the horizon, and the point towards it. I conceive the horizon as a fixed object both of sight and touch, with relation to which, objects are said to be high or low, erect or inverted; and when the question is asked, why I see the object erect, and not inverted, it is the same as if you should ask, why I see it in that position which it really hath, or why the eye shews the real position of objects, and doth not shew them in an inverted position, as they are seen by a common astronomical telescope, or as their pictures are seen upon the *retina* of an eye when it is dissected.

Section XII.

THE SAME SUBJECT CONTINUED.

It is impossible to give a satisfactory answer to this question, otherwise than by pointing out the laws of nature which take place in vision; for by these the phænomena of vision must be regulated.

Therefore, I answer, First, That, by a law of nature, the rays of light proceed from every point of the object to the pupil of the eye, in straight lines; Secondly, That, by the laws of nature, the rays coming from any one point of the object to the various parts of the pupil, are so refracted as to meet again in one point of the *retina;* and the rays from different points of the object, first crossing each other, and then proceeding to as many different points of the *retina*, form an inverted picture of the object.

So far the principles of optics carry us; and experience further assures us, that, if there is no such picture upon the *retina*, there is no vision; and that such as the picture on the *retina* is, such is the appearance of the object, in colour and figure, distinctness or indistinctness, brightness or faintness.

It is evident, therefore, that the pictures upon the *retina* are, by the laws of nature, a mean of vision; but in what way they accomplish their end, we are totally ignorant. Philosophers conceive, that the impression made on the *retina* by the rays of light, is communicated to the optic nerve, and by the optic nerve conveyed to some part of the brain, by them called the *sensorium;* and that the impression thus conveyed to the *sensorium* is immediately perceived by the mind, which is supposed to reside there. But we know nothing of the seat of the soul: and we are so far from perceiving immediately what is transacted in the brain, that of all parts of the human body we know least about it. It is indeed very probable, that the optic nerve is an instrument of vision no less necessary than the *retina;* and that some impression is made upon it, by means of the pictures on the *retina.* But of what kind this impression is, we know nothing.

There is not the least probability that there is any picture or image of the object either in the optic nerve or brain. The pictures on the *retina* are formed by the rays of light; and, whether we suppose, with some, that their impulse upon the *retina* causes some vibration of the fibres of the optic nerve, or, with others, that it gives motion to some subtile fluid contained in the nerve, neither that vibration nor this motion can resemble the visible object which is presented to the mind. Nor is there any probability that the mind perceives the pictures upon the *retina.* These pictures are no more objects of our perception, than the brain is, or the optic nerve. No man ever saw the pictures in his own eye, nor indeed the pictures in the eye of another, until it was taken out of the head and duly prepared.

It is very strange, that philosophers, of all ages, should have agreed in this notion, that the images of external objects are conveyed by the organs of sense to the brain, and are there perceived by the mind. Nothing can be more unphilosophical. For, First, This notion hath no foundation in fact and observation. Of all the organs of sense, the eye only, as far as we can discover, forms any kind of image of its object; and the images formed by the eye are not in the brain, but only in the bottom of the eye; nor are they at all perceived or felt by the mind. Secondly, It is as difficult to conceive how the mind perceives images in the brain, as how it perceives things more distant. If any man will shew how the mind may perceive images in the brain, I will undertake to shew how it may perceive the most distant objects; for, if we give eyes to the mind, to perceive what is transacted at home in its dark chamber, why may we not make these eyes a little longer-sighted? and then we shall have no occasion for that unphilosophical fiction of images in the brain. In a word, the manner and mechanism of the mind's perception is quite beyond our comprehension; and this way of explaining it, by images in the brain, seems to be founded upon very gross notions of the mind and its operations; as if the supposed images in the brain, by a kind of contact, formed similar impressions or images of objects upon the mind, of which impressions it is supposed to be conscious,

We have endeavoured to shew, throughout the course of this inquiry, that the impressions made upon the mind by means of the five senses, have not the least resemblance to the objects of sense; and, therefore, as we see no shadow of evidence that there are any such images in the brain, so we see no purpose, in philosophy, that the supposition of them can answer. Since the picture upon the *retina*, therefore, is neither itself seen by the mind, nor produces any impression upon the brain or *sensorium*, which is seen by the mind, nor makes any impression upon the mind that resembles the object, it may still be asked, How this picture upon the *retina* causes vision?

Before we answer this question, it is proper to observe, that, in the operations of the mind, as well as in those of bodies, we must often be satisfied with knowing that certain things are connected, and invariably follow one another, without being able to discover the chain that goes between them. It is to such connections that we give the name of *laws of nature*; and when we say that one thing produces another by a law of nature, this signifies no more, but that one thing, which we call in popular language *the cause*, is constantly and invariably followed by another, which we call *the effect;* and that we know not how they are connected. Thus, we see it is a fact, that bodies gravitate towards bodies; and that this gravitation is regulated by certain mathematical proportions, according to the distances of the bodies from each other, and their quantities of matter. Being unable to discover the cause of this gravitation, and presuming that it is the immediate operation, either of the Author of nature, or of some subordinate cause, which we have not hitherto been able to reach, we call it *a law of nature.* If any philosopher should hereafter be so happy, as to discover the cause of gravitation, this can only be done by discovering some more general law of nature, of which the gravitation of bodies is a necessary consequence. In every chain of natural causes, the highest link is a primary law of nature, and the highest link which we can trace, by just induction, is either this primary law of nature, or a necessary consequence of it. To trace out the laws of nature, by induction from the phænomena of nature, is all that true philosophy aims at, and all that it can ever reach.

There are laws of nature by which the operations of the mind are regulated, there are also laws of nature that govern the material system ; and, as the latter are the ultimate conclusions which the human faculties can reach in the philosophy of bodies, so the former are the ultimate conclusions we can reach in the philosophy of minds.

To return, therefore, to the question above proposed, we may see, from what hath been just now observed, that it amounts to this—By what law of nature is a picture upon the *retina* the mean or occasion of my seeing an external object of the same figure and colour in a contrary position, and in a certain direction from the eye?

It will, without doubt, be allowed that I see the whole object in the same manner and by the same law by which I see any one point of it. Now I know it to be a fact, that, in direct vision, I see every point of the object in the direction of the right line that passeth from the centre of the eye to that point of the object. And I know, likewise, from optics, that the ray of light that comes to the centre of my eye, passes on to the *retina* in the same direction. Hence, it appears to be a fact, *that every point of the object is seen in the direction of a right line passing from the picture of that point on the* retina, *through the centre of the eye.* As this is a fact that holds universally and invariably, it must either be a law of nature or the necessary consequence of some more general law of nature; and, according to the just rules of philosophising, we may hold it for a law of nature, until some more general law be discovered, whereof it is a necessary consequence—which, I suspect, can never be done.

Thus, we see that the phænomena of vision lead us by the hand to a law of nature, or a law of our constitution, of which law, our seeing objects erect by inverted images, is a necessary consequence. For it necessarily follows, from the law we have mentioned, that the object whose picture is lowest on the *retina* must be seen in the highest direction from the eye; and that the object whose picture is on the right of the *retina* must be seen on the left; so that, if the pictures had been erect in the *retina*, we should have seen the object inverted. My chief intention in handling this question, was to point out this law of nature, which, as it is a part of the constitution of the human mind, belongs properly to the subject of this inquiry. For this reason, I shall make some farther remarks upon it, after doing justice to the ingenious Dr. Porterfield, who long ago, in the "Medical Essays," or, more lately, in his "Treatise of the Eye," pointed out, as a primary law of our nature, That a visible object appears in the direction of a right line perpendicular to the *retina* at that point where its image is painted. If lines drawn from the centre of the eye to all parts of the *retina* be perpendicular to it, as they must be very nearly, this coincides with the law we have mentioned, and is the same in other words. In order, therefore, that we may have a more distinct notion of this law of our constitution, we may observe—

1. That we can give no reason why the *retina* is, of all parts of the body, the only one on which pictures made by the rays of light cause vision; and, therefore, we must resolve this solely into a law of our constitution. We may form such pictures by means of optical glasses, upon the hand, or upon any other part of the body; but they are not felt, nor do they produce anything like vision. A picture upon the *retina* is as little felt as one upon the hand; but it produces vision, for no other reason that we know, but because it is destined by the wisdom of nature to this purpose. The vibrations of the air strike upon the eye, the palate, and the olfactory membrane, with the same force as upon the *membrani tympani* of the ear. The impression they make upon the last produces the sensation of sound; but their impression upon any of the former produces no sensation at all. This may be extended to all the senses, whereof each hath its peculiar laws, according to which the impressions made upon the organ of that sense, produce sensations or perceptions in the mind, that cannot be produced by impressions made upon any other organ.

2. We may observe, that the laws of perception, by the different senses, are very different, not only in respect of the nature of the objects perceived by them, but likewise in respect of the notices they give us of the distance and situation of the object. In all of them the object is conceived * to be external, and to have real existence, independent of our perception: but in one, the distance, figure, and situation of the object, are all

* The common sense of mankind assures us that the object of sense, is not merely *conceived* to be external, but *perceived* in its externality; that we know the Non-Ego, not merely mediately, by a representation in the Ego, but immediately, as existing though only as existing in relation to our organs.—H.

presented to the mind: in another, the figure and situation, but not the distance; and in others, neither figure, situation, nor distance. In vain do we attempt to account for these varieties in the manner of perception by the different senses, from principles of anatomy or natural philosophy. They must at last be resolved into the will of our Maker, who intended that our powers of perception should have certain limits, and adapted the organs of perception, and the laws of nature by which they operate, to his wise purposes.

When we hear an unusual sound, the sensation indeed is in the mind, but we know that there is something external that produced this sound. At the same time, our hearing does not inform us whether the sounding body is near or at a distance, in this direction or that; and therefore we look round to discover it.

If any new phænomenon appears in the heavens, we see exactly its colour, its apparent place, magnitude, and figure; but we see not its distance. It may be in the atmosphere, it may be among the planets, or it may be in the sphere of the fixed stars, for anything the eye can determine.

The testimony of the sense of touch reaches only to objects that are contiguous to the organ, but, with regard to them, is more precise and determinate. When we feel a body with our hand, we know the figure, distance, and position of it, as well as whether it is rough or smooth, hard or soft, hot or cold.

The sensations of touch, of seeing, and hearing, are all in the mind, and can have no existence but when they are perceived. How do they all constantly and invariably suggest the conception and belief of external objects, which exist whether they are perceived or not? No philosopher can give any other answer to this, but that such is the constitution of our nature. How do we know that the object of touch is at the finger's end, and nowhere else?—that the object of sight is in such a direction from the eye, and in no other, but may be at any distance?—and that the object of hearing may be at any distance, and in any direction? Not by custom surely —not by reasoning, or comparing ideas—but by the constitution of our nature. How do we perceive visible objects in the direction of right lines perpendicular to that part of the *retina* on which the rays strike, while we do not perceive the objects of hearing in lines perpendicular to the *membrana tympani* upon which the vibrations of the air strike? Because such are the laws of our nature. How do we know the parts of our bodies affected by particular pains? Not by experience or by reasoning, but by the constitution of nature. The sensation of pain is, no doubt, in the mind, and cannot be said to have any relation, from its own nature, to any part of the body; but this sensation, by our constitution, gives a perception of some particular part of the body, whose disorder causes the uneasy sensation. If it were not so, a man who never before felt either the gout or the toothache, when he is first seized with the gout in his toe, might mistake it for the toothache.

Every sense, therefore, hath its peculiar laws and limits, by the constitution of our nature; and one of the laws of sight is, that we always see an object in the direction of a right line, passing from its image on the *retina* through the centre of the eye.

3. Perhaps some readers will imagine that it is easier, and will answer the purpose as well, to conceive a law of nature, by which we shall always see objects in the place in which they are, and in their true position, without having recourse to images on the *retina*, or to the optical centre of the eye.

To this I answer, that nothing can be a law of nature which is contrary to fact. The laws of nature are the most general facts we can discover in the operations of nature. Like other facts, they are not to be hit upon by a happy conjecture, but justly deduced from observation;

like other general facts, they are not to be drawn from a few particulars, but from a copious, patient, and cautious induction. That we see things always in their true place and position, is not fact; and therefore it can be no law of nature. In a plain mirror, I see myself, and other things, in places very different from those they really occupy. And so it happens in every instance wherein the rays coming from the object are either reflected or refracted before falling upon the eye. Those who know anything of optics, know that, in all such cases, the object is seen in the direction of a line passing from the centre of the eye, to the point where the rays were last reflected or refracted; and that upon this all the powers of the telescope and microscope depend.

Shall we say, then, that it is a law of nature, that the object is seen in the direction which the rays have when they fall on the eye, or rather in the direction contrary to that of the rays when they fall upon the eye? No. This is not true; and therefore it is no law of nature. For the rays, from any one point of the object, come to all parts of the pupil; and therefore must have different directions: but we see the object only in one of these directions—to wit, in the direction of the rays that come to the centre of the eye. And this holds true, even when the rays that should pass through the centre are stopped, and the object is seen by rays that pass at a distance from the centre.

Perhaps it may still be imagined, that, although we are not made so as to see objects always in their true place, nor so as to see them precisely in the direction of the rays when they fall upon the *cornea;* yet we may be so made as to see the object in the direction which the rays have when they fall upon the *retina,* after they have undergone all their refractions in the eye—that is, in the direction in which the rays pass from the crystalline to the *retina.* But neither is this true; and consequently it is no law of our constitution. In order to see that it is not true, we must conceive all the rays that pass from the crystalline to one point of the *retina*, as forming a small cone, whose base is upon the back of the crystalline, and whose vertex is a point of the *retina*. It is evident that the rays which form the picture in this point, have various directions, even after they pass the crystalline: yet the object is seen only in one of these directions —to wit, in the direction of the rays that come from the centre of the eye. Nor is this owing to any particular virtue in the central rays, or in the centre itself; for the central rays may be stopped. When they are stopped, the image will be formed upon the same point of the *retina* as before, by rays that are not central, nor have the same direction which the central rays had: and in this case the object is seen in the same direction as before, although there are now no rays coming in that direction.

From this induction we conclude, That our seeing an object in that particular direction in which we do see it, is not owing to any law of nature by which we are made to see it in the direction of the rays, either before their refractions in the eye, or after, but to a law of our nature, by which we see the object in the direction of the right line that passeth from the picture of the object upon the *retina* to the centre of the eye.

The facts upon which I ground this induction, are taken from some curious experiments of Scheiner, in his "Fundamentum Opticum," quoted by Dr. Porterfield, and confirmed by his experience. I have also repeated these experiments, and found them to answer. As they are easily made, and tend to illustrate and confirm the law of nature I have mentioned, I shall recite them as briefly and distinctly as I can.

Experiment 1. Let a very small object, such as the head of a pin, well illuminated, be fixed at such a distance from the eye as to be beyond the nearest limit and within the farthest limit of distinct vision. For a young eye, not near-sighted, the object may be placed at the distance of eighteen inches. Let the eye be kept steadily in one place, and take a distinct view of the object. We know, from the principles of optics, that the rays from any one point of this object, whether they pass through the centre of the eye, or at any distance from the centre which the breadth of the pupil will permit, do all unite again in one point of the *retina*. We know, also, that these rays have different directions, both before they fall upon the eye, and after they pass through the crystalline.

Now, we can see the object by any one small parcel of these rays, excluding the rest, by looking through a small pin-hole in a card. Moving this pin-hole over the various parts of the pupil, we can see the object, first by the rays that pass above the centre of the eye, then by the central rays, then by the rays that pass below the centre, and in like manner by the rays that pass on the right and left of the centre. Thus, we view this object, successively, by rays that are central, and by rays that are not central; by rays that have different directions, and are variously inclined to each other, both when they fall upon the *cornea*, and when they fall upon the *retina;* but always by rays which fall upon the same point of the *retina*. And what is the event? It is this—that the object is seen in the same individual direction, whether seen by all these rays together, or by any one parcel of them.

Experiment 2. Let the object above mentioned be now placed within the nearest limit of distinct vision—that is, for an eye that is not near-sighted, at the distance of four or five inches. We know that, in this case, the rays coming from one point of the object do not meet in one point of the *retina*, but spread over a small circular spot of it; the central rays occupying the centre of this circle, the rays that pass above the centre occupying the upper part of the circular spot, and so of the rest.

And we know that the object is, in this case, seen confused; every point of it being seen, not in one, but in various directions. To remedy this confusion, we look at the object through the pin-hole, and while we move the pin-hole over the various parts of the pupil, the object does not keep its place, but seems to move in a contrary direction.

It is here to be observed, that, when the pin-hole is carried upwards over the pupil, the picture of the object is carried upwards upon the *retina*, and the object, at the same time, seems to move downwards, so as to be always in the right line, passing from the picture through the centre of the eye. It is likewise to be observed, that the rays which form the upper and the lower pictures upon the *retina* do not cross each other, as in ordinary vision; yet, still, the higher picture shews the object lower, and the lower picture shews the object higher, in the same manner as when the rays cross each other. Whence we may observe, by the way, that this phænomenon of our seeing objects in a position contrary to that of their pictures upon the *retina*, does not depend upon the crossing of the rays, as Kepler and Des Cartes conceived.

Experiment 3. Other things remaining as in the last experiment, make three pin-holes in a straight line, so near that the rays coming from the object through all the holes may enter the pupil at the same time. In this case, we have a very curious phænomenon; for the object is seen triple with one eye. And if you make more holes within the breadth of the pupil, you will see as many objects as there are holes. However, we shall suppose them only three—one on the right, one in the middle and one on the left; in which case you see three objects standing in a line from right to left.

It is here to be observed, that there are three pictures on the *retina*; that on the left being formed by the rays which pass on the left of the eye's centre, the middle picture being formed by the central rays, and the right-hand picture by the rays which pass on the right of the eye's centre. It is farther to be observed, that the object which appears on the right, is not that which is seen through the hole on the right, but that which is seen through the hole on the left; and, in like manner, the left-hand object is seen through the hole on the right, as is easily proved by covering the holes successively: so that, whatever is the direction of the rays which form the right-hand and left-hand pictures, still the right-hand picture shews a left-hand object, and the left-hand picture shews a right-hand object.

Experiment 4. It is easy to see how the two last experiments may be varied, by placing the object beyond the farthest limit of distinct vision. In order to make this experiment, I looked at a candle at the distance of ten feet, and put the eye of my spectacles behind the card, that the rays from the same point of the object might meet and cross each other, before they reached the *retina*. In this case, as in the former, the candle was seen triple through the three pin-holes; but the candle on the right was seen through the hole on the right; and, on the contrary, the left-hand candle was seen through the hole on the left. In this experiment it is evident, from the principles of optics, that the rays forming the several pictures on the *retina* cross each other a little before they reach the *retina*; and, therefore, the left-hand picture is formed by the rays which pass through the hole on the right: so that the position of the pictures is contrary to that of the holes by which they are formed; and, therefore, is also contrary to that of their objects—as we have found it to be in the former experiments.

These experiments exhibit several uncommon phænomena, that regard the apparent place, and the direction of visible objects from the eye; phænomena that seem to be most contrary to the common rules of vision.

When we look at the same time through three holes that are in a right line, and at certain distances from each other, we expect that the objects seen through them should really be, and should appear to be, at a distance from each other. Yet, by the first experiment, we may, through three such holes, see the same object, and the same point of that object; and through all the three it appears in the same individual place and direction.

When the rays of light come from the object in right lines to the eye, without any reflection, inflection, or refraction, we expect that the object should appear in its real and proper direction from the eye; and so it commonly does. But in the second, third, and fourth experiments, we see the object in a direction which is not its true and real direction from the eye, although the rays come from the object to the eye, without any inflection, reflection, or refraction.

When both the object and the eye are fixed without the least motion, and the medium unchanged, we expect that the object should appear to rest, and keep the same place. Yet, in the second and fourth experiments, when both the eye and the object are at rest, and the medium unchanged, we make the object appear to move upwards or downwards, or in any direction we please.

When we look, at the same time and with the same eye, through holes that stand in a line from right to left, we expect that the object seen through the left-hand hole should appear on the left, and the object seen through the right-hand hole should appear on the right. Yet, in the third experiment, we find the direct contrary.

Although many instances occur in seeing the same object double with two eyes, we always expect that it should appear single when seen only by one eye. Yet, in the second and fourth experiments, we have instances wherein the same object may appear double, triple, or quadruple to one eye, without the help of a polyhedron or multiplying glass.

All these extraordinary phænomena, regarding the direction of visible objects from the eye, as well as those that are common and ordinary, lead us to that law of nature which I have mentioned, and are the necessary consequences of it. And, as there is no probability that we shall ever be able to give a reason why pictures upon the *retina* make us see external objects, any more than pictures upon the hand or upon the cheek; or, that we shall ever be able to give a reason, why we see the object in the direction of a line passing from its picture through the centre of the eye, rather than in any other direction—I am, therefore, apt to look upon this law as a primary law of our constitution.

To prevent being misunderstood, I beg the reader to observe, that I do not mean to affirm that the picture upon the *retina* will make us see an object in the direction mentioned, or in any direction, unless the optic nerve, and the other more immediate instruments of vision, be sound, and perform their function. We know not well what is the office of the optic nerve, nor in what manner it performs that office; but that it hath some part in the faculty of seeing, seems to be certain; because, in an *amaurosis*, which is believed to be a disorder of the optic nerve, the pictures on the *retina* are clear and distinct, and yet there is no vision.

We know still less of the use and function of the choroid membrane; but it seems likewise to be necessary to vision: for it is well known, that pictures upon that part of the *retina* where it is not covered by the choroid—I mean at the entrance of the optic nerve—produce no vision any more than a picture upon the hand. We acknowledge, therefore, that the *retina* is not the last and most immediate instrument of the mind in vision. There are other material organs, whose operation is necessary to seeing, even after the pictures upon the *retina* are formed. If ever we come to know the structure and use of the choroid membrane, the optic nerve, and the brain, and what impressions are made upon them by means of the pictures on the *retina*, some more links of the chain may be brought within our view, and a more general law of vision discovered; but, while we know so little of the nature and office of these more immediate instruments of vision, it seems to be impossible to trace its laws beyond the pictures upon the *retina*.

Neither do I pretend to say, that there may not be diseases of the eye, or accidents, which may occasion our seeing objects in a direction somewhat different from that mentioned above. I shall beg leave to mention one instance of this kind that concerns myself.

In May, 1761, being occupied in making an exact meridian, in order to observe the transit of Venus, I rashly directed to the sun, by my right eye, the cross hairs of a small telescope. I had often done the like in my younger days with impunity; but I suffered by it at last, which I mention as a warning to others.

I soon observed a remarkable dimness in that eye; and for many weeks, when I was in the dark, or shut my eyes, there appeared before the right eye a lucid spot, which trembled much like the image of the sun seen by reflection from water. This appearance grew fainter, and less frequent, by degrees; so that now there are seldom any remains of it. But some other very sensible effects of this hurt still remain. For, First, The sight of the right eye continues to be more dim than that of the left. Secondly, The nearest limit of distinct vision is more remote in the right eye than in the other; although, before the time mentioned, they were equal in both these respects, as I had found by many trials. But, thirdly, what I chiefly intended to mention is, That a straight line, in some circumstances, appears to the right eye to have a curvature in it. Thus, when I look upon a music book, and, shutting my left eye, direct the right to a point of the middle-line of the five which compose the staff of music, the middle line appears dim, indeed, at the point to which the eye is directed, but straight; at the same time, the two lines above it, and the two below it, appear to be bent outwards, and to be more distant from each other and from the middle line, than at other parts of the staff, to which the eye is not directed. Fourthly, Although I have repeated this experiment times innumerable, within these sixteen months, I do not find that custom and experience takes away this appearance of curvature in straight lines. Lastly, This appearance of curvature is perceptible when I look with the right eye only, but not when I look with both eyes; yet I see better with both eyes together, than even with the left eye alone.

I have related this fact minutely as it is, without regard to any hypothesis; because I think such uncommon facts deserve to be recorded. I shall leave it to others to conjecture the cause of this appearance. To me it seems most probable, that a small part of the *retina* toward the centre is shrunk, and that thereby the contiguous parts are drawn nearer to the centre, and to one another, than they were before; and that objects whose images fall on these parts, appear at that distance from each other which corresponds, not to the interval of the parts in their present preternatural contraction, but to their interval in their natural and sound state.

Section XIII.

OF SEEING OBJECTS SINGLE WITH TWO EYES.

Another phænomenon of vision which deserves attention, is our seeing objects single with two eyes. There are two pictures of the object, one on each *retina,* and each picture by itself makes us see an object in a certain direction from the eye; yet both together commonly make us see only one object. All the accounts or solutions of this phænomenon given by anatomists and philosophers seem to be unsatisfactory. I shall pass over the opinions of Galen, of Gassendus, of Baptista Porta, and of Rohault. The reader may see these examined and refuted by Dr. Porterfield. I shall examine Dr. Porterfield's own opinion, Bishop Berkeley's, and some others. But it will be necessary first to ascertain the facts; for, if we mistake the phænomena of single and double vision, it is ten to one that this mistake will lead us wrong in assigning the causes. This likewise we ought carefully to attend to, which is acknowledged in theory by all who have any true judgment or just taste in inquiries of this nature, but is very often overlooked in practice—namely, that, in the solution of natural phænomena, all the length that the human faculties can carry us, is only this, that, from particular phænomena, we may, by induction, trace out general phænomena, of which all the particular ones are necessary consequences. And when we have arrived at the most general phænomena we can reach, there we must stop. If it is asked, Why such a body gravitates towards the earth? all the answer that can be given is, Because all bodies gravitate towards the earth. This is resolving a particular phænomenon into a general one. If it should again be asked, Why do all bodies gravitate toward the earth? we can give no other solution of this phænomenon, but that all bodies whatsoever gravitate towards each other. This is resolving a general phænomenon into a more general one. If it should be asked, Why all bodies gravitate to one another? we cannot tell; but, if we could tell, it could only be by resolving this universal gravitation of bodies into some other phænomenon still more general, and of which the gravitation of all bodies is a particular instance. The most general phænomena we can reach, are what we call *laws of nature;* so that the laws of nature are nothing else but the most general facts relating to the operations of nature, which include a great many particular facts under them. And if, in any case, we should give the name of a law of nature to a general phænomenon, which human industry shall afterwards trace to one more general, there is no great harm done. The most general assumes the name of a law of nature when it is discovered, and the less general is contained and comprehended in it. Having premised these things, we proceed to consider the phænomena of single and double vision, in order to discover some general principle to which they all lead, and of which they are the necessary consequences. If we can discover any such general principle, it must either be a law of nature, or the necessary consequence of some law of nature; and its authority will be equal whether it is the first or the last.

1. We find that, when the eyes are sound and perfect, and the axes of both directed to one point, an object placed in that point is seen single—and here we observe, that in this case the two pictures which shew the object single, are in the centres of the *retina*. When two pictures of a small object are formed upon points of the *retina*, if they shew the objects single, we shall, for the sake of perspicuity, call such two points of the *retina*, *corresponding points;* and where the object is seen double, we shall call the points of the *retina* on which the pictures are formed, *points that do not correspond.* Now, in this first phænomenon, it is evident, that the two centres of the *retina* are corresponding points.

2. Supposing the same things as in the last phænomenon, other objects at the same distance from the eyes as that to which their axes are directed, do also appear single. Thus, if I direct my eyes to a candle placed at the distance of ten feet, and, while I look at this candle, another stands at the same distance from my eyes, within the field of vision, I can, while I look at the first candle, attend to the appearance which the second makes to the eye; and I find

that in this case it always appears single. It is here to be observed, that the pictures of the second candle do not fall upon the centres of the *retinæ*, but they both fall upon the same side of the centres—that is, both to the right, or both to the left; and both are at the same distance from the centres. This might easily be demonstrated from the principles of optics. Hence it appears, that in this second phænomenon of single vision, the corresponding points are points of the two *retinæ*, which are similarly situate with respect to the two centres, being both upon the same side of the centre, and at the same distance from it. It appears likewise, from this phænomenon, that every point in one *retina* corresponds with that which is similarly situate in the other.

3. Supposing still the same things, objects which are much nearer to the eyes, or much more distant from them, than that to which the two eyes are directed, appear double. Thus, if the candle is placed at the distance of ten feet, and I hold my finger at arms-length between my eyes and the candle—when I look at the candle, I see my finger double; and when I look at my finger, I see the candle double; and the same thing happens with regard to all other objects at like distances which fall within the sphere of vision. In this phænomenon, it is evident to those who understand the principles of optics, that the pictures of the objects which are seen double, do not fall upon the points of the *retinæ* which are similarly situate, but that the pictures of the objects seen single do fall upon points similarly situate. Whence we infer, that, as the points of the two *retinæ*, which are similarly situate with regard to the centres, do correspond, so those which are dissimilarly situate do not correspond.

4. It is to be observed, that, although, in such cases as are mentioned in the last phænomenon, we have been accustomed from infancy to see objects double which

we know to be single; yet custom, and experience of the unity of the object, never take away this appearance of duplicity.

5. It may, however, be remarked that the custom of attending to visible appearances has a considerable effect, and makes the phænomenon of double vision to be more or less observed and remembered. Thus you may find a man that can say, with a good conscience, that he never saw things double all his life; yet this very man, put in the situation above mentioned, with his finger between him and the candle, and desired to attend to the appearance of the object which he does not look at, will, upon the first trial, see the candle double, when he looks at his finger; and his finger double, when he looks at the candle. Does he now see otherwise than he saw before? No; surely; but he now attends to what he never attended to before. The same double appearance of an object hath been a thousand times presented to his eye before now, but he did not attend to it; and so it is as little an object of his reflection and memory, as if it had never happened.

When we look at an object, the circumjacent objects may be seen at the same time, although more obscurely and indistinctly: for the eye hath a considerable field of vision, which it takes in at once. But we attend only to the object we look at. The other objects which fall within the field of vision, are not attended to; and therefore are as if they were not seen. If any of them draws our attention, it naturally draws the eyes at the same time: for, in the common course of life, the eyes always follow the attention: or if at any time, in a revery, they are separated from it, we hardly at that time see what is directly before us. Hence we may see the reason why the man we are speaking of thinks that he never before saw an object double. When he looks at any object, he sees it single, and takes no notice of other visible objects at that time, whether they appear single or double. If any of them draws his attention, it draws his eyes at the same time; and, as soon as the eyes are turned towards it, it appears single. But, in order to see things double —at least, in order to have any reflection or remembrance that he did so—it is necessary that he should look at one object, and at the same time attend to the faint appearance of other objects which are within the field of vision. This is a practice which perhaps he never used, nor attempted; and therefore he does not recollect that ever he saw an object double. But when he is put upon giving this attention, he immediately sees objects double, in the same manner, and with the very same circumstances, as they who have been accustomed, for the greatest part of their lives, to give this attention.

There are many phænomena of a similar nature, which shew that the mind may not attend to, and thereby, in some sort, not perceive objects that strike the senses. I had occasion to mention several instances of this in the second chapter; and I have been assured, by persons of the best skill in music, that, in hearing a tune upon the harpsichord, when they give attention to the treble, they do not hear the bass; and when they attend to the bass, they do not perceive the air of the treble. Some persons are so near-sighted, that, in reading, they hold the book to one eye, while the other is directed to other objects. Such persons acquire the habit of attending, in this case, to the objects of one eye, while they give no attention to those of the other.

6. It is observable, that, in all cases, wherein we see an object double, the two appearances have a certain position with regard to one another, and a certain apparent or angular distance. This apparent distance is greater or less in different circumstances; but, in the same circumstances, it is always the same, not only to the same, but to different persons.

Thus, in the experiment above mentioned, if twenty different persons, who see perfectly with both eyes, shall place their finger and the candle at the distances above expressed, and hold their heads upright, looking at the finger, they will see two candles, one on the right, another on the left. That which is seen on the right, is seen by the right eye, and that which is seen on the left, by the left eye; and they will see them at the same apparent distance from each other. If, again, they look at the candle, they will see two fingers, one on the right, and the other on the left; and all will see them at the same apparent distance; the finger towards the left being seen by the right eye, and the other by the left. If the head is laid horizontally to one side, other circumstances remaining the same, one appearance of the object seen double, will be directly above the other. In a word, vary the circumstances as you please, and the appearances are varied to all the spectators in one and the same manner.

7. Having made many experiments in order to ascertain the apparent *distance* of the two appearances of an object seen double, I have found that in all cases this apparent distance is proportioned to the *distance* between the point of the *retina*, where the picture is made in one eye, and the point which is situated similarly to that on which the picture is made on the other eye; so that, as the apparent distance of two objects seen with one eye, is proportioned to the arch of the *retina*, which lies between their pictures, in like manner, when an object is seen double with the two eyes, the apparent distance of the two appearances is proportioned to the arch of either *retina*, which lies between the picture in that *retina*, and the point corresponding to that of the picture in the other *retina*.

8. As, in certain circumstances, we invariably see one obect appear double, so, in others, we as invariably see two objects unite into one, and, in appearance, lose their duplicity. This is evident in the appearance of the binocular telescope. And the same thing happens when any two similar tubes are applied to the two eyes in a

parallel direction; for, in this case, we see only one tube. And if two shillings are placed at the extremities of the two tubes, one exactly in the axis of one eye, and the other in the axis of the other eye, we shall see but one shilling. If two pieces of coin, or other bodies, of different colour, and of different figure be properly placed in the two axes of the eyes, and at the extremities of the tubes, we shall see both the bodies in one and the same place, each as it were spread over the other, without hiding it; and the colour will be that which is compounded of the two colours.

9. From these phænomena, and from all the trials I have been able to make, it appears evidently, that, in perfect human eyes, the centres of the two *retinæ* correspond and harmonize with one another, and that every other point in one *retina* doth correspond and harmonize with the point which is similarly situate in the other; in such manner, that pictures falling on the corresponding points of the two *retinæ*, shew only one object, even when there are really two; and pictures falling upon points of the *retinæ* which do not correspond, shew us two visible appearances, although there be but one object: so that pictures, upon corresponding points of the two *retinæ*, present the same appearance to the mind as if they had both fallen upon the same point of one *retina;* and pictures upon points of the two *retinæ*, which do not correspond, present to the mind the same apparent distance and position of two objects, as if one of those pictures was carried to the point corresponding to it in the other *retina*. This relation and sympathy between corresponding points of the two *retinæ*, I do not advance as an hypothesis, but as a general fact or phænomenon of vision. All the phænomena before mentioned, of single or double vision, lead to it, and are necessary consequences of it. It holds true invariably in all perfect human eyes, as far as I am able to collect from innumerable trials of various kinds made upon my own

eyes, and many made by others at my desire. Most of the hypotheses that have been contrived to resolve the phænomena of single and double vision, suppose this general fact, while their authors were not aware of it. Sir Isaac Newton, who was too judicious a philosopher, and too accurate an observer, to have offered even a conjecture which did not tally with the facts that had fallen under his observation, proposes a query with respect to the cause of it—"Optics," Query, 15. The judicious Dr. Smith, in his "Optics," Book I, § 137, hath confirmed the truth of this general phænomenon from his own experience, not only as to the apparent unity of objects whose pictures fall upon the corresponding points of the *retinæ*, but also as to the apparent distance of the two appearances of the same object when seen double.

This general phænomenon appears, therefore, to be founded upon a very full induction, which is all the evidence we can have for a fact of this nature. Before we make an end of this subject, it will be proper to inquire, First, Whether those animals whose eyes have an adverse position in their heads, and look contrary ways, have such corresponding points in their *retinæ?* Secondly, What is the position of the corresponding points in imperfect human eyes—I mean in those that squint? And, in the last place, Whether this harmony of the corresponding points in the *retinæ*, be natural and original, or the effect of custom? And, if it is original, Whether it can be accounted for by any of the laws of nature already discovered? or whether it is itself to be looked upon as a law of nature, and a part of the human constitution?

Section XIV.

OF THE LAWS OF VISION IN BRUTE ANIMALS.

It is the intention of nature, in giving eyes to animals, that they may perceive the situation of visible objects, or the direction in which they are placed—it is probable, therefore, that, in ordinary cases, every animal, whether it has many eyes or few, whether of one structure or of another, sees objects single, and in their true and proper direction. And, since there is a prodigious variety in the structure, the motions, and the number of eyes in different animals and insects, it is probable that the laws by which vision is regulated, are not the same in all, but various, adapted to the eyes which nature hath given them.

Mankind naturally turn their eyes always the same way, so that the axes of the two eyes meet in one point. They naturally attend to, or look at that object only which is placed in the point where the axes meet. And whether the object be more or less distant, the configuration of the eye is adapted to the distance of the object, so as to form a distinct picture of it.

When we use our eyes in this natural way, the two pictures of the object we look at are formed upon the centres of the two *retinæ;* and the two pictures of any contiguous object are formed upon the points of the *retinæ* which are similarly situate with regard to the centres. Therefore, in order to our seeing objects single, and in their proper direction, with two eyes, it is sufficient that we be so constituted, that objects whose pictures are formed upon the centres of the two *retinæ*, or upon points similarly situate with regard to these centres, shall be seen in the same visible place. And this is the constitution which nature hath actually given to human eyes.

When we distort our eyes from their parallel direction, which is an unnatural motion, but may be learned by practice; or when we direct the axes of the two eyes to one point, and at the same time direct our attention to some visible object much nearer or much more distant than that point, which is also unnatural, yet may be learned: in these cases, and in these only, we see one object double, or two objects confounded in one. In these cases, the two pictures of the same object are formed upon points of the *retinæ* which are not similarly situate, and so the object is seen double; or the two pictures of different objects are formed upon points of the *retinæ* which are similarly situate, and so the two objects are seen confounded in one place.

Thus it appears, that the laws of vision in the human constitution are wisely adapted to the natural use of human eyes, but not to that use of them which is unnatural. We see objects truly when we use our eyes in the natural way; but have false appearances presented to us when we use them in a way that is unnatural. We may reasonably think that the case is the same with other animals. But is it not unreasonable to think, that those animals which naturally turn one eye towards one object, and another eye towards another object, must thereby have such false appearances presented to them, as we have when we do so against nature?

Many animals have their eyes by nature placed adverse and immovable, the axes of the two eyes being always directed to opposite points. Do objects painted on the centres of the two *retinæ* appear to such animals as they do to human eyes, in one and the same visible place? I think it is highly probable that they do not; and that they appear, as they really are, in opposite places.

If we judge from analogy in this case, it will lead us to think that there is a certain correspondence between points of the two *retinæ* in such animals, but of a different kind from that which we have found in human eyes. The centre of one *retina* will correspond with the centre of the other, in such manner that the objects whose pictures are formed upon the secorresponding points, shall appear not to be in the same place, as in human eyes, but in opposite places. And in the same manner will the superior part of one *retina* correspond with the inferior part of the other, and the anterior part of one with the posterior part of the other.

Some animals, by nature, turn their eyes with equal facility, either the same way or different ways, as we turn our hands and arms. Have such animals corresponding points in their *retinæ*, and points which do not correspond, as the human kind has? I think it is probable that they have not; because such a constitution in them could serve no other purpose but to exhibit false appearances.

If we judge from analogy, it will lead us to think, that, as such animals move their eyes in a manner similar to that in which we move our arms, they have an immediate and natural perception of the direction they give to their eyes, as we have of the directions we give to our arms; and perceive the situation of visible objects by their eyes, in a manner similar to that in which we perceive the situation of tangible objects with our hands.

We cannot teach brute animals to use their eyes in any other way than in that which nature hath taught them; nor can we teach them to communicate to us the appearances which visible objects make to them, either in ordinary or in extraordinary cases. We have not, therefore, the same means of discovering the laws of vision in them, as in our own kind, but must satisfy ourselves with probable conjectures; and what we have said upon this subject, is chiefly intended to shew, that animals to which nature hath given eyes differing in their number, in their position, and in their natural motions, may very probably be subjected to different laws of vision, adapted to the peculiarities of their organs of vision.

Section XV.

SQUINTING CONSIDERED HYPOTHETICALLY.

Whether there be corresponding points in the *retinæ*, of those who have an involuntary squint? and if there are, whether they be situate in the same manner as in those who have no squint? are not questions of mere curiosity. They are of real importance to the physician who attempts the cure of a squint, and to the patient who submits to the cure. After so much has been said of the *strabismus*, or squint, both by medical and by optical writers, one might expect to find abundance of facts for determining these questions. Yet, I confess, I have been disappointed in this expectation, after taking some pains both to make observations, and to collect those which have been made by others.

Nor will this appear very strange, if we consider, that to make the observations which are necessary for determining these questions, knowledge of the principles of optics, and of the laws of vision, must concur with opportunities rarely to be met with.

Of those who squint, the far greater part have no distinct vision with one eye. When this is the case, it is impossible, and indeed of no importance, to determine the situation of the corresponding points. When both eyes are good, they commonly differ so much in their direction, that the same object cannot be seen by both at the same time; and, in this case, it will be very difficult to determine the situation of the corresponding points; for such persons will probably attend only to the objects of one eye, and the objects of the other will be as little regarded as if they were not seen.

We have before observed, that, when we look at a near object, and attend to it, we do not perceive the double appearances of more distant objects, even when they are in the same direction, and are presented to the eye at the same time. It is probable that a squinting person, when he attends to the objects of one eye, will, in like manner, have his attention totally diverted from the objects of the other; and that he will perceive them as little as we perceive the double appearances of objects when we use our eyes in the natural way. Such a person, therefore, unless he is so much a philosopher as to have acquired the habit of attending very accurately to the visible appearances of objects, and even of objects which he does not look at, will not be able to give any light to the questions now under consideration.

It is very probable that hares, rabbits, birds, and fishes, whose eyes are fixed in an adverse position, have the natural faculty of attending at the same time to visible objects placed in different, and even in contrary directions; because, without this faculty, they could not have those advantages from the contrary direction of their eyes, which nature seems to have intended. But it is not probable that those who squint have any such natural faculty; because we find no such faculty in the rest of the species. We naturally attend to objects placed in the point where the axes of the two eyes meet, and to them only. To give attention to an object in a different direction is unnatural and not to be learned without pains and practice.

A very convincing proof of this may be drawn from a fact now well known to philosophers : when one eye is shut, there is a certain space within the field of vision, where we can see nothing at all—the space which is directly opposed to that part of the bottom of the eye where the optic nerve enters. This defect of sight, in one part of the eye, is common to all human eyes, and hath been so from the beginning of the world; yet it was never known, until the sagacity of the Abbé Mariotte discovered it in the last century. And now when it is known, it cannot be perceived, but by means of some particular experiments, which require care and attention to make them succeed.

What is the reason that so remarkable a defect of sight, common to all mankind, was so long unknown, and is now perceived with so much difficulty? It is surely this—That the defect is at some distance from the axis of the eye, and consequently in a part of the field of vision to which we never attend naturally, and to which we cannot attend at all, without the aid of some particular circumstances.

From what we have said, it appears, that, to determine the situation of the corresponding points in the eyes of those who squint, is impossible, if they do not see distinctly with both eyes; and that it will be very difficult, unless the two eyes differ so little in their direction, that the same object may be seen with both at the same time. Such patients I apprehend are rare; at least there are very few of them with whom I have had the fortune to meet: and therefore, for the assistance of those who may have happier opportunities, and inclination to make the proper use of them, we shall consider the case of squinting, hypothetically, pointing out the proper articles of inquiry, the observations that are wanted, and the conclusions that may be drawn from them.

1. It ought to be inquired, Whether the squinting person sees equally well with both eyes? and, if there be a defect in one, the nature and degree of that defect ought to be remarked. The experiments by which this may be done, are so obvious, that I need not mention them. But I would advise the observer to make the proper experiments, and not to rely upon the testimony of the patient; because I have found many instances, both of persons that squinted, and others who were found, upon trial, to have a great defect in the sight of one eye, although they were never aware of it before. In all the following articles, it is supposed that the patient sees with both eyes so well as to be able to read with either, when the other is covered.

2. It ought to be inquired, Whether, when one eye is covered, the other is turned directly to the object? This ought to be tried in both eyes successively. By this observation, as a touchstone, we may try the hypothesis concerning squinting, invented by M. de la Hire, and adopted by Boerhaave, and many others of the medical faculty.

The hypothesis is, That, in one eye of a squinting person, the greatest sensibility and the most distinct vision is not, as in other men, in the centre of the *retina*, but upon one side of the centre; and that he turns the axis of this eye aside from the object, in order that the picture of the object may fall upon the most sensible part of the *retina*, and thereby give the most distinct vision. If this is the cause of squinting, the squinting eye will be turned aside from the object, when the other eye is covered, as well as when it is not.

A trial so easy to be made, never was made for more than forty years; but the hypothesis was very generally received—so prone are men to invent hypotheses, and so backward to examine them by facts. At last, Dr. Jurin having made the trial, found that persons who squint turn the axis of the squinting eye directly to the object, when the other eye is covered. This fact is confirmed by Dr. Porterfield; and I have found it verified in all the instances that have fallen under my observation.

3. It ought to be inquired, Whether the axes of the two eyes follow one another, so as to have always the same inclination, or make the same angle, when the person looks to the right or to the left, upward or downward, or straight forward. By this observation we may judge whether a squint is owing to any defect in the muscles which move the eye, as some have supposed. In the following articles, we suppose that the inclination of the axes of the eyes is found to be always the same.

4. It ought to be inquired, Whether the person that squints sees an object single or double?

If he sees the object double, and if the two appearances have an angular distance, equal to the angle which the axes of his eyes make with each other, it may be concluded that he hath corresponding points in the *retinæ* of his eyes, and that they have the same situation as in those who have no squint. If the two appearances should have an angular distance which is always the same, but manifestly greater or less than the angle contained under the optic axes, this would indicate corresponding points in the *retinæ*, whose situation is not the same as in those who have no squint; but it is difficult to judge accurately of the angle which the optic axes make.

A squint too small to be perceived, may occasion double vision of objects: for, if we speak strictly, every person squints more or less, whose optic axes do not meet exactly in the object which he looks at. Thus, if a man can only bring the axes of his eyes to be parallel, but cannot make them converge in the least, he must have a small squint in looking at near objects, and will see them double, while he sees very distant objects single. Again, if the optic axes always converge, so as to meet eight or ten feet before the face at farthest, such a person will see near objects single; but when he looks at very distant objects, he will squint a little, and see them double.

An instance of this kind is related by Aguilonius in his "Optics," who says, that he had seen a young man to whom near objects appeared single, but distant objects appeared double.

Dr. Briggs, in his "Nova Visionis Theoria," having collected from authors several instances of double vision, quotes this from Aguilonius, as the most wonderful and unaccountable of all, insomuch that he suspects some imposition on the part of the young man: but to those who understand the laws by which single and double vision are regulated, it appears to be the natural effect of a very small squint.

Double vision may always be owing to a small squint, when the two appearances are seen at a small angular distance, although no squint was observed: and I do not remember any instances of double vision recorded by authors, wherein any account is given of the angular distance of the appearances.

In almost all the instances of double vision, there is reason to suspect a squint or distortion of the eyes, from the concomitant circumstances, which we find to be one or other of the following—the approach of death or of a *deliquium*, excessive drinking or other intemperance, violent headache, blistering the head, smoking tobacco, blows or wounds in the head. In all these cases, it is reasonable to suspect a distortion of the eyes, either from spasm, or paralysis in the muscles that move them. But, although it be probable that there is always a squint greater or less where there is double vision, yet it is certain that there is not double vision always where there is a squint. I know no instance of double vision that continued for life, or even for a great number of years. We shall therefore suppose, in the following articles, that the squinting person sees objects single.

5. The next inquiry, then, ought to be, Whether the object is seen with both eyes at the same time, or only with the eye whose axes is directed to it? It hath been taken for granted, by the writers upon the *strabismus*, before Dr. Jurin, that those who squint commonly see objects single with both eyes at the same time; but I know not one fact advanced by any writer which proves it. Dr. Jurin is of a contrary opinion; and, as it is of consequence, so it is very easy, to determine this point, in particular instances, by this obvious experiment. While the person that squints looks steadily at an object, let the observer carefully remark the direction of both his eyes, and observe their motions; and let an opaque body be interposed between the object and the two eyes successively. If the patient, notwithstanding this interposition, and without changing the direction of his eyes, continues to see the object all the time, it may be concluded that he saw it with both eyes at once. But, if the interposition of the body between one eye and the object makes it disappear, then we may be certain that it was seen by that eye only. In the two following articles, we shall

suppose the first to happen, according to the common hypothesis.

6. Upon this supposition, it ought to be inquired, Whether the patient sees an object double in those circumstances wherein it appears double to them who have no squint? Let him, for instance, place a candle at the distance of ten feet; and holding his finger at arm's-length between him and the candle, let him observe, when he looks at the candle, whether he sees his finger with both eyes, and whether he sees it single or double; and when he looks at his finger, let him observe whether he sees the candle with both eyes and whether single or double.

By this observation, it may be determined, whether to this patient, the phænomena of double as well as of single vision are the same as to them who have no squint. If they are not the same—if he sees objects single with two eyes, not only in the cases wherein they appear single, but in those also wherein they appear double to other men—the conclusion to be drawn from this supposition is, that his single vision does not arise from corresponding points in the *retinæ* of his eyes: and that the laws of vision are not the same in him as in the rest of mankind.

7. If, on the other hand, he sees objects double in those cases wherein they appear double to others, the conclusion must be, that he hath corresponding points in the *retinæ* of his eyes, but unnaturally situate. And their situation may be thus determined.

When he looks at an object, having the axis of one eye directed to it, and the axis of the other turned aside from it, let us suppose a right line to pass from the object through the centre of the diverging eye. We shall, for the sake of perspicuity, call this right line, *the natural axis of the eye;* and it will make an angle with the real axis, greater or less, according as his squint is greater or less. We shall also call that point of the *retina* in which the natural axis cuts it, *the natural centre of the retina;* which will be more or less distant from the real centre, according as the squint is greater or less.

Having premised these definitions, it will be evident to those who understand the principles of optics, that in this person the natural centre of one *retina* corresponds with the real centre of the other, in the very same manner as the two real centres correspond in perfect eyes; and that the points similarly situate with regard to the real centre in one *retina*, and the natural centre in the other, do likewise correspond, in the very same manner as the points similarly situate with regard to the two real centres correspond in perfect eyes.

If it is true, as has been commonly affirmed, that one who squints sees an object with both eyes at the same time, and yet sees it single, the squint will most probably be such as we have described in this article. And we may further conclude, that, if a person affected with such a squint as we have supposed, could be brought to the habit of looking straight, his sight would thereby be greatly hurt; for he would then see everything double which he saw with both eyes at the same time; and objects distant from one another would appear to be confounded together. His eyes are made for squinting, as much as those of other men are made for looking straight; and his sight would be no less injured by looking straight, than that of another man by squinting. He can never see perfectly when he does not squint, unless the corresponding points of his eyes should by custom change their place; but how small the probability of this is will appear in the 17th section.

Those of the medical faculty who attempt the cure of a squint, would do well to consider whether it is attended with such symptoms as are above described. If it is, the cure would be worse than the malady: for, every one will readily acknowledge that it is better to put up with the deformity of a squint, than to purchase the cure by the loss of perfect and distinct vision.

8. We shall now return to Dr. Jurin's hypothesis, and suppose that our patient, when he saw objects single notwithstanding his squint, was found, upon trial, to have seen them only with one eye.

We would advise such a patient to endeavor, by repeated efforts, to lessen his squint, and to bring the axes of his eyes nearer to a parallel direction. We have naturally the power of making small variations in the inclination of the optic axes ; and this power may be greatly increased by exercise.

In the ordinary and natural use of our eyes, we can direct their axes to a fixed star; in this case they must be parallel: we can direct them also to an object six inches distant from the eye; and in this case the axes must make an angle of fifteen or twenty degrees. We see young people in their frolics learn to squint, making their eyes either converge or diverge, when they will, to a very considerable degree. Why should it be more difficult for a squinting person to learn to look straight when he pleases? If once, by an effort of his will, he can but lessen his squint, frequent practice will make it easy to lessen it, and will daily increase his power. So that, if he begins this practice in youth, and perseveres in it, he may probably, after some time, learn to direct both his eyes to one object.

When he hath acquired this power, it will be no difficult matter to determine, by proper observations, whether the centres of the *retina*, and other points similarly situate with regard to the centres, correspond, as in other men.

9. Let us now suppose that he finds this to be the case ; and that he sees an object single with both eyes, when the axes of both are directed to it. It will then concern him to acquire the habit of looking straight, as he hath got the power, because he will thereby not only remove a deformity, but improve his sight ; and I conceive this habit, like all others, may be got by frequent

exercise. He may practise before a mirror when alone, and in company he ought to have those about him who will observe and admonish him when he squints.

10. What is supposed in the 9th article is not merely imaginary; it is really the case of some squinting persons, as will appear in the next section. Therefore, it ought further to be inquired, How it comes to pass that such a person sees an object which he looks at, only with one eye, when both are open? In order to answer this question, it may be observed, first, Whether, when he looks at an object, the diverging eye is not drawn so close to the nose, that it can have no distinct images? Or, secondly, whether the pupil of the diverging eye is not covered wholly, or in part, by the upper eyelid? Dr. Jurin observed instances of these cases in persons that squinted, and assigns them as causes of their seeing the object only with one eye. Thirdly, it may be observed, whether the diverging eye is not so directed, that the picture of the object falls upon that part of the *retina* where the optic nerve enters, and where there is no vision? This will probably happen in a squint wherein the axes of the eyes converge so as to meet about six inches before the nose.

11. In the last place, it ought to be inquired, Whether such a person hath any distinct vision at all with the diverging eye, at the time he is looking at an object with the other?

It may seem very improbable that he should be able to read with the diverging eye when the other is covered, and yet, when both are open, have no distinct vision with it at all. But this, perhaps, will not appear so improbable if the following considerations are duly attended to.

Let us suppose that one who saw perfectly, gets, by a blow on the head, or some other accident, a permanent and involuntary squint. According to the laws of vision, he will see objects double, and will see objects distant from one another confounded together; but, such vision being very disagreeable, as well as inconvenient, he will do everything in his power to remedy it. For alleviating such distresses, nature often teaches men wonderful expedients, which the sagacity of a philosopher would be unable to discover. Every accidental motion, every direction or conformation of his eyes, which lessens the evil, will be agreeable; it will be repeated until it be learned to perfection, and become habitual, even without thought or design. Now, in this case, what disturbs the sight of one eye is the sight of the other; and all the disagreeable appearances in vision would cease if the light of one eye was extinct. The sight of one eye will become more distinct and more agreeable, in the same proportion as that of the other becomes faint and indistinct. It may, therefore, be expected, that every habit will, by degrees, be acquired which tends to destroy distinct vision in one eye while it is preserved in the other. These habits will be greatly facilitated if one eye was at first better than the other; for, in that case, the best eye will always be directed to the object which he intends to look at, and every habit will be acquired which tends to hinder his seeing it at all, or seeing it distinctly by the other at the same time.

I shall mention one or two habits that may probably be acquired in such a case; perhaps there are others which we cannot so easily conjecture. First, By a small increase or diminution of his squint, he may bring it to correspond with one or other of the cases mentioned in the last article. Secondly, The diverging eye may be brought to such a conformation as to be extremely short-sighted, and consequently to have no distinct vision of objects at a distance. I knew this to be the case of one person that squinted; but cannot say whether the short-sightedness of the diverging eye was original, or acquired by habit.

We see, therefore, that one who squints, and originally saw objects double by reason of that squint, may acquire such habits that, when he looks at an object, he shall see it only with one eye; nay, he may acquire such habits that, when he looks at an object with his best eye, he shall have no distinct vision with the other at all. Whether this is really the case—being unable to determine in the instances that have fallen under my observation—I shall leave to future inquiry.

I have endeavoured, in the foregoing articles, to delineate such a process as is proper in observing the phænomena of squinting. I know well by experience, that this process appears more easy in theory than it will be found to be in practice; and that, in order to carry it on with success, some qualifications of mind are necessary in the patient, which are not always to be met with. But, if those who have proper opportunities and inclination to observe such phænomena, attend duly to this process, they may be able to furnish facts less vague and uninstructive than those we meet with, even in authors of reputation. By such facts, vain theories may be exploded, and our knowledge of the laws of nature, which regard the noblest of our senses, enlarged.

Section XVI.

FACTS RELATING TO SQUINTING.

Having considered the phænomena of squinting, hypothetically, and their connection with corresponding points in the *retinæ*. I shall now mention the facts I have had occasion to observe myself, or have met with in authors, that can give any light to this subject.

Having examined above twenty persons that squinted, I found in all of them a defect in the sight of one eye. Four only had so much of distinct vision in the weak eye, as to be able to read with it, when the other was covered. The rest saw nothing at all distinctly with one eye.

Dr. Porterfield says, that this is generally the case of

people that squint; and I suspect it is so more generally than is commonly imagined. Dr. Jurin, in a very judicious dissertation upon squinting, printed in Dr. Smith's "Optics," observes, that those who squint, and see with both eyes, never see the same object with both at the same time; that, when one eye is directed straight forward to an object, the other is drawn so close to the nose that the object cannot at all be seen by it, the images being too oblique and too indistinct to affect the eye. In some squinting persons, he observed the diverging eye drawn under the upper eyelid, while the other was directed to the object. From these observations, he concludes that "the eye is thus distorted, not for the sake of seeing better with it, but rather to avoid seeing at all with it as much as possible." From all the observations he had made, he was satisfied that there is nothing peculiar in the structure of a squinting eye; that the fault is only in its wrong direction; and that this wrong direction is got by habit. Therefore, he proposes that method of cure which we have described in the eighth and ninth articles of the last section. He tells us, that he had attempted a cure, after this method, upon a young gentleman, with promising hopes of success; but was interrupted by his falling ill of the small-pox, of which he died.

It were to be wished that Dr. Jurin had acquainted us whether he ever brought the young man to direct the axes of both eyes to the same object, and whether, in that case, he saw the object single, and saw it with both eyes; and that he had likewise acquainted us, whether he saw objects double when his squint was diminished. But as to these facts he is silent.

I wished long for an opportunity of trying Dr. Jurin's method of curing a squint, without finding one; having always, upon examination, discovered so great a defect in the sight of one eye of the patient as discouraged the attempt.

But I have lately found three young gentlemen, with whom I am hopeful this method may have suceess, if they have patience and perseverance in using it. Two of them are brothers, and, before I had access to examine them, had been practising this method by the direction of their tutor, with such success, that the elder looks straight when he is upon his guard; the younger can direct both his eyes to one object; but they soon return to their usual squint.

A third young gentleman, who had never heard of this method before, by a few days' practice, was able to direct both his eyes to one object, but could not keep them long in that direction. All the three agree in this, that, when both eyes are directed to one object, they see it and the adjacent objects single; but, when they squint, they see objects sometimes single and sometimes double. I observed of all the three, that when they squinted most —that is, in the way they had been accustomed to—the axes of their eyes converged so as to meet five or six inches before the nose. It is probable that, in this case, the picture of the object in the diverging eye, must fall upon that part of the *retina* where the optic nerve enters; and therefore, the object could not be seen by the eye.

All the three have some defect in the sight of one eye, which none of them knew until I put them upon making trials; and when they squint, the best eye is always directed to the object, and the weak eye is that which diverges from it. But when the best eye is covered, the weak eye is turned directly to the object. Whether this defect of sight in one eye, be the effect of its having been long disused, as it must have been when they squinted; or whether some original defect in one eye might be the occasion of their squinting, time may discover. The two brothers have found the sight of the weak eye improved by using to read with it while the other is covered. The elder can read an ordinary print with the weak eye; the other, as well as the third gentleman, can only read a large print with the weak eye. I have met with one other person only who squinted, and yet could read a large print with the weak eye. He is a young man, whose eyes are both tender and weak-sighted, but the left much weaker than the right. When he looks at any object, he always directs the right eye to it, and then the left is turned towards the nose so much that it is impossible for him to see the same object with both eyes at the same time. When the right eye is covered, he turns the left directly to the object; but he sees it indistinctly, and as if it had a mist about it.

I made several experiments, some of them in the company and with the assistance of an ingenious physician, in order to discover whether objects that were in the axes of the two eyes, were seen in one place confounded together, as in those who have no involuntary squint. The object placed in the axis of the weak eye was a lighted candle, at the distance of eight or ten feet. Before the other eye was placed a printed book, at such a distance as that he could read upon it. He said, that while he read upon the book, he saw the candle but very faintly. And from what we could learn, these two objects did not appear in one place, but had all that angular distance in appearance which they had in reality.

If this was really the case, the conclusion to be drawn from it is, that the corresponding points in his eyes are not situate in the same manner as in other men; and that, if he could be brought to direct both eyes to one object, he would see it double. But, considering that the young man had never been accustomed to observations of this kind, and that the sight of one eye was so imperfect, I do not pretend to draw this conclusion with certainty from this single instance.

All that can be inferred from these facts is, that, of four persons who squint, three appear to have nothing preternatural in the structure of their eyes. The centres of their *retinæ*, and the points similarly situate with regard to the centres, do certainly correspond in the same manner as in other men—so that, if they can be brought to the habit of directing their eyes right to an object, they will not only remove a deformity, but improve their sight. With regard to the fourth, the case is dubious, with some probability of a deviation from the usual course of nature in the situation of the corresponding points of his eyes.

Section XVII.

OF THE EFFECT OF CUSTOM IN SEEING OBJECTS SINGLE.

It appears from the phænomena of single and double vision, recited in § 13, that our seeing an object single with two eyes, depends upon these two things:—First, Upon that mutual correspondence of certain points of the *retina* which we have often described; Secondly, Upon the two eyes being directed to the object so accurately that the two images of it fall upon corresponding points. These two things must concur in order to our seeing an object single with two eyes; and, as far as they depend upon custom, so far only can single vision depend upon custom.

With regard to the second—that is, the accurate direction of both eyes to the object—I think it must be acknowledged that this is only learned by custom. Nature hath wisely ordained the eyes to move in such manner that their axes shall always be nearly parallel; but hath left it in our power to vary their inclination a little, according to the distance of the object we look at. Without this power, objects could appear single at one particular distance only; and, at distances much less or much greater, would always appear double. The wisdom of nature is conspicuous in giving us this power, and no less conspicuous in making the extent of it exactly adequate to the end.

The parallelism of the eyes, in general, is therefore the work of nature; but that precise and accurate direction, which must be varied according to the distance of the object, is the effect of custom. The power which nature hath left us of varying the inclination of the optic axes a little, is turned into a habit of giving them always that inclination which is adapted to the distance of the object.

But it may be asked, What gives rise to this habit? The only answer that can be given to this question is, that it is found necessary to perfect and distinct vision. A man who hath lost the sight of one eye, very often loses the habit of directing it exactly to the object he looks at, because that habit is no longer of use to him. And if he should recover the sight of his eye, he would recover this habit, by finding it useful. No part of the human constitution is more admirable than that whereby we acquire habits which are found useful, without any design or intention. Children must see imperfectly at first; but, by using their eyes, they learn to use them in the best manner, and acquire, without intending it, the habits necessary for that purpose. Every man becomes most expert in that kind of vision which is most useful to him in his particular profession and manner of life. A miniature painter, or an engraver, sees very near objects better than a sailor; but the sailor sees very distant objects much better than they. A person that is short-sighted, in looking at distant objects, gets the habit of contracting the aperture of his eyes, by almost closing his eyelids. Why? For no other reason, but because this makes him see the object more distinct. In like manner, the reason why every man acquires the habit of directing both eyes accurately to the object, must be, because thereby he sees it more perfectly and distinctly.

It remains to be considered, whether that correspondence between certain points of the *retinæ*, which is likewise necessary to single vision, be the effect of custom, or an original property of human eyes.

A strong argument for its being an original property, may be drawn from the habit, just now mentioned, of directing the eyes accurately to an object. This habit is got by our finding it necessary to perfect and distinct vision. But why is it necessary? For no other reason but this, because thereby the two images of the object falling upon corresponding points, the eyes assist each other in vision, and the object is seen better by both together, than it could be by one; but when the eyes are not accurately directed, the two images of an object fall upon points that do not correspond, whereby the sight of one eye disturbs the sight of the other, and the object is seen more indistinctly with both eyes than it would be with one. Whence it is reasonable to conclude, that this correspondence of certain points of the *retinæ*, is prior to the habits we acquire in vision, and consequently is natural and original. We have all acquired the habit of directing our eyes always in a particular manner, which causes single vision. Now, if nature hath ordained that we should have single vision only, when our eyes are thus directed, there is an obvious reason why all mankind should agree in the habit of directing them in this manner. But, if single vision is the effect of custom, any other habit of directing the eyes would have answered the purpose; and no account can be given why this particular habit should be so universal; and it must appear very strange, that no one instance hath been found of a person who had acquired the habit of seeing objects single with both eyes, while they were directed in any other manner.

The judicious Dr. Smith, in his excellent system of optics, maintains the contrary opinion, and offers some reasonings and facts in proof of it. He agrees with Bishop Berkeley in attributing it entirely to custom, that we see objects single with two eyes, as well as that we see objects erect by inverted images. Having considered Bishop Berkeley's reasonings in the 11th section, we shall now beg leave to make some remarks on what Dr. Smith hath said upon this subject, with the respect due to an author to whom the world owes, not only many valuable discoveries of his own, but those of the brightest mathematical genius of this age, which, with great labour, he generously redeemed from oblivion.

He observes, that the question, Why we see objects single with two eyes? is of the same sort with this, Why we hear sounds single with two ears?—and that the same answer must serve both. The inference intended to be drawn from this observation is, that, as the second of these phænomena is the effect of custom, so likewise is the first.

Now, I humbly conceive that the questions are not so much of the same sort, that the same answer must serve for both; and, moreover, that our hearing single with two ears, is not the effect of custom.

Two or more visible objects, although perfectly similar, and seen at the very same time, may be distinguished by their visible places; but two sounds perfectly similar, and heard at the same time, cannot be distinguished; for, from the nature of sound, the sensations they occasion must coalesce into one, and lose all distinction. If, therefore, it is asked, Why we hear sounds single with two ears? I answer, Not from custom; but because two sounds which are perfectly like and synchronous, have nothing by which they can be distinguished. But will this answer fit the other question? I think not.

The object makes an appearance to each eye, as the sound makes an impression upon each ear: so far the two senses agree. But the visible appearances may be distinguished by place, when perfectly like in other respects; the sounds cannot be thus distinguished: and herein the two senses differ. Indeed, if the two appearances have the same visible place, they are, in that case, as incapable of distinction as the sounds were, and we see the object single. But when they have not the same visible place, they are perfectly distinguishable, and we see the object double. We see the object single only, when the eyes are directed in one particular manner; while there are many other ways of directing them within the sphere of our power, by which we see the object double.

Dr. Smith justly attributes to custom that well-known fallacy in feeling, whereby a button pressed with two opposite sides of two contiguous fingers laid across, is felt double. I agree with him, that the cause of this appearance is, that those opposite sides of the fingers have never been used to feel the same object, but two different objects, at the same time. And I beg leave to add, that, as custom produces this phænomenon, so a contrary custom destroys it; for, if a man frequently accustoms himself to feel the button with his fingers across, it will at last be felt single; as I have found by experience.

It may be taken for a general rule, that things which are produced by custom, may be undone or changed by disuse, or by a contrary custom. On the other hand, it is a strong argument, that an effect is not owing to custom, but to the constitution of nature, when a contrary custom, long continued, is found neither to change nor weaken it. I take this to be the best rule by which we can determine the question presently under consideration. I shall, therefore, mention two facts brought by Dr. Smith, to prove that the corresponding points of the *retinæ* have been changed by custom; and then I shall mention some facts tending to prove, that there are corresponding points of the *retinæ* of the eyes originally, and that custom produces no change in them.

"One fact is related upon the authority of Martin Folkes, Esq., who was informed by Dr. Hepburn of Lynn, that the Rev. Mr. Foster of Clinchwharton, in that neighbourhood, having been blind for some years of a *gutta serena*, was restored to sight by salivation; and that, upon his first beginning to see, all objects appeared to him double; but afterwards, the two appearances approaching by degrees, he came at last to see single, and as distinctly as he did before he was blind."

Upon this case, I observe, First, That it does not prove any change of the corresponding points of the eyes, unless we suppose, what is not affirmed, that Mr. Foster directed his eyes to the object at first, when he saw double, with the same accuracy, and in the same manner, that he did afterwards, when he saw single. Secondly, If we should suppose this, no account can be given, why at first the two appearances should be seen at one certain angular distance rather than another; or why this angular distance should gradually decrease, until at last the appearances coincided. How could this effect be produced by custom? But, Thirdly, Every circumstance of this case may be accounted for on the supposition that Mr. Foster had corresponding points in the *retinæ* of his eyes from the time he began to see, and that custom made no change with regard to them. We need only further suppose, what is common in such cases, that, by some years' blindness, he had lost the habit of directing his eyes accurately to an object, and that he gradually recovered this habit when he came to see.

The second fact mentioned by Dr. Smith, is taken from Mr. Cheselden's "Anatomy," and is this:—"A gentleman who, from a blow on the head, had one eye distorted, found every object appear double; but, by degrees, the most familiar ones became single; and, in time, all objects became so without any amendment of the distortion."

I observe here, that it is not said that the two appearances gradually approached, and at last united, without any amendment of the distortion. This would indeed have been a decisive proof of a change in the corresponding points of the *retinæ*, and yet of such a change as could not be accounted for from custom. But this is not said; and, if it had been observed, a circumstance so remarkable would have been mentioned by Mr. Cheselden, as it was in the other case by Dr. Hepburn. We may, therefore, take it for granted, that one of the appearances vanished by degrees, without approaching to the other. And this I conceive might happen several ways. First, The sight of the distorted eye might gradually decay by the hurt; so the appearances presented by that eye would gradually vanish. Secondly, A small and unperceived change in the manner of directing the eyes, might occasion his not seeing the object with the distorted eye, as appears from § 15, Art. 10. Thirdly, By acquiring the habit of directing one and the same eye always to the object, the faint and oblique appearance presented by the other eye, might be so little attended to when it became familiar, as not to be perceived. One of these causes, or more of them concurring, might produce the effect mentioned, without any change of the corresponding points of the eyes.

For these reasons, the facts mentioned by Dr. Smith, although curious, seem not to be decisive.

The following facts ought to be put in the opposite scale. First, in the famous case of the young gentleman couched by Mr. Cheselden, after having had cataracts on both eyes until he was [above] thirteen years of age, it appears that he saw objects single from the time he began to see with both eyes. Mr. Cheselden's words are, "And now, being lately couched of his other eye, he says, that objects, at first, appeared large to this eye, but not so large as they did at first to the other; and, looking upon the same object with both eyes, he thought it looked about twice as large as with the first couched eye only, but not double, that we can anywise discover."

Secondly, The three young gentlemen mentioned in the last section, who had squinted, as far as I know, from infancy, as soon as they learned to direct both eyes to an object, saw it single. In these four cases, it appears evident that the centres of the *retinæ* corresponded originally, and before custom could produce any such effect; for Mr. Cheselden's young gentleman had never been accustomed to see at all before he was couched; and the other three had never been accustomed to direct the axes of both eyes to the object.

Thirdly, from the facts recited in § 13, it appears, that, from the time we are capable of observing the phænomena of single and double vision, custom makes no change in them.

I have amused myself with such observations for more than thirty years; and in every case wherein I saw the object double at first, I see it so to this day, notwithstanding the constant experience of its being single. In other cases, where I know there are two objects, there appears only one, after thousands of experiments.

Let a man look at a familiar object through a polyhedron, or multiplying-glass, every hour of his life, the number of visible appearances will be the same at last as at first; nor does any number of experiments, or length of time, make the least change.

Effects produced by habit, must vary according as the acts by which the habit is acquired are more or less frequent; but the phænomena of single and double vision are so invariable and uniform in all men, are so exactly regulated by mathematical rules, that I think we have good reason to conclude that they are not the effect of custom, but of fixed and immutable laws of nature.

Section XVIII.

OF DR. PORTERFIELD'S ACCOUNT OF SINGLE AND DOUBLE VISION.

Bishop Berkeley and Dr. Smith seem to attribute too much to custom in vision, Dr. Porterfield too little.

This ingenious writer thinks, that, by an original law

of our nature, antecedent to custom and experience, we perceive visible objects in their true place, not only as to their direction, but likewise as to their distance from the eye; and, therefore, he accounts for our seeing objects single, with two eyes, in this manner. Having the faculty of perceiving the object with each eye in its true place, we must perceive it with both eyes in the same place; and, consequently, must perceive it single.

He is aware that this principle, although it accounts for our seeing objects single with two eyes, yet does not at all account for our seeing objects double; and, whereas other writers on this subject take it to be a sufficient cause for double vision that we have two eyes, and only find it difficult to assign a cause for single vision, on the contrary, Dr. Porterfield's principle throws all the difficulty on the other side.

Therefore, in order to account for the phænomena of double vision, he advances another principle, without signifying whether he conceives it to be an original law of our nature, or the effect of custom. It is, That our natural perception of the distance of objects from the eye, is not extended to all the objects that fall within the field of vision, but limited to that which we directly look at; and that the circumjacent objects, whatever be their real distance, are seen at the same distance with the object we look at; as if they were all in the surface of a sphere, whereof the eye is the centre.

Thus, single vision is accounted for by our seeing the true distance of an object which we look at; and double vision, by a false appearance of distance in objects which we do not directly look at.

We agree with this learned and ingenious author, that it is by a natural and original principle that we see visible objects in a certain direction from the eye, and honour him as the author of this discovery: but we cannot assent to either of those principles by which he explains single and double vision—for the following reasons:—

1. Our having a natural and original perception of the distance of objects from the eye, appears contrary to a well-attested fact: for the young gentleman couched by Mr. Cheselden imagined, at first, that whatever he saw touched his eye, as what he felt touched his hand.

2. The perception we have of the distance of objects from the eye, whether it be from nature or custom, is not so accurate and determined as is necessary to produce single vision. A mistake of the twentieth or thirtieth part of the distance of a small object, such as a pin, ought, according to Dr. Porterfield's hypothesis, to make it appear double. Very few can judge of the distance of a visible object with such accuracy. Yet we never find double vision produced by mistaking the distance of the object. There are many cases in vision, even with the naked eye, wherein we mistake the distance of an object by one half or more: why do we see such objects single? When I move my spectacles from my eyes toward a small object, two or three feet distant, the object seems to approach, so as to be seen at last at about half its real distance; but it is seen single at that apparent distance, as well as when we see it with the naked eye at its real distance. And when we look at an object with a binocular telescope, properly fitted to the eyes, we see it single, while it appears fifteen or twenty times nearer than it is. There are then few cases wherein the distance of an object from the eye is seen so accurately as is necessary for single vision, upon this hypothesis: this seems to be a conclusive argument against the account given of single vision. We find, likewise, that false judgments or fallacious appearances of the distance of an object, do not produce double vision: this seems to be a conclusive argument against the account given of double vision.

3. The perception we have of the linear distance of objects seems to be wholly the effect of experience.

This, I think, hath been proved by Bishop Berkeley and by Dr. Smith; and when we come to point out the means of judging of distance by sight, it will appear that they are all furnished by experience.

4. Supposing that, by a law of our nature, the distance of objects from the eye were perceived most accurately, as well as their direction, it will not follow that we must see the object single. Let us consider what means such a law of nature would furnish for resolving the question, Whether the objects of the two eyes are in one and the same place, and consequently are not two, but one?

Suppose then, two right lines, one drawn from the centre of one eye to its object, the other drawn, in like manner, from the centre of the other eye to its object. This law of nature gives us the direction or position of each of these right lines, and the length of each; and this is all that it gives. These are geometrical *data*, and we may learn from geometry what is determined by their means. Is it, then, determined by these *data*, Whether the two right lines terminate in one and the same point, or not? No, truly. In order to determine this, we must have three other *data*. We must know whether the two right lines are in one plane; we must know what angle they make; and we must know the distance between the centres of the eyes. And when these things are known, we must apply the rules of trigonometry, before we can resolve the question, Whether the objects of the two eyes are in one and the same place; and, consequently, whether they are two or one?

5. That false appearance of distance into which double vision is resolved, cannot be the effect of custom, for constant experience contradicts it. Neither hath it the features of a law of nature, because it does not answer any good purpose, nor, indeed, any purpose at all, but to deceive us. But why should we seek for arguments, in a question concerning what appears to us, or does not appear? The question is, At what distance do the ob-

jects now in my eye appear? Do they all appear at one distance, as if placed in the concave surface of a sphere, the eye being in the centre? Every man, surely, may know this with certainty; and, if he will but give attention to the testimony of his eyes, needs not ask a philosopher how visible objects appear to him. Now, it is very true, that, if I look up to a star in the heavens, the other stars that appear at the same time, do appear in this manner: yet this phænomenon does not favour Dr. Porterfield's hypothesis; for the stars and heavenly bodies do not appear at their true distances when we look directly to them, any more than when they are seen obliquely: and if this phænomenon be an argument for Dr. Porterfield's second principle, it must destroy the first.

The true cause of this phænomenon will be given afterwards; therefore, setting it aside for the present, let us put another case. I sit in my room, and direct my eyes to the door, which appears to be about sixteen feet distant: at the same time, I see many other objects faintly and obliquely—the floor, floor-cloth, the table which I write upon, papers, standish, candle, &c. Now, do all these objects appear at the same distance of sixteen feet? Upon the closest attention I find they do not.

Section XIX.

OF DR BRIGGS'S THEORY AND SIR ISAAC NEWTON'S CONJECTURE ON THIS SUBJECT.

I am afraid the reader, as well as the writer, is already tired of the subject of single and double vision. The multitude of theories advanced by authors of great name, and the multitude of facts, observed without sufficient skill in optics, or related without attention to the most material and decisive circumstances, have equally contributed to perplex it.

In order to bring it to some issue, I have, in the 13th section, given a more full and regular deduction than had been given heretofore, of the phænomena of single and double vision, in those whose sight is perfect; and have traced them up to one general principle, which appears to be a law of vision in human eyes that are perfect and in their natural state.

In the 14th section, I have made it appear, that this law of vision, although excellently adapted to the fabric of human eyes, cannot answer the purposes of vision in some other animals; and therefore, very probably is not common to all animals. The purpose of the 15th and 16th sections is, to inquire, Whether there be any deviation from this law of vision in those who squint?—a question which is of real importance in the medical art, as well as in the philosophy of vision; but which, after all that hath been observed and written on the subject, seems not to be ripe for a determination, for want of proper observations. Those who have had skill to make proper observations, have wanted opportunities; and those who have had opportunities, have wanted skill or attention. I have therefore thought it worth while to give a distinct account of the observations necessary for the determination of this question, and what conclusions may be drawn from the facts observed. I have likewise collected, and set in one view, the most conclusive facts that have occurred in authors, or have fallen under my own observation.

It must be confessed that these facts, when applied to the question in hand, make a very poor figure; and the gentlemen of the medical faculty are called upon, for the honour of their profession, and for the benefit of mankind, to add to them.

All the medical, and all the optical writers upon the *strabismus* that I have met with, except Dr. Jurin, either affirm, or take it for granted, that squinting persons see the object with both eyes, and yet see it single. Dr.

Jurin affirms that squinting persons never see the object with both eyes; and that, if they did, they would see it double. If the common opinion be true, the cure of a squint would be as pernicious to the sight of the patient, as the causing of a permanent squint would be to one who naturally had no squint; and therefore, no physician ought to attempt such a cure, no patient ought to submit to it. But, if Dr. Jurin's opinion be true, most young people that squint may cure themselves, by taking some pains; and may not only remove the deformity, but, at the same time, improve their sight. If the common opinion be true, the centres, and other points of the two *retinæ*, in squinting persons, do not correspond, as in other men, and Nature, in them, deviates from her common rule. But, if Dr. Jurin's opinion be true, there is reason to think that the same general law of vision, which we have found in perfect human eyes, extends also to those which squint.

It is impossible to determine, by reasoning, which of these opinions is true; or whether one may not be found true in same patients, and the other in others. Here, experience and observation are our only guides; and a deduction of instances is the only rational argument. It might, therefore, have been expected, that the patrons of the contrary opinions should have given instances in support of them that are clear and indisputable; but I have not found one such instance on either side of the question, in all the authors I have met with. I have given three instances from my own observation, in confirmation of Dr. Jurin's opinion, which admit of no doubt; and one which leans rather to the other opinion, but is dubious. And here I must leave the matter to further observation.

In the 17th section, I have endeavoured to shew that the correspondence and [or] sympathy of certain points of the two *retinæ*, into which we have resolved all the phænomena of single and double vision, is not, as Dr.

Smith conceived, the effect of custom, nor can [it] be changed by custom, but is a natural and original property of human eyes; and, in the last section, that it is not owing to an original and natural perception of the true distance of objects from the eye, as Dr. Porterfield imagined. After this recapitulation, which is intended to relieve the attention of the reader, shall we enter into more theories upon this subject?

That of Dr. Briggs—first published in English, in the "Philosophical Transactions," afterwards in Latin, under the title of "Nova Visionis Theoria," with a prefatory epistle of Sir Isaac Newton to the author—amounts to this, That the fibres of the optic nerves, passing from corresponding points of the *retinæ* to the *thalami nervorum opticorum*, having the same length, the same tension, and a similar situation, will have the same tone; and, therefore, their vibrations, excited by the impression of the rays of light, will be like unisons in music, and will present one and the same image to the mind: but the fibres passing from parts of the *retinæ* which do not correspond, having different tensions and tones, will have discordant vibrations; and, therefore, present different images to the mind.

I shall not enter upon a particular examination of this theory. It is enough to observe, in general, that it is a system of conjectures concerning things of which we are entirely ignorant; and that all such theories in philosophy deserve rather to be laughed at, than to be seriously refuted.

From the first dawn of philosophy to this day, it hath been believed that the optic nerves are intended to carry the images of visible objects from the bottom of the eye to the mind; and that the nerves belonging to the organs of the other senses have a like office. But how do we know this? We conjecture it; and, taking this conjecture for a truth, we consider how the nerves may best answer this purpose. The system of the nerves, for many ages, was taken to be a hydraulic engine, consisting of a bundle of pipes, which carried to and fro a liquor called *animal spirits*. About the time of Dr. Briggs, it was thought rather to be a stringed instrument, composed of vibrating chords, each of which had its proper tension and tone. But some, with as great probability, conceived it to be a wind instrument, which played its part by the vibrations of an elastic æther in the nervous fibrils.

These, I think, are all the engines into which the nervous system hath been moulded by philosophers, for conveying the images of sensible things from the organ to the *sensorium*. And, for all that we know of the matter, every man may freely choose which he thinks fittest for the purpose; for, from fact and experiment, no one of them can claim preference to another. Indeed, they all seem so unhandy engines for carrying images, that a man would be tempted to invent a new one.

Since, therefore, a blind man may guess as well in the dark as one that sees, I beg leave to offer another conjecture touching the nervous system, which, I hope, will answer the purpose as well as those we have mentioned, and which recommends itself by its simplicity. Why may not the optic nerves, for instance, be made up of empty tubes, opening their mouths wide enough to receive the rays of light which form the image upon the *retinæ*, and gently conveying them safe, and in their proper order, to the very seat of the soul, until they flash in her face? It is easy for an ingenious philosopher to fit the caliber of these empty tubes to the diameter of the particles of light, so as they shall receive no grosser kind of matter; and, if these rays should be in danger of mistaking their way, an expedient may also be found to prevent this; for it requires no more than to bestow upon the tubes of the nervous system a peristaltic motion, like that of the alimentary tube.

It is a peculiar advantage of this hypothesis, that, although all philosophers believe that the species or images of things are conveyed by the nerves to the soul, yet none of their hypotheses shew how this may be done. For how can the images of sound, taste, smell, colour, figure, and all sensible qualities, be made out of the vibrations of musical chords, or the undulations of animal spirits, or of æther? We ought not to suppose means inadequate to the end. Is it not as philosophical, and more intelligible, to conceive, that, as the stomach receives its food, so the soul receives her images by a kind of nervous deglutition? I might add, that we need only continue this peristaltic motion of the nervous tubes from the *sensorium* to the extremities of the nerves that serve the muscles, in order to account for muscular motion.

Thus Nature will be consonant to herself: and, as sensation will be the conveyance of the ideal aliment to the mind, so muscular motion will be the expulsion of the recrementitious part of it. For who can deny, that the images of things conveyed by sensation, may, after due concoction, become fit to be thrown off by muscular motion? I only give hints of these things to the ingenious, hoping that in time this hypothesis may be wrought up into a system as truly philosophical as that of animal spirits, or the vibration of nervous fibres.

To be serious: In the operations of nature, I hold the theories of a philosopher, which are unsupported by fact, in the same estimation with the dreams of a man asleep, or the ravings of a madman. We laugh at the Indian philosopher, who, to account for the support of the earth, contrived the hypothesis of a huge elephant, and, to support the elephant, a huge tortoise. If we will candidly confess the truth, we know as little of the operation of the nerves, as he did of the manner in which the earth is supported; and our hypotheses about animal spirits, or about the tension and vibrations of the nerves, are as like to be true, as his about the support of the earth. His elephant was a hypothesis, and our hypotheses are elephants. Every theory in philosophy, which is built on pure conjecture, is an elephant; and every theory that is supported partly by fact, and partly by conjecture, is like Nebuchadnezzar's image, whose feet were partly of iron and partly of clay.

The great Newton first gave an example to philosophers, which always ought to be, but rarely hath been followed, by distinguishing his conjectures from his conclusions, and putting the former by themselves, in the modest form of queries. This is fair and legal; but all other philosophical traffic in conjecture ought to be held contraband and illicit. Indeed, his conjectures have commonly more foundation in fact, and more verisimilitude, than the dogmatical theories of most other philosophers; and, therefore, we ought not to omit that which he hath offered concerning the cause of our seeing objects single with two eyes, in the 15th query annexed to his "Optics."

"Are not the species of objects seen with both eyes, united where the optic nerves meet before they come into the brain, the fibres on the right side of both nerves uniting there, and after union going thence into the brain in the nerve which is on the right side of the head, and the fibres on the left side of both nerves uniting in the same place, and after union going into the brain in the nerve which is on the left side of the head, and these two nerves meeting in the brain in such a manner that their fibres make but one entire species or picture, half of which on the right side of the *sensorium* comes from the right side of both eyes through the right side of both optic nerves, to the place where the nerves meet, and from thence on the right side of the head into the brain, and the other half on the left side of the *sensorium* comes, in like manner, from the left side of both eyes? For the optic nerves of such animals as look the same way with both eyes (as men, dogs, sheep, oxen, &c.) meet before they come into the brain; but the optic nerves of such animals as do not look the same way with both eyes (as of fishes, and of the chameleon) do not meet, if I am rightly informed."

I beg leave to distinguish this query into two, which are of very different natures; one being purely anatomical, the other relating to the carrying species or pictures of visible objects to the *sensorium*.

The first question is, Whether the fibres coming from corresponding points of the two *retinæ* do not unite at the place where the optic nerves meet, and continue united from thence to the brain; so that the right optic nerve, after the meeting of the two nerves, is composed of the fibres coming from the right side of both *retinæ*, and the left, of the fibres coming from the left side of both *retinæ*?

This is undoubtedly a curious and rational question; because, if we could find ground from anatomy to answer it in the affirmative, it would lead us a step forward in discovering the cause of the correspondence and sympathy which there is between certain points of the two *retinæ*. For, although we know not what is the particular function of the optic nerves, yet it is probable that some impression made upon them, and communicated along their fibres, is necessary to vision; and, whatever be the nature of this impression, if two fibres are united into one, an impression made upon one of them, or upon both, may probably produce the same effect. Anatomists think it a sufficient account of a sympathy between two parts of the body, when they are served by branches of the same nerve; we should, therefore, look upon it as an important discovery in anatomy, if it were found that the same nerve sent branches to the corresponding points of the *retinæ*.

But hath any such discovery been made? No, not so much as in one subject, as far as I can learn; but, in several subjects, the contrary seems to have been discovered. Dr. Porterfield hath given us two cases at length from Vesalius, and one from Cæsalpinus, wherein the optic nerves, after touching one another as usual, appeared to be reflected back to the same side whence they came, without any mixture of their fibres. Each of these persons had lost an eye some time before his death, and the optic nerve belonging to that eye was shrunk, so that it could be distinguished from the other at the place where they met. Another case, which the same author gives from Vesalius, is still more remarkable; for in it the optic nerves did not touch at all; and yet, upon inquiry, those who were most familiar with the person in his lifetime, declared that he never complained of any defect of sight, or of his seeing objects double. Diemerbroeck tells us, that Aquapendens [ab Aquapendente] and Valverda likewise affirm, that they have met with subjects wherein the optic nerves did not touch.

As these observations were made before Sir Isaac Newton put this query, it is uncertain whether he was ignorant of them, or whether he suspected some inaccuracy in them, and desired that the matter might be more carefully examined. But, from the following passage of the most accurate Winslow, it does not appear that later observations have been more favorable to his conjecture. "The union of these (optic) nerves, by the small curvatures of their *cornua*, is very difficult to be unfolded in human bodies. This union is commonly found to be very close; but, in some subjects, it seems to be no more than a strong adhesion—in others, to be partly made by an intersection or crossing of fibres. They have been found quite separate; and, in other subjects, one of them has been found to be very much altered both in size and colour through its whole passage, the other remaining in its natural state."

When we consider this conjecture of Sir Isaac Newton by itself, it appears more ingenious, and to have more verisimilitude, than anything that has been offered upon the subject; and we admire the caution and modesty of the author, in proposing it only as a subject of inquiry: but when we compare it with the observations of anatomists which contradict it, we are naturally led to this reflection, That, if we trust to the conjectures of men of the greatest genius in the operations of nature, we have only the chance of going wrong in an ingenious manner.

The second part of the query is, Whether the two species of objects from the two eyes are not, at the place where the optic nerves meet, united into one species or picture, half of which is carried thence to the *sensorium* in the right optic nerve, and the other half in the left? and whether these two halves are not so put together again at the *sensorium*, as to make one species or picture?

Here it seems natural to put the previous question, What reason have we to believe that pictures of objects are at all carried to the *sensorium*, either by the optic nerves, or by any other nerves? Is it not possible that this great philosopher, as well as many of a lower form, having been led into this opinion at first by education, may have continued in it, because he never thought of calling it in question? I confess this was my own case for a considerable part of my life. But since I was led by accident to think seriously what reason I had to believe it, I could find none at all. It seems to be a mere hypothesis, as much as the Indian philosopher's elephant. I am not conscious of any pictures of external objects in my *sensorinm*, any more than in my stomach: the things which I perceive by my senses, appear to be external, and not in any part of the brain; and my sensations, properly so called, have no resemblance of external objects.

The conclusion from all that hath been said, in no less than seven sections, upon our seeing objects single with two eyes, is this—That, by an original property of human eyes, objects painted upon the centres of the two *retinæ*, or upon points similarly situate with regard to the centres, appear in the same visible place; that the most plausible attempts to account for this property of the eyes, have been unsuccessful; and, therefore, that it must be either a primary law of our constitution, or the consequence of some more general law, which is not yet discovered.

We have now finished what we intended to say, both of the visible appearances of things to the eye, and of the laws of our constitution by which those appearances are exhibited. But it was observed, in the beginning of this chapter, that the visible appearances of objects serve only as signs of their distance, magnitude, figure, and other tangible qualities. The visible appearance is that which is presented to the mind by nature, according to those laws of our constitution which have been explained. But the thing signified by that appearance, is that which is presented to the mind by custom.

When one speaks to us in a language that is familiar, we hear certain sounds, and this is all the effect that his discourse has upon us by nature; but by custom we understand the meaning of these sounds; and, therefore, we fix our attention, not upon the sounds, but upon the things signified by them. In like manner, we see only the visible appearance of objects by nature; but we learn by custom to interpret these appearances, and to understand their meaning. And when this visual language is learned, and becomes familiar, we attend only to the things signified; and cannot, without great difficulty, attend to the signs by which they are presented. The mind passes from one to the other so rapidly and so familiarly, that no trace of the sign is left in the memory, and we seem immediately, and without the intervention of any sign, to perceive the thing signified.

When I look at the apple-tree which stands before my window, I perceive, at the first glance, its distance and magnitude, the roughness of its trunk, the disposition of its branches, the figure of its leaves and fruit. I seem to perceive all these things immediately. The visible appearance which presented them all to the mind, has entirely escaped me; I cannot, without great difficulty, and painful abstraction, attend to it, even when it stands before me. Yet it is certain that this visible appearance only is presented to my eye by nature, and that I learned by custom to collect all the rest from it. If I had never seen before now, I should not perceive either the distance or tangible figure of the tree; and it would have required the practice of seeing for many months, to change that original perception which nature gave me by my eyes, into that which I now have by custom.

The objects which we see naturally and originally, as hath been before observed, have length and breadth, but no thickness nor distance from the eye. Custom, by a kind of legerdemain, withdraws gradually these original and proper objects of sight, and substitutes in their place objects of touch, which have length, breadth, and thickness, and a determinate distance from the eye. By what means this change is brought about, and what principles of the human mind concur in it, we are next to inquire.

Section XX.

OF PERCEPTION IN GENERAL.

Sensation, and the perception * of external objects by the senses, though very different in their nature, have commonly been considered as one and the same thing.†

* On the distinction of *Sensation proper*, from *Perception proper*, see "Essays on the Intellectual Powers," Essay II., chap 16. Reid himself, especially in this work, has not been always rigid in observing their discrimination —H.

† Not only are they different, but—what has escaped our philosophers—the law of their manifestation is, that, while both are co-existent, each is always in the inverse ratio of the other. Perception is the objective, Sensation the subjective, element. This by the way.—H.

The purposes of common life do not make it necessary to distinguish them, and the received opinions of philosophers tend rather to confound them; but, without attending carefully to this distinction, it is impossible to have any just conception of the operations of our senses. The most simple operations of the mind, admit not of a logical definition: all we can do is to describe them, so as to lead those who are conscious of them in themselves, to attend to them, and reflect upon them; and it is often very difficult to describe them so as to answer this intention.

The same mode of expression is used to denote sensation and perception; and, therefore, we are apt to look upon them as things of the same nature. Thus, *I feel a pain; I see a tree:* the first denoteth a sensation, the last a perception. The grammatical analysis of both expressions is the same: for both consist of an active verb and an object. But if we attend to the things signified by these expressions, we shall find that, in the first, the distinction between the act and the object is not real but grammatical; in the second, the distinction is not only grammatical but real.

The form of the expression, *I feel pain*, might seem to imply that the feeling is something distinct from the pain felt; yet, in reality, there is no distinction. As *thinking a thought* is an expression which could signify no more than *thinking*, so *feeling a pain* signifies no more than *being pained.* What we have said of pain is applicable to every other mere sensation. It is difficult to give instances, very few of our sensations having names; and, where they have, the name being common to the sensation, and to something else which is associated with it. But, when we attend to the sensation by itself, and separate it from other things which are conjoined with it in the imagination, it appears to be something which can have no existence but in a sentient mind, no distinction from the act of the mind by which it is felt.

Perception, as we here understand it, hath always an object distinct from the act by which it is perceived; an object which may exist whether it be perceived or not. I perceive a tree that grows before my window; there is here an object which is perceived, and an act of the mind by which it is perceived; and these two are not only distinguishable, but they are extremely unlike in their natures. The object is made up of a trunk, branches, and leaves; but the act of the mind by which it is perceived hath neither trunk, branches, nor leaves. I am conscious of this act of my mind, and I can reflect upon it; but it is too simple to admit of an analysis, and I cannot find proper words to describe it. I find nothing that resembles it so much as the remembrance of the tree, or the imagination of it. Yet both these differ essentially from perception: they differ likewise one from another. It is in vain that a philosopher assures me, that the imagination of the tree, the remembrance of it, and the perception of it, are all one, and differ only in degree of vivacity. I know the contrary; for I am as well acquainted with all the three as I am with the apartments of my own house. I know this also, that the perception of an object implies both a conception of its form, and a belief of its present existence.* I know, moreover, that this belief is not the effect of argumenta-

* It is to be observed that Reid himself does not discriminate *perception* and *imagination* by any essential difference. According to him, perception is only the conception (imagination) of an object, accompanied with a belief of its present existence; and even this last distinction, a mere "faith without knowledge," is surrendered by Mr. Stewart. Now, as conception (imagination) is only immediately cognisant of the *ego*, so must perception on this doctrine be a knowledge purely *subjective*. Perception must be wholly different in kind from Conception, if we are to possess a faculty informing us of the existence and qualities of an external world; and, unless we are possessed of such a faculty, we shall never be competent to vindicate more than an ideal reality to the objects of our cognitions.—H.

tion and reasoning; it is the immediate effect of my constitution.

I am aware that this belief which I have in perception stands exposed to the strongest batteries of scepticism. But they make no great impression upon it. The sceptic asks me, Why do you believe the existence of the external object which you perceive? This belief, sir, is none of my manufacture; it came from the mint of Nature; it bears her image and superscription; and, if it is not right, the fault is not mine: I even took it upon trust, and without suspicion. Reason, says the sceptic, is the only judge of truth, and you ought to throw off every opinion and every belief that is not grounded on reason. Why, sir, should I believe the faculty of reason more than that of perception?—they came both out of the same shop, and were made by the same artist; and if he puts one piece of false ware into my hands, what should hinder him from putting another?*

Perhaps the sceptic will agree to distrust reason, rather than give any credit to perception. For, says he, since, by your own concession, the object which you perceive, and that act of your mind by which you perceive it, are quite different things, the one may exist without the other; and, as the object may exist without being perceived, so the perception may exist without an object. There is nothing so shameful in a philosopher as to be deceived and deluded; and, therefore, you ought to resolve firmly to withhold assent, and to throw off this belief of external objects, which may be all delusion. For my part, I will never attempt to throw it off; and, although the sober part of mankind will not be

* This argument would be good in favour of our belief, that we are really percipient of a *non-ego*: it is not good in favour of our belief that a *non-ego* really exists, our perception of its real existence being abandoned. Mankind have the latter belief only as they have the former; and, if we are deceived by our Nature touching the one, it is absurd to appeal to her veracity in proof of the other.—H.

very anxious to know my reasons, yet, if they can be of use to any sceptic, they are these:—

First, because it is not in my power: why, then, should I make a vain attempt? It would be agreeable to fly to the moon, and to make a visit to Jupiter and Saturn; but, when I know that Nature has bound me down by the law of gravitation to this planet which I inhabit, I rest contented, and quietly suffer myself to be carried along in its orbit. My belief is carried along by perception, as irresistibly as my body by the earth. And the greatest sceptic will find himself to be in the same condition. He may struggle hard to disbelieve the informations of his senses, as a man does to swim against a torrent; but, ah! it is in vain. It is in vain that he strains every nerve, and wrestles with nature, and with every object that strikes upon his senses. For, after all, when his strength is spent in the fruitless attempt, he will be carried down the torrent with the common herd of believers.

Secondly, I think it would not be prudent to throw off this belief, if it were in my power. If Nature intended to deceive me, and impose upon me by false appearances, and I, by my great cunning and profound logic, have discovered the imposture, prudence would dictate to me, in this case, even to put up [with] this indignity done me, as quietly as I could, and not to call her an impostor to her face, lest she should be even with me in another way. For what do I gain by resenting this injury? You ought at least not to believe what she says. This indeed seems reasonable, if she intends to impose upon me. But what is the consequence? I resolve not to believe my senses. I break my nose against a post that comes in my way; I step into a dirty kennel; and, after twenty such wise and rational actions, I am taken up and clapped into a mad-house. Now, I confess I would rather make one of the credulous fools whom Nature imposes upon, than of those wise and rational philosophers who resolve to withhold assent at all this expense. If a man pretends to be a sceptic with regard to the informations of sense, and yet prudently keeps out of harm's way as other men do, he must excuse my suspicion, that he either acts the hypocrite, or imposes upon himself. For, if the scale of his belief were so evenly poised as to lean no more to one side than to the contrary, it is impossible that his actions could be directed by any rules of common prudence.*

Thirdly, Although the two reasons already mentioned are perhaps two more than enough, I shall offer a third. I gave implicit belief to the informations of Nature by my senses, for a considerable part of my life, before I had learned so much logic as to be able to start a doubt concerning them. And now, when I reflect upon what is past, I do not find that I have been imposed upon by this belief. I find that without it I must have perished by a thousand accidents. I find that without it I should have been no wiser now than when I was born. I should not even have been able to acquire that logic which suggests these sceptical doubts with regard to my senses. Therefore, I consider this instinctive belief as one of the best gifts of Nature. I thank the Author of my being, who bestowed it upon me before the eyes of my reason were opened, and still bestows it upon me, to be my guide where reason leaves me in the dark. And now I yield to the direction of my senses, not from instinct only, but from confidence and trust in a faithful and beneficent Monitor, grounded upon the experience of his paternal care and goodness.

In all this, I deal with the Author of my being, no otherwise than I thought it reasonable to deal with my parents and tutors. I believed by instinct whatever they told me, long before I had the idea of a lie, or thought

* This is not a fair consequence of Idealism; therefore, it is not a *reductio ad absurdum*.—H.

of the possibility of their deceiving me. Afterwards, upon reflection, I found they had acted like fair and honest people, who wished me well. I found that, if I had not believed what they told me, before I could give a reason of my belief, I had to this day been little better than a changeling. And although this natural credulity hath sometimes occasioned my being imposed upon by deceivers, yet it hath been of infinite advantage to me upon the whole; therefore, I consider it as another good gift of Nature. And I continue to give that credit, from reflection, to those of whose integrity and veracity I have had experience, which before I gave from instinct.

There is a much greater similitude than is commonly imagined, between the testimony of nature given by our senses, and the testimony of men given by language. The credit we give to both is at first the effect of instinct only. When we grow up, and begin to reason about them, the credit given to human testimony is restrained and weakened, by the experience we have of deceit. But the credit given to the testimony of our senses, is established and confirmed by the uniformity and constancy of the laws of nature.

Our perceptions are of two kinds: some are natural and original; others acquired, and the fruit of experience. When I perceive that this is the taste of cyder, that of brandy; that this is the smell of an apple, that of an orange; that this is the noise of thunder, that the ringing of bells; this the sound of a coach passing, that the voice of such a friend: these perceptions, and others of the same kind, are not original—they are acquired. But the perception which I have, by touch, of the hardness and softness of bodies, of their extension, figure, and motion, is not acquired—it is original.

In all our senses, the acquired perceptions are many more than the original, especially in sight. By this sense we perceive originally the visible figure and colour of bodies only, and their visible place: * but we learn to perceive by the eye, almost everything which we can perceive by touch. The original perceptions of this sense serve only as signs to introduce the acquired.

The signs by which objects are presented to us in perception, are the language of Nature to man; and as, in many respects, it hath great affinity with the language of man to man, so particularly in this, that both are partly natural and original, partly acquired by custom. Our original or natural perceptions are analogous to the natural language of man to man, of which we took notice in the fourth chapter; and our acquired perceptions are analogous to artificial language, which, in our mother-tongue, is got very much in the same manner with our acquired perceptions—as we shall afterwards more fully explain.

Not only men, but children, idiots, and brutes, acquire by habit many perceptions which they had not originally. Almost every employment in life hath perceptions of this kind that are peculiar to it. The shepherd knows every sheep of his flock, as we do our acquaintance, and can pick them out of another flock one by one. The butcher knows by sight the weight and quality of his beeves and sheep before they are killed. The farmer perceives by his eye, very nearly, the quantity of hay in a rick, or of corn in a heap. The sailor sees the burthen, the built, and the distance of a ship at sea, while she is a great way off. Every man accustomed to writing, distinguishes his acquaintance by their handwriting, as he does by their faces. And the painter distinguishes, in the works of his art, the style of all the great masters. In a word, acquired perception is very different in different persons, according to the diversity of objects about which they are employed, and the application they bestow in observing them.

* In this passage Reid admits Figure and Place (consequently, Extension) to be *original* perceptions of vision.

Perception ought not only to be distinguished from sensation, but likewise from that knowledge of the objects of sense which is got by reasoning. There is no reasoning in perception, as hath been observed. The belief which is implied in it, is the effect of instinct. But there are many things, with regard to sensible objects, which we can infer from what we perceive; and such conclusions of reason ought to be distinguished from what is merely perceived. When I look at the moon, I perceive her to be sometimes circular, sometimes horned, and sometimes gibbous. This is simple perception, and is the same in the philosopher and in the clown: but from these various appearances of her enlightened part, I infer that she is really of a spherical figure. This conclusion is not obtained by simple perception, but by reasoning. Simple perception has the same relation to the conclusions of reason drawn from our perceptions, as the axioms in mathematics have to the propositions. I cannot demonstrate that two quantities which are equal to the same quantity, are equal to each other; neither can I demonstrate that the tree which I perceive, exists. But, by the constitution of my nature, my belief is irresistibly carried along by my apprehension of the axiom; and, by the constitution of my nature, my belief is no less irresistibly carried along by my perception of the tree. All reasoning is from principles. The first principles of mathematical reasoning are mathematical axioms and definitions; and the first principles of all our reasoning about existences, are our perceptions. The first principles of every kind of reasoning are given us by Nature, and are of equal authority with the faculty of reason itself, which is also the gift of Nature. The conclusions of reason are all built upon first principles, and can have no other foundation. Most justly, therefore, do such principles disdain to be tried by reason, and laugh at all the artillery of the logician, when it is directed against them.

When a long train of reasoning is necessary in demonstrating a mathematical proposition, it is easily distinguished from an axiom; and they seem to be things of a very different nature. But there are some propositions which lie so near to axioms, that it is difficult to say whether they ought to be held as axioms, or demonstrated as propositions. The same thing holds with regard to perception, and the conclusions drawn from it. Some of these conclusions follow our perceptions so easily, and are so immediately connected with them, that it is difficult to fix the limit which divides the one from the other.

Perception, whether original or acquired, implies no exercise of reason; and is common to men, children, idiots, and brutes. The more obvious conclusions drawn from our perceptions, by reason, make what we call *common understanding;* by which men conduct themselves in the common affairs of life, and by which they are distinguished from idiots. The more remote conclusions which are drawn from our perceptions, by reason, make what we commonly call *science* in the various parts of nature, whether in agriculture, medicine, mechanics, or in any part of natural philosophy. When I see a garden in good order, containing a great variety of things of the best kinds, and in the most flourishing condition, I immediately conclude from these signs the skill and industry of the gardener. A farmer, when he rises in the morning, and perceives that the neighbouring brook overflows his field, concludes that a great deal of rain hath fallen in the night. Perceiving his fence broken, and his corn trodden down, he concludes that some of his own or his neighbours' cattle have broke loose. Perceiving that his stable-door is broke open, and some of his horses gone, he concludes that a thief has carried them off. He traces the prints of his horses' feet in the soft ground, and by them discovers which road the thief hath taken. These are instances of common understanding, which dwells so near to perception that it is difficult to trace the line which divides the one from the other. In like manner the science of nature dwells so near to common understanding that we cannot discern where the latter ends and the former begins. I perceive that bodies lighter than water swim in water, and that those which are heavier sink. Hence I conclude, that, if a body remains wherever it is put under water, whether at the top or bottom, it is precisely of the same weight with water. If it will rest only when part of it is above water, it is lighter than water. And the greater the part above water is, compared with the whole, the lighter is the body. If it had no gravity at all, it would make no impression upon the water, but stand wholly above it. Thus, every man, by common understanding, has a rule by which he judges of the specific gravity of bodies which swim in water; and a step or two more leads him into the science of hydrostatics.

All that we know of nature, or of existences, may be compared to a tree, which hath its root, trunk, and branches. In this tree of knowledge, perception is the root, common understanding is the trunk, and the sciences are the branches.

Section XXI.

OF THE PROCESS OF NATURE IN PERCEPTION.

Although there is no reasoning in perception, yet there are certain means and instruments, which, by the appointment of nature, must intervene between the object and our perception of it: and, by these, our perceptions are limited and regulated. First, if the object is not in contact with the organ of sense, there must be some medium which passes between them. Thus, in vision, the rays of light; in hearing, the vibrations of elastic air; in smelling, the effluvia of the body smelled—must pass from the object to the organ; otherwise we have no perception.* Secondly, There must be some action or impression upon the organ of sense, either by the immediate application of the object, or by the medium that goes between them. Thirdly, The nerves which go from the brain to the organ must receive some impression by means of that which was made upon the organ; and, probably, by means of the nerves, some impression must be made upon the brain. Fourthly, The impression made upon the organ, nerves, and brain, is followed by a sensation. And, last of all, This sensation is followed by the perception of the object.

Thus, our perception of objects is the result of a train of operations; some of which affect the body only, others affect the mind. We know very little of the nature of some of these operations; we know not at all how they are connected together, or in what way they contribute to that perception which is the result of the whole; but, by the laws of our constitution, we perceive objects in this and in no other way.

There may be other beings who can perceive external objects without rays of light, or vibrations of air, or effluvia of bodies—without impressions on bodily organs, or even without sensations; but we are so framed by the Author of Nature, that even when we are surrounded by external objects, we may perceive none of them Our faculty of perceiving an object lies dormant, until it is roused and stimulated by a certain corresponding sensation. Nor is this sensation always at hand to perform its office; for it enters into the mind only in consequence of a certain corresponding impression made on the organ of sense by the object.

* The only object of *perception* is the *immediate* object. The distant reality—the mediate object, or object simply of Reid and other philosophers—is unknown to the perception of sense, and only reached by reasoning.—H.

Let us trace this correspondence of impressions, sensations, and perceptions, as far as we can—beginning with that which is first in order, the impression made upon the bodily organ. But, alas! we know not of what nature these impressions are, far less how they excite sensations in the mind.

We know that one body may act upon another by pressure, by percussion, by attraction, by repulsion, and, probably, in many other ways which we neither know nor have names to express. But in which of these ways objects, when perceived by us, act upon the organs of sense, these organs upon the nerves, and the nerves upon the brain, we know not. Can any man tell me how in vision, the rays of light act upon the *retina*, how the *retina* acts upon the optic nerve, and how the optic nerve acts upon the brain? No man can. When I feel the pain of the gout in my toe, I know that there is some unusual impression made upon that part of my body. But of what kind is it? Are the small vessels distended with some redundant elastic, or unelastic fluid? Are the fibres unusually stretched? Are they torn asunder by force, or gnawed and corroded by some acrid humour? I can answer none of these questions. All that I feel is pain, which is not an impression upon the body, but upon the mind; and all that I perceive by this sensation is, that some distemper in my toe occasions this pain. But as I know not the natural temper and texture of my toe when it is at ease, I know as little what change or disorder of its parts occasions this uneasy sensation. In like manner, in every other sensation, there is, without doubt, some impression made upon the organ of sense; but an impression of which we know not the nature. It is too subtile to be discovered by our senses, and we may make a thousand conjectures without coming near the truth. If we understood the structure of our organs of sense so minutely as to discover what effects are produced upon them by external objects, this knowledge would contribute nothing to our perception of the object; for they perceive as distinctly who know least about the manner of perception, as the greatest adepts. It is necessary that the impression be made upon our organs, but not that it be known. Nature carries on this part of the process of perception, without our consciousness or concurrence.

But we cannot be unconscious of the next step in this process—the sensation of the mind, which always immediately follows the impression made upon the body. It is essential to a sensation to be felt, and it can be nothing more than we feel it to be. If we can only acquire the habit of attending to our sensations, we may know them perfectly. But how are the sensations of the mind produced by impressions upon the body? Of this we are absolutely ignorant, having no means of knowing how the body acts upon the mind, or the mind upon the body. When we consider the nature and attributes of both, they seem to be so different, and so unlike, that we can find no handle by which the one may lay hold of the other. There is a deep and a dark gulf between them, which our understanding cannot pass; and the manner of their correspondence and intercourse is absolutely unknown.

Experience teaches us, that certain impressions upon the body are constantly followed by certain sensations of the mind; and that, on the other hand, certain determinations of the mind are constantly followed by certain motions in the body; but we see not the chain that ties these things together. Who knows but their connection may be arbitrary, and owing to the will of our Maker? Perhaps the same sensations might have been connected with other impressions, or other bodily organs. Perhaps we might have been so made as to taste with our fingers, to smell with our ears, and to hear by the nose. Perhaps we might have been so made as to have all the sensations and perceptions which we have, without any impression made upon our bodily organs at all.

However these things may be, if Nature had given us nothing more than impressions made upon the body, and sensations in our minds corresponding to them, we should, in that case, have been merely sentient, but not percipient beings. We should never have been able to form a conception of any external object, far less a belief of its existence. Our sensations have no resemblance to external objects; nor can we discover, by our reason, any necessary connection between the existence of the former, and that of the latter.

We might, perhaps, have been made of such a constitution as to have our present perceptions connected with other sensations. We might, perhaps, have had the perception of external objects, without either impressions upon the organs of sense, or sensations. Or, lastly, The perceptions we have, might have been immediately connected with the impressions upon our organs, without any intervention of sensations. This last seems really to be the case in one instance—to wit, in our perception of the visible figure of bodies, as was observed in the eighth section of this chapter.

The process of Nature, in perception by the senses, may, therefore, be conceived as a kind of drama, wherein some things are performed behind the scenes, others are represented to the mind in different scenes, one succeeding another. The impression made by the object upon the organ, either by immediate contact or by some intervening medium, as well as the impression made upon the nerves and brain, is performed behind the scenes, and the mind sees nothing of it. But every such impression, by the laws of the drama, is followed by a sensation, which is the first scene exhibited to the mind; and this scene is quickly succeeded by another, which is the perception of the object.

In this drama, Nature is the actor, we are the spectators. We know nothing of the machinery by means of which every different impression upon the organ, nerves, and brain, exhibits its corresponding sensation; or of the machinery by means of which each sensation exhibits its corresponding perception. We are inspired with the sensation, and we are inspired with the corresponding perception, by means unknown.* And, because the mind passes immediately from the sensation to that conception and belief of the object which we have in perception, in the same manner as it passes from signs to the things signified by them, we have, therefore, called our sensations *signs of external objects;* finding no word more proper to express the function which Nature hath assigned them in perception, and the relation which they bear to their corresponding objects.

There is no necessity of a resemblance between the sign and the thing signified ; and indeed no sensation can resemble any external object. But there are two things necessary to our knowing things by means of signs. First, That a real connection between the sign and thing signified be established, either by the course of nature, or by the will and appointment of men. When they are connected by the course of nature, it is a natural sign; when by human appointment, it is an artificial sign. Thus, smoke is a natural sign of fire; certain features are natural signs of anger: but our words, whether expressed by articulate sounds or by writing, are artificial signs of our thoughts and purposes.

Another requisite to our knowing things by signs is, that the appearance of the sign to the mind, be followed by the conception and belief of the thing signified. Without this, the sign is not understood or interpreted; and, therefore, is no sign to us, however fit in its own nature for that purpose.

Now, there are three ways in which the mind passes from the appearance of a natural sign to the conception

* On perception as a revelation—"a miraculous revelation"—see Jacobi's "David Hume."—H.

and belief of the thing signified—by *original principles of our constitution*, by *custom* and by *reasoning*.

Our original perceptions are got in the first of these ways, our acquired perceptions in the second, and all that reason discovers of the course of nature, in the third. In the first of these ways, Nature, by means of the sensations of touch, informs us of the hardness and softness of bodies; of their extension, figure, and motion; and of that space in which they move and are placed—as hath been already explained in the fifth chapter of this inquiry. And, in the second of these ways, she informs us, by means of our eyes, of almost all the same things which originally we could perceive only by touch.

In order, therefore, to understand more particularly how we learn to perceive so many things by the eye, which originally could be perceived only by touch, it will be proper, First, To point out the signs by which those things are exhibited to the eye, and their connection with the things signified by them; and, Secondly, To consider how the experience of this connection produces that habit by which the mind, without any reasoning or reflection, passes from the sign to the conception and belief of the thing signified.

Of all the acquired perceptions which we have by sight, the most remarkable is the perception of the distance of objects from the eye; we shall, therefore, particularly consider the signs by which this perception is exhibited, and only make some general remarks with regard to the signs which are used in other acquired perceptions.

Section XXII.

OF THE SIGNS BY WHICH WE LEARN TO PERCEIVE DISTANCE FROM THE EYE.

It was before observed in general, that the original perceptions of sight are signs which serve to introduce those that are acquired; but this is not to be understood as if no other signs were employed for that purpose. There are several motions of the eyes, which, in order to distinct vision, must be varied, according as the object is more or less distant; and such motions being by habit connected with the corresponding distances of the object, become signs of those distances. These motions were at first voluntary and unconfined; but, as the intention of nature was to produce perfect and distinct vision by their means, we soon learn by experience to regulate them according to that intention only, without the least reflection.

A ship requires a different trim for every variation of the direction and strength of the wind; and, if we may be allowed to borrow that word, the eyes require a different trim for every degree of light, and for every variation of the distance of the object, while it is within certain limits. The eyes are trimmed for a particular object, by contracting certain muscles and relaxing others; as the ship is trimmed for a particular wind by drawing certain ropes and slackening others. The sailor learns the trim of his ship, as we learn the trim of our eyes, by experience. A ship, although the noblest machine that human art can boast, is far inferior to the eye in this respect, that it requires art and ingenuity to navigate her; and a sailor must know what ropes he must pull, and what he must slacken, to fit her to a particular wind; but with such superior wisdom is the fabric of the eye, and the principles of its motion contrived, that it requires no art nor ingenuity to see by it. Even that part of vision which is got by experience, is attained by idiots. We need not know what muscles we are to contract, and what we are to relax, in order to fit the eye to a particular distance of the object.

But, although we are not conscious of the motions we perform, in order to fit the eyes to the distance of the object, we are conscious of the effort employed in producing these motions; and probably have some sensation which accompanies them, to which we give as little attention as to other sensations. And thus, an effort consciously exerted, or a sensation consequent upon that effort, comes to be conjoined with the distance of the object which gave occasion to it, and by this conjunction becomes a sign of that distance. Some instances of this will appear in considering the means or signs by which we learn to see the distance of objects from the eye. In the enumeration of these, we agree with Dr. Porterfield, notwithstanding that distance from the eye, in his opinion, is perceived originally, but, in our opinion, by experience only.

In general, when a near object affects the eye in one manner, and the same object, placed at a greater distance, affects it in a different manner, these various affections of the eye become signs of the corresponding distances. The means of perceiving distance by the eye will therefore be explained by shewing in what various ways objects affect the eye differently, according to their proximity or distance.

1. It is well known, that, to see objects distinctly at various distances, the form of the eye must undergo some change: and nature hath given us the power of adapting it to near objects, by the contraction of certain muscles, and to distant objects by the contraction of other muscles. As to the manner in which this is done, and the muscular parts employed, anatomists do not altogether agree. The ingenious Dr. Jurin, in his excellent essay on distinct and indistinct vision, seems to have given the most probable account of this matter; and to him I refer the reader.

But, whatever be the manner in which this change of the form of the eye is effected, it is certain that young people have commonly the power of adapting their eyes to all distances of the object, from six or seven inches, to fifteen or sixteen feet; so as to have perfect and distinct vision at any distance within these limits. From this it follows, that the effort we consciously employ to adapt the eye to any particular distance of objects within these limits, will be connected and associated with that distance, and will become a sign of it. When the object is removed beyond the farthest limit of distinct vision, it will be seen indistinctly; but, more or less so, according as its distance is greater or less; so that the degrees of indistinctness of the object may become the signs of distances considerably beyond the farthest limit of distinct vision.

If we had no other mean but this, of perceiving distance of visible objects, the most distant would not appear to be above twenty or thirty feet from the eye, and the tops of houses and trees would seem to touch the clouds; for, in that case, the signs of all greater distances being the same, they have the same signification, and give the same perception of distance.

But it is of more importance to observe, that, because the nearest limit of distinct vision in the time of youth, when we learn to perceive distance by the eye, is about six or seven inches, no object seen distinctly ever appears to be nearer than six or seven inches from the eye. We can, by art, make a small object appear distinct, when it is in reality not above half an inch from the eye; either by using a single microscope, or by looking through a small pin-hole in a card. When, by either of these means, an object is made to appear distinct, however small its distance is in reality, it seems to be removed at least to the distance of six or seven inches—that is, within the limits of distinct vision.

This observation is the more important, because it affords the only reason we can give why an object is magnified either by a single microscope, or by being seen through a pin-hole; and the only mean by which we can ascertain the degree in which the object will be magnified by either. Thus, if the object is really half an inch distant from the eye, and appears to be seven inches distant, its diameter will seem to be enlarged in the same proportion as its distance—that is, fourteen times.

2. In order to direct both eyes to an object, the optic axes must have a greater or less inclination, according as the object is nearer or more distant. And, although we are not conscious of this inclination, yet we are conscious of the effort employed in it. By this mean we perceive small distances more accurately than we could do by the conformation of the eye only. And, therefore, we find, that those who have lost the sight of one eye are apt, even within arms-length, to make mistakes in the distance of objects, which are easily avoided by those who see with both eyes. Such mistakes are often discovered in snuffing a candle, in threading a needle, or in filling a tea-cup.

When a picture is seen with both eyes, and at no great distance, the representation appears not so natural as when it is seen only with one. The intention of painting being to deceive the eye, and to make things appear at different distances which in reality are upon the same piece of canvass, this deception is not so easily put upon both eyes as upon one; because we perceive the distance of visible objects more exactly and determinately with two eyes than with one. If the shading and relief be executed in the best manner, the picture may have almost the same appearance to one eye as the objects themselves would have; but it cannot have the same appearance to both. This is not the fault of the artist, but an unavoidable imperfection in the art. And it is owing to what we just now observed, that the perception we have of the distance of objects by one eye is more uncertain, and more liable to deception, than that which we have by both.

The great impediment, and I think the only invincible impediment, to that agreeable deception of the eye which the painter aims at, is the perception which we have of the distance of visible objects from the eye, partly by means of the conformation of the eye, but chiefly by means of the inclination of the optic axes. If this perception could be removed, I see no reason why a picture might not be made so perfect as to deceive the eye in reality, and to be mistaken for the original object. Therefore, in order to judge of the merit of a picture, we ought, as much as possible, to exclude these two means of perceiving the distance of the several parts of it.

In order to remove this perception of distance, the connoisseurs in painting use a method which is very proper. They look at the picture with one eye, through a tube which excludes the view of all other objects. By this method, the principal mean whereby we perceive the distance of the object—to wit, the inclination of the optic axes—is entirely excluded. I would humbly propose, as an improvement of this method of viewing pictures, that the aperture of the tube next to the eye should be very small. If it is as small as a pin-hole, so much the better, providing there be light enough to see the picture clearly. The reason of this proposal is, that, when we look at an object through a small aperture, it will be seen distinctly, whether the conformation of the eye be adapted to its distance or not; and we have no mean left to judge of the distance, but the light and colouring, which are in the painter's power. If, therefore, the artist performs his part properly, the picture will by this method affect the eye in the same manner that the object represented would do; which is the perfection of this art.

Although this second mean of perceiving the distance of visible objects be more determinate and exact than the first, yet it hath its limits, beyond which it can be of no use. For when the optic axes directed to an object are so nearly parallel that, in directing them to an object yet more distant, we are not conscious of any new effort, nor have any different sensation, there our perception of distance stops; and, as all more distant objects affect the eye in the same manner, we perceive them to be at the same distance. This is the reason why the sun, moon, planets, and fixed stars, when seen not near the horizon, appear to be all at the same distance, as if they touched the concave surface of a great sphere. The surface of this celestial sphere is at that distance beyond which all objects affect the eye in the same manner. Why this celestial vault appears more distant towards the horizon, than towards the zenith, will afterwards appear.

3. The colours of objects, according as they are more distant, become more faint and languid, and are tinged more with the azure of the intervening atmosphere: to this we may add, that their minute parts become more indistinct, and their outline less accurately defined. It is by these means chiefly, that painters can represent objects at very different distances, upon the same canvass. And the diminution of the magnitude of an object would not have the effect of making it appear to be at a great distance, without this degradation of colour, and indistinctness of the outline, and of the minute parts. If a painter should make a human figure ten times less than other human figures that are in the same piece, having the colours as bright, and the outline and minute parts as accurately defined, it would not have the appearance of a man at a great distance, but of a pigmy or Liliputian.

When an object hath a known variety of colours, its distance is more clearly indicated by the gradual dilution of the colours into one another, than when it is of one uniform colour. In the steeple which stands before me at a small distance, the joinings of the stones are clearly perceptible; the grey colour of the stone, and the white cement are distinctly limited: when I see it at a greater distance, the joinings of the stones are less distinct, and the colours of the stone and of the cement begin to dilute into one another: at a distance still greater, the joinings disappear altogether, and the variety of colour vanishes.

In an apple-tree which stands at the distance of about twelve feet, covered with flowers, I can perceive the figure and the color of the leaves and petals; pieces of branches, some larger, others smaller, peeping through the intervals of the leaves—some of them enlightened by the sun's rays, others shaded; and some openings of the sky are perceived through the whole. When I gradually remove from this tree, the appearance, even as to colour, changes every minute. First, the smaller parts, then the larger, are gradually confounded and mixed. The colours of leaves, petals, branches, and sky, are gradually diluted into each other, and the colour of the whole becomes more and more uniform. This change of appearance, corresponding to the several distances, marks the distance more exactly than if the whole object had been of one colour.

Dr. Smith, in his "Optics," gives us a very curious observation made by Bishop Berkeley, in his travels through Italy and Sicily. He observed, That, in those countries, cities and palaces seen at a great distance appeared nearer to him by several miles than they really were: and he very judiciously imputed it to this cause. That the purity of the Italian and Sicilian air, gave to very distant objects that degree of brightness and distinctness which, in the grosser air of his own country, was to be seen only in those that are near. The purity of the Italian air hath been assigned as the reason why the Italian painters commonly give a more lively colour to the sky than the Flemish. Ought they not, for the same reason, to give less degradation of the colours, and less indistinctness of the minute parts, in the representation of very distant objects?

It is very certain that, as in air uncommonly pure, we are apt to think visible objects nearer and less than they really are, so, in air uncommonly foggy, we are apt to think them more distant and larger than the truth. Walking by the sea-side in a thick fog, I see an object which seems to me to be a man on horseback, and at the distance of about half a mile. My companion, who has better eyes, or is more accustomed to see such objects in such circumstances, assures me that it is a sea-gull, and not a man on horseback. Upon a second view, I immediately assent to his opinion; and now it appears to me to be a sea-gull, and at the distance only of seventy or eighty yards. The mistake made on this occasion, and the correction of it, are both so sudden, that we are at a loss whether to call them by the name of *judgment*, or by that of *simple perception*.

It is not worth while to dispute about names; but it is evident that my belief, both first and last, was produced rather by signs than by arguments, and that the mind proceeded to the conclusion in both cases by habit, and not by ratiocination. And the process of the mind seems to have been this—First, Not knowing, or not minding, the effect of a foggy air on the visible appearance of objects, the object seems to me to have that degradation of colour, and that indistinctness of the outline, which objects have at the distance of half a mile; therefore, from the visible appearance as a sign, I immediately proceed to the belief that the object is half a mile distant. Then, this distance, together with the visible magnitude, signify to me the real magnitude, which, supposing the distance to be half a mile, must be equal to that of a man on horseback; and the figure, considering the indistinctness of the outline, agrees with that of a man on horseback. Thus the deception is brought about. But when I am assured that it is a sea-gull, the real magnitude of a sea-gull, together with the visible magnitude presented to the eye, immediately suggest the distance, which, in this case, cannot be above seventy or eighty yards: the indistinctness of the figure likewise suggests the fogginess of the air as its cause; and now the whole chain of signs, and things signified, seems stronger and better connected than it was before; the half mile vanishes to eighty yards; the man on horse-back dwindles to a sea-gull; I get a new perception, and wonder how I got the former, or what is become of it; for it is now so entirely gone, that I cannot recover it.

It ought to be observed that, in order to produce such deceptions from the clearness or fogginess of the air, it must be uncommonly clear or uncommonly foggy; for we learn, from experience, to make allowance for that variety of constitutions of the air which we have been accustomed to observe, and of which we are aware. Bishop Berkeley therefore committed a mistake, when he attributed the large appearance of the horizontal moon to the faintness of her light, occasioned by its passing through a larger tract of atmosphere:* for we are so much accustomed to see the moon in all degrees of faintness and brightness, from the greatest to the least, that we learn to make allowance for it; and do not imagine her magnitude increased by the faintness of her appearance. Besides, it is certain that the horizontal moon seen through a tube which cuts off the view of the interjacent ground, and of all terrestrial objects, loses all that unusual appearance of magnitude.

4. We frequently perceive the distance of objects, by means of intervening or contiguous objects, whose distance or magnitude is otherwise known. When I perceive certain fields or tracts of ground to lie between me and an object, it is evident that these may become signs of its distance. And although we have no particular information of the dimensions of such fields or tract, yet their similitude to others which we know, suggests their dimensions.

* This explanation was not original to Berkeley.—H.

We are so much accustomed to measure with our eye the ground which we travel, and to compare the judgments of distances formed by sight, with our experience or information, that we learn by degrees, in this way, to form a more accurate judgment of the distance of terrestrial objects, than we could do by any of the means before mentioned. An object placed upon the top of a high building, appears much less than when placed upon the ground, at the same distance. When it stands upon the ground, the intervening tract of ground serves as a sign of its distance; and the distance, together with the visible magnitude, serves as a sign of its real magnitude. But when the object is placed on high, this sign of its distance is taken away: the remaining signs lead us to place it at a less distance: and this less distance, together with the visible magnitude, becomes a sign of a less real magnitude.

The two first means we have mentioned, would never of themselves make a visible object appear above a hundred and fifty, or two hundred feet, distant; because, beyond that there is no sensible change, either of the conformation of the eyes, or of the inclination of their axes. The third mean is but a vague and undeterminate sign, when applied to distances above two or three hundred feet, unless we know the real colour and figure of the objeet; and the fifth mean, to be afterwards mentioned, can only be applied to objects which are familiar, or whose real magnitude is known. Hence it follows, that, when unknown objects, upon or near the surface of the earth, are perceived to be at the distance of some miles, it is always by this fourth mean that we are led to that conclusion.

Dr. Smith hath observed, very justly, that the known distance of the terrestrial objects which terminate our view, makes that part of the sky which is towards the horizon appear more distant than that which is towards the zenith. Hence it comes to pass, that the apparent figure of the sky is not that of a hemisphere, but rather a less segment of a sphere. And, hence, likewise, it comes to pass, that the diameter of the sun or moon, or the distance between two fixed stars, seen contiguous to a hill, or to any distant terrestrial object, appears much greater than when no such object strikes the eye at the same time.

These observations have heen sufficiently explained and confirmed by Dr. Smith. I beg leave to add, that, when the visible horizon is terminated by very distant objects, the celestial vault seems to be enlarged in all its dimensions. When I view it from a confined street or lane, it bears some proportion to the buildings that surround me; but, when I view it from a large plain, terminated on all hands by hills which rise one above another to the distance of twenty miles from the eye, methinks I see a new heaven, whose magnificence declares the greatness of its Author, and puts every human edifice out of countenance; for now the lofty spires and the gorgeous palaces shrink into nothing before it, and bear no more proportion to the celestial dome than their makers bear to its Maker.

5. There remains another mean by which we perceive the distance of visible objects—and that is the diminution of their visible or apparent magnitude. By experience, I know what figure a man, or any other known object, makes to my eye at the distance of ten feet—I perceive the gradual and proportional diminution of this visible figure, at the distance of twenty, forty, a hundred feet, and at greater distances, until it vanish altogether. Hence a certain visible magnitude of a known object becomes the sign of a certain determinate distance, and carries along with it the conception and belief of that distance.

In this process of the mind, the sign is not a sensation; it is an original perception. We perceive the visible figure and visible magnitude of the object, by the original powers of vision ; but the visible figure is used only as a sign of the real figure, and the visible magnitude is used only as a sign either of the distance, or of the real magnitude, of the object : and, therefore, these original perceptions, like other mere signs, pass through the mind without any attention or reflection.

This last mean of perceiving the distance of known objects, serves to explain some very remarkable phænomena in optics, which would otherwise appear very mysterious. When we view objects of known dimensions through optical glasses, there is no other mean left of determining their distance, but this fifth. Hence it follows, that known objects seen through glasses, must seem to be brought nearer, in proportion to the magnifying power of the glass, or to be removed to a greater distance in proportion to the diminishing power of the glass.

If a man who had never before seen objects through a telescope, were told that the telescope, which he is about to use, magnifies the diameter of the object ten times ; when he looks through this telescope at a man six feet high, what would he expect to see ? Surely he would very naturally expect to see a giant sixty feet high. But he sees no such thing. The man appears no more than six feet high, and consequently no bigger than he really is ; but he appears ten times nearer than he is. The telescope indeed magnifies the image of this man upon the *retina* ten times in diameter, and must, therefore, magnify his visible figure in the same proportion; and, as we have been accustomed to see him of this visible magnitude when he was ten times nearer than he is presently, and in no other case, this visible magnitude, therefore, suggests the conception and belief of that distance of the object with which it hath been always connected. We have been accustomed to conceive this amplification of the visible figure of a known object, only as the effect or sign of its being brought nearer : and we have annexed a certain determinate distance to every degree of visible magnitude of the object; and, therefore, any particular degree of visible magnitude, whether seen by the naked eye or by glasses, brings along with it the conception and belief of the distance which corresponds to it. This is the reason why a telescope seems not to magnify known objects, but to bring them nearer to the eye.

When we look through a pin-hole, or a single microscope, at an object which is half an inch from the eye, the picture of the object upon the *retina* is not enlarged, but only rendered distinct; neither is the visible figure enlarged: yet the object appears to the eye twelve or fourteen times more distant, and as many times larger in diameter, than it really is. Such a telescope as we have mentioned amplifies the image on the *retina*, and the visible figure of the object, ten times in diameter, and yet makes it seem no bigger, but only ten times nearer. These appearances had been long observed by the writers on topics; they tortured their invention to find the causes of them from optical principles; but in vain: they must be resolved into habits of perception, which are acquired by custom, but are apt to be mistaken for original perceptions. The Bishop of Cloyne first furnished the world with the proper key for opening up these mysterious appearances; but he made considerable mistakes in the application of it. Dr. Smith, in his elaborate and judicious treatise of "Optics," hath applied it to the apparent distance of objects seen with glasses, and to the apparent figure of the heavens, with such happy success, that there can be no more doubt about the causes of these phenomena.

Section XXIII.

OF THE SIGNS USED IN OTHER ACQUIRED PERCEPTIONS.

The distance of objects from the eye is the most important lesson in vision. Many others are easily learned in consequence of it. The distance of the object, joined with its visible magnitude, is a sign of its real magnitude: and the distance of the several parts of an object, joined with its visible figure, becomes a sign of its real figure. Thus, when I look at a globe which stands before me, by the original powers of sight I perceive only something of a circular form, variously coloured. The visible figure hath no distance from the eye, no convexity, nor hath it three dimensions; even its length and breadth are incapable of being measured by inches, feet, or other linear measures. But, when I have learned to perceive the distance of every part of this object from the eye, this perception gives it convexity, and a spherical figure; and adds a third dimension to that which had but two before. The distance of the whole object makes me likewise perceive the real magnitude; for, being accustomed to observe how an inch or a foot of length affects the eye at that distance, I plainly perceive by my eye the linear dimensions of the globe, and can affirm with certainty that its diameter is about one foot and three inches.

It was shewn in the 7th section of this chapter that the visible figure of a body may, by mathematical reasoning, be inferred from its real figure, distance, and position, with regard to the eye: in like manner, we may, by mathematical reasoning, from the visible figure, together with the distance of the several parts of it from the eye, infer the real figure and position. But this last inference is not commonly made by mathematical reasoning, nor, indeed, by reasoning of any kind, but by custom.

The original appearance which the colour of an object makes to the eye, is a sensation for which we have no name, because it is used merely as a sign, and is never made an object of attention in common life: but this appearance, according to the different circumstances, signifies various things. If a piece of cloth, of one uniform colour, is laid so that part of it is in the sun, and part in the shade, the appearance of colour, in these different parts, is very different: yet we perceive the colour to be the same; we interpret the variety of appearance as a sign of light and shade, and not as a sign of real difference in colour. But, if the eye could be so far deceived as not to perceive the difference of light in the two parts of the cloth, we should, in that case, interpret the variety of appearance to signify a variety of colour in the parts of the cloth.

Again, if we suppose a piece of cloth placed as before, but having the shaded part so much brighter in the colour that it gives the same appearance to the eye as the more enlightened part, the sameness of appearance will here be interpreted to signify a variety of colour, because we shall make allowance for the effect of light and shade.

When the real colour of an object is known, the appearance of it indicates, in some circumstances, the degree of light or shade; in others, the colour of the circumambient bodies, whose rays are reflected by it; and, in other circumstances, it indicates the distance or proximity of the object—as was observed in the last section; and by means of these, many other things are suggested to the mind. Thus, an unusual appearance in the colour of familiar objects may be the diagnostic of a disease in the spectator. The appearance of things in my room may indicate sunshine or cloudy weather, the earth covered with snow or blackened with rain. It hath been observed, that the colour of the sky, in a piece of painting, may indicate the country of the painter, because the Italian sky is really of a different colour from the Flemish.

It was already observed, that the original and acquired perceptions which we have by our senses, are the language of nature to man, which, in many respects, hath a great affinity to human languages. The instances which we have given of acquired perceptions, suggest this affinity—that, as, in human languages, ambiguities are often found, so this language of nature in our acquired perceptions is not exempted from them. We have seen, in vision particularly, that the same appearance to the eye, may, in different circumstances, indicate different things. Therefore, when the circumstances are unknown upon which the interpretation of the signs depends, their meaning must be ambiguous; and when the circumstances are mistaken, the meaning of the signs must also be mistaken.

This is the case in all the phænomena which we call *fallacies of the senses;* and particularly in those which are called *fallacies in vision.* The appearance of things to the eye always corresponds to the fixed laws of Nature; therefore, if we speak properly, there is no fallacy in the senses. Nature always speaketh the same language, and useth the same signs in the same circumstances; but we sometimes mistake the meaning of the signs, either through ignorance of the laws of Nature, or through ignorance of the circumstances which attend the signs.

To a man unacquainted with the principles of optics, almost every experiment that is made with the prism, with the magic lanthorn, with the telescope, with the microscope, seems to produce some fallacy in vision. Even the appearance of a common mirror, to one altogether unacquainted with the effects of it, would seem most remarkably fallacious. For how can a man be more imposed upon, than in seeing that before him which is really behind him? How can he be more imposed upon, than in being made to see himself several yards removed from himself? Yet children, even before they can speak their mother tongue, learn not to be deceived by these appearances. These, as well as all the other surprising appearances produced by optical glasses, are a part of the visual language, and, to those who understand the laws of Nature concerning light and colours, are in nowise fallacious, but have a distinct and true meaning.

Section XXIV.

OF THE ANALOGY BETWEEN PERCEPTION AND THE CREDIT WE GIVE TO HUMAN TESTIMONY.

The objects of human knowledge are innumerable; but the channels by which it is conveyed to the mind are few. Among these, the perception of external things by our senses, and the informations which we receive upon human testimony, are not the least considerable; and so remarkable is the analogy between these two, and the analogy between the principles of the mind which are subservient to the one and those which are subservient to the other, that, without further apology, we shall consider them together.

In the testimony of Nature given by the senses, as well as in human testimony given by language, things are signified to us by signs: and in one as well as the other, the mind, either by original principles or by custom, passes from the sign to the conception and belief of the things signified.

We have distinguished our perceptions into original and acquired; and language, into natural and artificial. Between acquired perception and artificial language, there is a great analogy; but still a greater between original perception and natural language.

The signs in original perception are sensations, of which Nature hath given us a great variety, suited to the variety of the things signified by them. Nature hath established a real connection between the signs and the things signified; and Nature hath also taught us the interpretation of the signs—so that, previous to experience, the sign suggests the thing signified, and creates the belief of it.

The signs in natural language are features of the face, gestures of the body, and modulations of the voice; the variety of which is suited to the variety of the things signified by them. Nature hath established a real connection between these signs, and the thoughts and dispositions of the mind which are signified by them; and Nature hath taught us the interpretation of these signs; so that, previous to experience, the signs suggest the thing signified, and create the belief of it.

A man in company, without doing good or evil, without uttering an articulate sound, may behave himself gracefully, civilly, politely; or, on the contrary, meanly, rudely, and impertinently. We see the dispositions of his mind by their natural signs in his countenance and behavior, in the same manner as we perceive the figure and other qualities of bodies by the sensations which nature hath connected with them.

The signs in the natural language of the human countenance and behaviour, as well as the signs in our original perceptions, have the same signification in all climates and in all nations; and the skill of interpreting them is not acquired, but innate.

In acquired perception, the signs are either sensations, or things which we perceive by means of sensations. The connection between the sign and the thing signified, is established by nature; and we discover this connection by experience; but not without the aid of our original perceptions, or of those which we have already acquired. After this connection is discovered, the sign, in like manner as in original perception, always suggests the thing signified, and creates the belief of it.

In artificial language, the signs are articulate sounds, whose connection with the things signified by them, is established by the will of men; and, in learning our mother tongue, we discover this connection by experience; but not without the aid of natural language, or of what we had before attained of artificial language. And, after this connection is discovered, the sign, as in natural language, always suggests the thing signified, and creates the belief of it.

Our original perceptions are few, compared with the acquired; but, without the former, we could not possibly attain the latter. In like manner, natural language is scanty, compared with artificial; but, without the former we could not possibly attain the latter.

Our original perceptions, as well as the natural language of human features and gestures, must be resolved into particular principles of the human constitution. Thus, it is by one particular principle of our constitution that certain features express anger; and, by another particular principle, that certain features express benevolence. It is, in like manner, by one particular principle of our constitution that a certain sensation signifies hardness in the body which I handle; and it is by another particular principle that a certain sensation signifies motion in that body.

But our acquired perceptions, and the information we receive by means of artificial language, must be resolved into general principles of the human constitution. When a painter perceives that this picture is the work of Raphael, that the work of Titian; a jeweller, that this is a true diamond, that a counterfeit; a sailor, that this is a ship of five hundred ton, that of four hundred; these different acquired perceptions are produced by the same general principles of the human mind, which have a different operation in the same person, according as they are variously applied, and in different persons according to the diversity of their education and manner of life. In like manner, when certain articulate sounds convey to my mind the knowledge of the battle of Pharsalia, and others, the knowledge of the battle of Poltowa—when a Frenchman and an Englishman receive the same information by different articulate sounds—the signs used in these different cases, produce the knowledge and belief of the things signified, by means of the same general principles of the human constitution.

Now, if we compare the general principles of our constitution, which fit us for receiving information from our fellow-creatures by language, with the general principles which fit us for acquiring the perception of things by our senses, we shall find them to be very similar in their nature and manner of operation.

When we begin to learn our mother tongue, we perceive, by the help of natural language, that they who speak to us use certain sounds to express certain things, we imitate the same sounds when we would express the same things; and find that we are understood.

But here a difficulty occurs which merits our attention, because the solution of it leads to some original principles of the human mind, which are of great importance, and of very extensive influence. We know by experience that men *have* used such words to express such things; but all experience is of the *past*, and can, of itself, give no notion or belief of what is *future*. How come we, then, to believe, and to rely upon it with assurance, that men, who have it in their power to do otherwise, will continue to use the same words when they think the same things? Whence comes this knowledge and belief—this foresight, we ought rather to call it—of the future and voluntary actions of our fellow-creatures? Have they promised that they will never impose upon us by equivocation or falsehood? No, they have not. And, if they had, this would not solve the difficulty; for such promise must be expressed by words or by other signs; and, before we can rely upon it, we must be assured that they put the usual meaning upon the signs which express that promise. No man of common sense ever thought of taking a man's own word for his honesty; and it is evident that we take his veracity for granted when we lay any stress upon his word or promise. I might add, that this reliance upon the declarations and testimony of men is found in children long before they know what a promise is.

There is, therefore, in the human mind an early anticipation, neither derived from experience, nor from reason, nor from any compact or promise, that our fellow-creatures will use the same signs in language, when they have the same sentiments.

This is, in reality, a kind of prescience of human actions; and it seems to me to be an original principle of the human constitution, without which we should be incapable of language, and consequently incapable of instruction.

The wise and beneficent Author of Nature, who intended that we should be social creatures, and that we should receive the greatest and most important part of our knowledge by the information of others, hath, for these purposes, implanted in our natures two principles that tally with each other.

The first of these principles is, a propensity to speak truth, and to use the signs of language so as to convey our real sentiments. This principle has a powerful operation, even in the greatest liars; for, where they lie once, they speak truth a hundred times. Truth is always uppermost, and is the natural issue of the mind. It requires no art or training, no inducement or temptation, but only that we yield to a natural impulse. Lying, on the contrary, is doing violence to our nature; and is never practised, even by the worst men, without some temptation. Speaking truth is like using our natural food, which we would do from appetite, although it answered no end; but lying is like taking physic, which is nauseous to the taste, and which no man takes but for some end which he cannot otherwise attain.

If it should be objected, That men may be influenced by moral or political considerations to speak truth, and, therefore, that their doing so is no proof of such an original principle as we have mentiond—I answer, First,

That moral or political considerations can have no influence until we arrive at years of understanding and reflection; and it is certain, from experience, that children keep to truth invariably, before they are capable of being influenced by such considerations. Secondly, When we are influenced by moral or political considerations, we must be conscious of that influence, and capable of perceiving it upon reflection. Now, when I reflect upon my actions most attentively, I am not conscious that, in speaking truth, I am influenced on ordinary occasions by any motive, moral or political. I find that truth is always at the door of my lips, and goes forth spontaneously, if not held back. It requires neither good nor bad intention to bring it forth, but only that I be artless and undesigning. There may indeed be temptations to falsehood, which would be too strong for the natural principle of veracity, unaided by principles of honor or virtue; but where there is no such temptation, we speak truth by instinct—and this instinct is the principle I have been explaining.

By this instinct, a real connection is formed between our words and our thoughts, and thereby the former became fit to be signs of the latter, which they could not otherwise be. And although this connection is broken in every instance of lying and equivocation, yet these instances being comparatively few, the authority of human testimony is only weakened by them, but not destroyed.

Another original principle implanted in us by the Supreme Being, is a disposition to confide in the veracity of others, and to believe what they tell us. This is the counterpart to the former; and, as that may be called *the principle of veracity*, we shall, for want of a more proper name, call this *the principle of credulity*. It is unlimited in children, until they meet with instances of deceit and falsehood; and it retains a very considerable degree of strength through life.

If Nature had left the mind of the speaker *in æquilibrio*,

without any inclination to the side of truth more than to that of falsehood, children would lie as often as they speak truth, until reason was so far ripened as to suggest the imprudence of lying, or conscience, as to suggest its immorality. And if Nature had left the mind of the hearer *in æquilibrio,* without any inclination to the side of belief more than to that of disbelief, we should take no man's word until we had positive evidence that he spoke truth. His testimony would, in this case, have no more authority than his dreams; which may be true or false, but no man is disposed to believe them, on this account, that they were dreamed. It is evident that, in the matter of testimony, the balance of human judgment is by nature inclined to the side of belief; and turns to that side of itself, when there is nothing put into the opposite scale. If it was not so, no proposition that is uttered in discourse would be believed, until it was examined and tried by reason; and most men would be unable to find reasons for believing the thousandth part of what is told them. Such distrust and incredulity would deprive us of the greatest benefits of society, and place us in a worse condition than that of savages.

Children, on this supposition, would be absolutely incredulous, and, therefore, absolutely incapable of instruction: those who had little knowledge of human life, and of the manners and characters of men, would be in the next degree incredulous: and the most credulous men would be those of greatest experience, and of the deepest penetration; because, in many cases, they would be able to find good reasons for believing testimony, which the weak and the ignorant could not discover.

In a word, if credulity were the effect of reasoning and experience, it must grow up and gather strength, in the same proportion as reason and experience do. But, if it is the gift of Nature, it will be strongest in childhood, and limited and restrained by experience; and the most superficial view of human life shews, that the last is really the case, and not the first.*

It is the intention of Nature, that we should be carried in arms before we are able to walk upon our legs; and it is likewise the intention of Nature, that our belief should be guided by the authority and reason of others, before it can be guided by our own reason. The weakness of the infant, and the natural affection of the mother, plainly indicate the former; and the natural credulity of youth, and authority of age, as plainly indicate the latter. The infant, by proper nursing and care, acquires strength to walk without support. Reason hath likewise her infancy, when she must be carried in arms: then she leans entirely upon authority, by natural instinct, as if she was conscious of her own weakness; and, without this support, she becomes vertiginous. When brought to maturity by proper culture, she begins to feel her own strength, and leans less upon the reason of others: she learns to suspect testimony in some cases, and to disbelieve it in others; and sets bounds to that authority to which she was at first entirely subject. But still, to the end of life, she finds a necessity of borrowing light from testimony, where she has none within herself, and of leaning, in some degree, upon the reason of others, where she is conscious of her own imbecility.

And as, in many instances, Reason, even in her maturity, borrows aid from testimony, so in others she mutually gives aid to it, and strengthens its authority. For, as we find good reason to reject testimony in some cases, so in others we find good reason to reply upon it with perfect security, in our most important concerns. The character, the number, and the disinterestedness of witnesses, the impossibility of collusion, and the incredibility of their concurring in their testimony without col-

* See, *contra*, Priestley's "Examination," p. 86. "Brown's Lect," lect. lxxxiv.

lusion, may give an irresistible strength to testimony, compared to which its native and intrinsic authority is very inconsiderable.

Having now considered the general principles of the human mind which fit us for receiving information from our fellow-creatures, by the means of language, let us next consider the general principles which fit us for receiving the information of Nature by our acquired perceptions.

It is undeniable, and indeed is acknowledged by all, that when we have found two things to have been constantly conjoined in the course of nature, the appearance of one of them is immediately followed by the conception and belief of the other. The former becomes a natural sign of the latter; and the knowledge of their constant conjunction in time past, whether got by experience or otherwise, is sufficient to make us rely with assurance upon the continuance of that conjunction.

This process of the human mind is so familiar that we never think of inquiring into the principles upon which it is founded. We are apt to conceive it as a self-evident truth, that what is to come must be similar to what is past. Thus, if a certain degree of cold freezes water to-day, and has been known to do so in all time past, we have no doubt but the same degree of cold will freeze water to-morrow, or a year hence. That this is a truth which all men believe as soon as they understand it, I readily admit; but the question is, Whence does its evidence arise? Not from comparing the ideas, surely. For, when I compare the idea of cold with that of water hardened into a transparent solid body, I can perceive no connection between them: no man can shew the one to be the necessary effect of the other; no man can give a shadow of reason why Nature hath conjoined them. But do we not learn their conjunction from experience? True; experience informs us that they have been conjoined in time *past;* but no man ever had any experience of what is *future:* and this is the very question to be resolved, How we come to believe that the *future* will be like the *past?* Hath the Author of nature promised this? Or were we admitted to his council, when he established the present laws of nature, and determined the time of their continuance. No, surely. Indeed, if we believe that there is a wise and good Author of nature, we may see a good reason why he should continue the same laws of nature, and the same connections of things, for a long time: because, if he did otherwise, we could learn nothing from what is past, and all our experience would be of no use to us. But, though this consideration, when we come to the use of reason, may confirm our belief of the continuance of the present course of nature, it is certain that it did not give rise to this belief; for children and idiots have this belief as soon as they know that fire will burn them. It must, therefore, be the effect of instinct, not of reason.*

The wise Author of our nature intended, that a great and necessary part of our knowledge should be derived from experience, before we are capable of reasoning, and he hath provided means perfectly adequate to this intention. For, First, He governs nature by fixed laws, so that we find innumerable connections of things which continue from age to age. Without this stability of the course of nature, there could be no experience; or, it would be a false guide, and lead us into error and mischief. If there were not a principle of veracity in the human mind, men's words would not be signs of their thoughts: and if there were no regularity in the course of nature, no one thing could be a natural sign of another. Secondly, He hath implanted in human minds

*Compare Stewart's "Elements," vol. I., chap. iv. § 5, p. 205, sixth edition; "Philosophical Essays," p. 74, sqq., fourth edition; Royer Collard, in Jouffroy's "Oeuvres de Reid," t. IV. p. 279, sqq.; with Priestley's "Examination," p. 86. sqq. I merely refer to works relative to *Reid's* doctrine.—H.

an original principle by which we believe and expect the continuance of the course of nature, and the continuance of those connections which we have observed in time past. It is by this general principle of our nature, that, when two things have been found connected in time past, the appearance of the one produces the belief of the other.

I think the ingenious author of the "Treatise of Human Nature" first observed, That our belief of the continuance of the laws of nature cannot be founded either upon knowledge or probability: but, far from conceiving it to be an original principle of the mind, he endeavours to account for it from his favourite hypothesis, That belief is nothing but a certain degree of vivacity in the idea of the thing believed. I made a remark upon this curious hypothesis in the second chapter, and shall now make another.

The belief which we have in perception, is a belief of the present existence of the object; that which we have in memory, is a belief of its past existence; the belief of which we are now speaking is a belief of its future existence; and in imagination there is no belief at all. Now, I would gladly know of this author, how one degree of vivacity fixes the existence of the object to the present moment; another carries it back to time past; a third, taking a contrary direction, carries it into futurity; and a fourth carries it out of existence altogether. Suppose, for instance, that I see the sun rising out of the sea; I remember to have seen him rise yesterday; I believe he will rise to-morrow near the same place; I can likewise imagine him rising in that place, without any belief at all. Now, according to this sceptical hypothesis, this perception, this memory, this foreknowledge, and this imagination, are all the same idea, diversified only by different degrees of vivacity. The perception of the sun rising is the most lively idea; the memory of his rising yesterday is the same idea a little more faint; the belief of his rising to-morrow is the same idea yet fainter; and the imagination of his rising is still the same idea, but faintest of all. One is apt to think, that this idea might gradually pass through all possible degrees of vivacity without stirring out of its place. But, if we think so, we deceive ourselves: for no sooner does it begin to grow languid than it moves backward into time past. Supposing this to be granted, we expect, at least, that, as it moves backward by the decay of its vivacity, the more that vivacity decays it will go back the farther, until it remove quite out of sight. But here we are deceived again; for there is a certain period of this declining vivacity when, as if it had met an elastic obstacle in its motion backward, it suddenly rebounds from the past to the future, without taking the present in its way. And now, having got into the regions of futurity, we are apt to think that it has room enough to spend all its remaining vigour: but still we are deceived: for, by another sprightly bound, it mounts up into the airy region of imagination. So that ideas, in the gradual declension of their vivacity, seem to imitate the inflection of verbs in grammar. They begin with the present, and proceed in order to the preterite, the future, and the indefinite. This article of the *sceptical creed* is indeed so full of mystery, on whatever side we view it, that they who hold that creed are very injuriously charged with incredulity; for, to me, it appears to require as much faith as that of St. Athanasius.

However, we agree with the author of the "Treatise of Human Nature," in this, That our belief of the continuance of nature's laws is not derived from reason. It is an instinctive prescience of the operations of nature very like to that prescience of human actions which makes us rely upon the testimony of our fellow-creatures; and as, without the latter, we should be incapable of receiving information from men by language, so, without the former, we should be incapable of receiving the information of nature by means of experience.

All our knowledge of nature beyond our original perceptions, is got by experience, and consists in the interpretation of natural signs. The constancy of nature's laws connects the sign with the thing signified; and, by the natural principle just now explained, we rely upon the continuance of the connections which experience hath discovered; and thus the appearance of the sign is followed by the belief of the thing signified.

Upon this principle of our constitution, not only acquired perception, but all inductive reasoning, and all our reasoning from analogy, is grounded; and, therefore, for want of another name, we shall beg leave to call it *the inductive principle.* It is from the force of this principle that we immediately assent to that axiom upon which all our knowledge of nature is built, That effects of the same kind must have the same cause; for *effects* and *causes*, in the operations of nature, mean nothing but signs and the things signified by them. We perceive no proper causality or efficiency in any natural cause; but only a connection established by the course of nature between it and what is called its effect. Antecedently to all reasoning, we have, by our constitution, an anticipation that there is a fixed and steady course of nature: and we have an eager desire to discover this course of nature. We attend to every conjunction of things which presents itself, and expect the continuance of that conjunction. And, when such a conjunction has been often observed, we conceive the things to be naturally connected, and the appearance of one, without any reasoning or reflection, carries along with it the belief of the other.

If any reader should imagine that the inductive principle may be resolved into what philosophers usually call the *association of ideas*, let him observe, that, by this principle, natural signs are not associated with the idea only, but with the belief of the things signified. Now, this can with no propriety be called an association of ideas, unless ideas and belief be one and the same thing. A child has found the prick of a pin conjoined with pain; hence he believes, and knows, that these things are naturally connected; he knows that the one will always follow the other. If any man will call this only an association of ideas, I dispute not about words, but I think he speaks very improperly. For, if we express it in plain English, it is a prescience that things which he hath found conjoined in time past, will be conjoined in time to come. And this prescience is not the effect of reasoning, but of an original principle of human nature, which I have called *the inductive principle.*

This principle, like that of credulity, is unlimited in infancy, and gradually restrained and regulated as we grow up. It leads us often into mistakes; but is of infinite advantage upon the whole. By it, the child once burnt shuns the fire; by it, he likewise runs away from the surgeon by whom he was inoculated. It is better that he should do the last, than that he should not do the first.

But the mistakes we are led into by these two natural principles, are of a different kind. Men sometimes lead us into mistakes, when we perfectly understand their language, by speaking lies. But Nature never misleads us in this way: her language is always true; and it is only by misinterpreting it that we fall into error. There must be many accidental conjunctions of things, as well as natural connections; and the former are apt to be mistaken for the latter. Thus, in the instance above mentioned, the child connected the pain of inoculation with the surgeon; whereas it was really connected with the incision only. Philosophers, and men of science are not exempted from such mistakes; indeed, all false reasoning in philosophy is owing to them; it is drawn from experience and analogy, as well as just reasoning, otherwise it could have no verisimilitude; but the one is an unskilful and rash, the other a just and legitimate interpretation of natural signs. If a child, or a man of common understanding, were put to interpret a book of science, written in his mother tongue, how many blunders and mistakes would he be apt to fall into? Yet he knows as much of this language as is necessary for his manner of life.

The language of Nature is the universal study; and the students are of different classes. Brutes, idiots, and children employ themselves in this study, and owe to it all their acquired perceptions. Men of common understanding make a greater progress, and learn, by a small degree of reflection, many things of which children are ignorant.

Philosophers fill up the highest form in this school, and are critics in the language of nature. All these different classes have one teacher—Experience, enlightened by the inductive principle. Take away the light of this inductive principle, and Experience is as blind as a mole: she may, indeed, feel what is present, and what immediately touches her; but she sees nothing that is either before or behind, upon the right hand or upon the left, future or past.

The rules of inductive reasoning, or of a just interpretation of Nature, as well as the fallacies by which we are apt to misinterpret her language, have been, with wonderful sagacity, delineated by the great genius of Lord Bacon: so that his "*Novum Organum*" may justly be called "A Grammar of the Language of Nature." It adds greatly to the merit of this work, and atones for its defects, that, at the time it was written, the world had not seen any tolerable model of inductive reasoning, from which the rules of it might be copied. The arts of poetry and eloquence were grown up to perfection when

Aristotle described them; but the art of interpreting Nature was yet *in embryo* when Bacon delineated its manly features and proportions. Aristotle drew his rules from the best models of those arts that have yet appeared; but the best models of inductive reasoning that have yet appeared, which I take to be the third book of the "Principia," and the "Optics," of Newton, were drawn from Bacon's rules. The purpose of all those rules, is to teach us to distinguish seeming, or apparent connections of things, in the course of nature, from such as are real.

They that are unskilful in inductive reasoning, are more apt to fall into error in their *reasonings* from the phænomena of nature than in their *acquired perceptions;* because we often reason from a few instances, and thereby are apt to mistake accidental conjunctions of things for natural connections: but that habit of passing, without reasoning, from the sign to the thing signified, which constitutes acquired perception, must be learned by many instances or experiments; and the number of experiments serves to disjoin those things which have been accidentally conjoined, as well as to confirm our belief of natural connections.

From the time that children begin to use their hands, Nature directs them to handle everything over and over, to look at it while they handle it, and to put it in various positions, and at various distances from the eye. We are apt to excuse this as a childish diversion, because they must be doing something, and have not reason to entertain themselves in a more manly way. But, if we think more justly, we shall find, that they are engaged in the most serious and important study; and, if they had all the reason of a philosopher, they could not be more properly employed. For it is this childish employment that enables them to make the proper use of their eyes. They are thereby every day acquiring habits of perception, which are of greater importance than anything we can teach them. The original perceptions which Nature gave them are few, and insufficient for the purposes of life; and, therefore, she made them capable of acquiring many more perceptions by habit. And, to complete her work, she hath given them an unwearied assiduity in applying to the exercises by which those perceptions are acquired.

This is the education which Nature gives to her children. And, since we have fallen upon this subject, we may add, that another part of Nature's education is, That, by the course of things, children must often exert all their muscular force, and employ all their ingenuity, in order to gratify their curiosity, and satisfy their little appetites. What they desire is only to be obtained at the expense of labour and patience, and many disappointments. By the exercise of body and mind necessary for satisfying their desires, they acquire agility, strength, and dexterity in their motions, as well as health and vigour to their constitutions; they learn patience and perseverance; they learn to bear pain without dejection, and disappointment without despondence. The education of Nature is most perfect in savages, who have no other tutor; and we see that, in the quickness of all their senses, in the agility of their motions, in the hardiness of their constitutions, and in the strength of their minds to bear hunger, thirst, pain, and disappointment, they commonly far exceed the civilized. A most ingenious writer, on this account, seems to prefer the savage life to that of society. But the education of Nature could never of itself produce a Rousseau. It is the intention of Nature that human education should be joined to her institution, in order to form the man. And she hath fitted us for human education, by the natural principles of imitation and credulity, which discover themselves almost in infancy, as well as by others which are of later growth.

When the education which we receive from men, does

not give scope to the education of Nature, it is wrong directed; it tends to hurt our faculties of perception, and to enervate both the body and mind. Nature hath her way of rearing men, as she hath of curing their diseases. The art of medicine is to follow Nature, to imitate and to assist her in the cure of diseases; and the art of education is to follow Nature, to assist and to imitate her in her way of rearing men. The ancient inhabitants of the Baleares followed Nature in the manner of teaching their children to be good archers, when they hung their dinner aloft by a thread, and left the younkers to bring it down by their skill in archery.

The education of Nature, without any more human care than is necessary to preserve life, makes a perfect savage. Human education, joined to that of Nature, may make a good citizen, a skilful artisan, or a well-bred man; but reason and reflection must superadd their tutory, in order to produce a Rousseau, a Bacon, or a Newton.

Notwithstanding the innumerable errors committed in human education, there is hardly any education so bad as to be worse than none. And I apprehend that, if even Rousseau were to choose whether to educate a son among the French, the Italians, the Chinese, or among the Eskimaux, he would not give the preference to the last.

When Reason is properly employed, she will confirm the documents of Nature, which are always true and wholesome; she will distinguish, in the documents of human education, the good from the bad, rejecting the last with modesty, and adhering to the first with reverence.

Most men continue all their days to be just what Nature and human education made them. Their manners, their opinions, their virtues, and their vices, are all got by habit, imitation, and instruction; and reason has little or no share in forming them.

CHAPTER VII.

CONCLUSION.

CONTAINING REFLECTIONS UPON THE OPINIONS OF PHILOSOPHERS ON THIS SUBJECT.

THERE are two ways in which men may form their notions and opinions concerning the mind, and concerning its powers and operations. The first is the only way that leads to truth; but it is narrow and rugged, and few have entered upon it. The second is broad and smooth, and hath been much beaten, not only by the vulgar, but even by philosophers; it is sufficient for common life, and is well adapted to the purposes of the poet and orator: but, in philosophical disquisitions concerning the mind, it leads to error and delusion.

We may call the first of these ways, *the way of reflection.* When the operations of the mind are exerted, we are conscious of them; and it is in our power to attend to them; and to reflect upon them, until they become familiar objects of thought. This is the only way in which we can form just and accurate notions of those operations. But this attention and reflection is so difficult to man, surrounded on all hands by external objects which constantly solicit his attention, that it has been very little practised, even by philosophers. In the course of this inquiry, we have had many occasions to shew how little attention hath been given to the most familiar operations of the senses.

The second, and the most common way, in which men form their opinions concerning the mind and its operations, we may call *the way of analogy.* There is nothing in the course of nature so singular, but we can find some resemblance, or at least some analogy, between it and other things with which we are acquainted. The mind naturally delights in hunting after such analogies, and attends to them with pleasure. From them, poetry and wit derive a great part of their charms; and eloquence, not a little of its persuasive force.

Besides the pleasure we receive from analogies, they are of very considerable use, both to facilitate the conception of things, when they are not easily apprehended without such a handle, and to lead us to probable conjectures about their nature and qualities, when we want the means of more direct and immediate knowledge. When I consider that the planet Jupiter, in like manner as the earth, rolls round his own axis, and revolves round the sun, and that he is enlightened by several secondary planets, as the earth is enlightened by the moon, I am apt to conjecture, from analogy, that, as the earth by these means is fitted to be the habitation of various orders of animals, so the planet Jupiter is, by the like means, fitted for the same purpose; and, having no argument more direct and conclusive to determine me in this point, I yield, to this analogical reasoning, a degree of assent proportioned to its strength. When I observe that the potato plant very much resembles the *solanum* in its flower and fructification, and am informed that the last is poisonous, I am apt from analogy to have some suspicion of the former: but, in this case, I have access to more direct and certain evidence; and, therefore, ought not to trust to analogy, which would lead me into an error.

Arguments from analogy are always at hand, and grow up spontaneously in a fruitful imagination; while arguments that are more direct and more conclusive often require painful attention and application; and therefore mankind in general have been very much disposed to trust to the former. If one attentively examines the systems of the ancient philosophers, either concerning the material world, or concerning the mind, he will find them to be built solely upon the foundation of analogy. Lord Bacon first delineated the strict and severe method of induction; since his time, it has been applied with very happy success in some parts of natural philosophy—and hardly in anything else. But there is no subject in which mankind are so much disposed to trust to the analogical way of thinking and reasoning, as in what concerns the mind and its operations; because, to form clear and distinct notions of those operations in the direct and proper way, and to reason about them, requires a habit of attentive reflection, of which few are capable, and which, even by those few, cannot be attained without much pains and labour.

Every man is apt to form his notions of things difficult to be apprehended, or less familiar, from their analogy to things which are more familiar. Thus, if a man bred to the seafaring life, and accustomed to think and talk only of matters relating to navigation, enters into discourse upon any other subject, it is well known that the language and the notions proper to his own profession are infused into every subject, and all things are measured by the rules of navigation; and, if he should take it into his head to philosophize concerning the faculties of the mind, it cannot be doubted but he would draw his notions from the fabric of his ship, and would find in the mind, sails, masts, rudder, and compass.*

Sensible objects, of one kind or other; do no less occupy and engross the rest of mankind, than things relating to navigation the seafaring man. For a considerable part of life, we can think of nothing but the objects of sense; and, to attend to objects of another na-

* See "Essays on the Intellectual Powers," Ess. VI., ch. viii., Nos. 2 and 6.—H.

ture, so as to form clear and distinct notions of them, is no easy matter, even after we come to years of reflection. The condition of mankind, therefore, affords good reason to apprehend that their language, and their common notions concerning the mind and its operations, will be analogical, and derived from the objects of sense; and that these analogies will be apt to impose upon philosophers, as well as upon the vulgar, and to lead them to materialize the mind and its faculties: and experience abundantly confirms the truth of this.

How generally men of all nations, and in all ages of the world, have conceived the soul, or thinking principle in man, to be some subtile matter, like breath or wind, the names given to it almost in all languages sufficiently testify. We have words which are proper, and not analogical, to express the various ways in which we perceive external objects by the senses—such as *feeling, sight, taste;* but we are often obliged to use these words analogically, to express other powers of the mind which are of a very different nature. And the powers which imply some degree of reflection, have generally no names but such as are analogical. The objects of thought are said to be *in the mind*—to be *apprehended, comprehended, conceived, imagined, retained, weighed, ruminated.*

It does not appear that the notions of the ancient philosophers, with regard to the nature of the soul, were much more refined than those of the vulgar, or that they were formed in any other way. We shall distinguish the philosophy that regards our subject into the *old* and the *new.* The old reached down to Des Cartes, who gave it a fatal blow, of which it has been gradually expiring ever since, and is now almost extinct. Des Cartes is the father of the new philosophy that relates to this subject; but it hath been gradually improving since his time, upon the principles laid down by him. The old philosophy seems to have been purely analogical; the new is more derived from reflection, but still with a very considerable mixture of the old analogical notions.

Because the objects of sense consist of *matter* and *form*, the ancient philosophers conceived everything to belong to one of these, or to be made up of both. Some, therefore, thought that the soul is a particular kind of subtile matter, separable from our gross bodies; others thought that it is only a particular form of the body, and inseparable from it. For there seem to have been some among the ancients, as well as among the moderns, who conceived that a certain structure or organization of the body, is all that is necessary to render it sensible and intelligent. The different powers of the mind were, accordingly, by the last sect of philosophers, conceived to belong to different parts of the body—as the heart, the brain, the liver, the stomach, the blood.

They who thought that the soul is a subtile matter, separable from the body, disputed to which of the four elements it belongs—whether to earth, water, air, or fire. Of the three last, each had its particular advocates. But some were of opinion, that it partakes of all the elements; that it must have something in its composition similar to everything we perceive; and that we perceive earth by the earthly part; water, by the watery part; and fire, by the fiery part of the soul. Some philosophers, not satisfied with determining of what kind of matter the soul is made, inquired likewise into its figure, which they determined to be spherical, that it might be the more fit for motion. The most spiritual and sublime notion concerning the nature of the soul, to be met with among the ancient philosophers, I conceive to be that of the Platonists, who held that it is made of that celestial and incorruptible matter of which the fixed stars were made, and, therefore, has a natural tendency to rejoin its proper element. I am at a loss to say, in which of these classes of philosophers Aristotle ought to be placed. He defines the soul to be, *The first* ἐντελέχεια *of a natural body which has potential life.* I beg to be excused from translating the Greek word, because I know not the meaning of it.

The notions of the ancient philosophers with regard to the operations of the mind, particularly with regard to perception and ideas, seem likewise to have been formed by the same kind of analogy.

Plato, of the writers that are extant, first introduced the word *idea* into philosophy; but his doctrine upon this subject had somewhat peculiar. He agreed with the rest of the ancient philosophers in this—that all things consist of matter and form; and that the matter of which all things were made, existed from eternity, without form: but he likewise believed that there are eternal forms of all possible things which exist, without matter; and to these eternal and immaterial forms he gave the name of *ideas;* maintaining that they are the only object of true knowledge. It is of no great moment to us, whether he borrowed these notions from Parmenides, or whether they were the issue of his own creative imagination. The latter Platonists seem to have improved upon them, in conceiving those ideas, or eternal forms of things, to exist not of themselves, but in the divine mind, and to be the models and patterns according to which all things were made:—

> "Then liv'd the Eternal One; then, deep retir'd
> In his unfathom'd essence, view'd at large
> The uncreated images of things."

To these Platonic notions, that of Malebranche is very nearly allied. This author seems, more than any other, to have been aware of the difficulties attending the common hypothesis concerning ideas—to wit, That ideas of all objects of thought are in the human mind; and, therefore, in order to avoid those difficulties, makes the ideas which are the immediate objects of human thought, to be the ideas of things in the Divine mind, who, being intimately present to every human mind, may discover his ideas to it, as far as pleaseth him.

The Platonists and Malebranche excepted, all other philosophers, as far as I know, have conceived that there are ideas or images of every object of thought in the human mind, or, at least, in some part of the brain, where the mind is supposed to have its residence.

Aristotle had no good affection to the word *idea*, and seldom or never uses it but in refuting Plato's notions about ideas. He thought that matter may exist without form; but that forms cannot exist without matter. But, at the same time, he taught, That there can be no sensation, no imagination, nor intellection, without forms, phantasms, or species in the mind; and that things sensible are perceived by sensible species, and things intelligible by intelligible species. His followers taught, more explicitly, that those sensible and intelligible species are sent forth by the objects, and make their impressions upon the passive intellect; and that the active intellect perceives them in the passive intellect. And this seems to have been the common opinion while the Peripatetic philosophy retained its authority.

The Epicurean doctrine, as explained by Lucretius, though widely different from the Peripatetic in many things, is almost the same in this. He affirms, that slender films or ghosts *(tenuia rerum simulacra)* are still going off from all things, and flying about; and that these, being extremely subtile, easily penetrate our gross bodies, and, striking upon the mind, cause thought and imagination.

After the Peripatetic system had reigned above a thousand years in the schools of Europe, almost without a rival, it sunk before that of Des Cartes; the perspicuity of whose writings and notions, contrasted with the obscurity of Aristotle and his commentators, created a strong prejudice in favor of this new philosophy. The characteristic of Plato's genius was sublimity, that of Aristotle's, subtilty; but Des Cartes far excelled both in perspicuity, and bequeathed this spirit to his successors. The system which is now generally received, with regard to the mind and its operations, derives not only its spirit from Des Cartes, but its fundamental principles; and, after all the improvements made by Malebranche, Locke, Berkeley, and Hume, may still be called *the Cartesian system:* we shall, therefore, make some remarks upon its spirit and tendency in general, and upon its doctrine concerning ideas in particular.

1. It may be observed, That the method which Des Cartes pursued, naturally led him to attend more to the operations of the mind by accurate reflection, and to trust less to analogical reasoning upon this subject, than any philosopher had done before him. Intending to build a system upon a new foundation, he began with a resolution to admit nothing but what was absolutely certain and evident. He supposed that his senses, his memory, his reason, and every other faculty to which we trust in common life, might be fallacious; and resolved to disbelieve everything, until he was compelled by irresistible evidence to yield assent.

In this method of proceeding, what appeared to him, first of all, certain and evident, was, That he thought—that he doubted—that he deliberated. In a word, the operations of his own mind, of which he was conscious, must be real, and no delusion; and, though all his other faculties should deceive him, his consciousness could not.* This, therefore, he looked upon as the first of all truths. This was the first firm ground upon which he set his foot, after being tossed in the ocean of scepticism; and he resolved to build all knowledge upon it, without seeking after any more first principles.

* Des Cartes did not commit Reid's error of making consciousness a co-ordinate and special faculty.—H.

As every other truth, therefore, and particularly the existence of the objects of sense, was to be deduced by a train of strict argumentation from what he knew by consciousness, he was naturally led to give attention to the operations of which he was conscious, without borrowing his notions of them from external things.

It was not in the way of analogy, but of attentive reflection, that he was led to observe, That thought, volition, remembrance, and the other attributes of the mind, are altogether unlike to extension, to figure, and to all the attributes of body; that we have no reason, therefore, to conceive thinking substances to have any resemblance to extended substances; and that, as the attributes of the thinking substance are things of which we are conscious, we may have a more certain and immediate knowledge of them by reflection, than we can have of external objects by our senses.

These observations, as far as I know, were first made by Des Cartes; and they are of more importance, and throw more light upon the subject, than all that had been said upon it before. They ought to make us diffident and jealous of every notion concerning the mind and its operations, which is drawn from sensible objects in the way of analogy, and to make us rely only upon accurate reflection, as the source of all real knowledge upon this subject.

2. I observe that, as the Peripatetic system has a tendency to materialize the mind and its operations, so the Cartesian has a tendency to spiritualize body and its qualities. One error, common to both systems, leads to the first of these extremes in the way of analogy, and to the last in the way of reflection. The error I mean is, That we can know nothing about body, or its qualities, but as far as we have sensations which resemble those qualities. Both systems agreed in this: but according to their differing methods of reasoning, they drew very different conclusions from it; the Peripatetic

drawing his notions of sensation from the qualities of body; the Cartesian, on the contrary, drawing his notions of the qualities of body from his sensations.

The Peripatetic, taking it for granted that bodies and their qualities do really exist, and are such as we commonly take them to be, inferred from them the nature of his sensations, and reasoned in this manner:—Our sensations are the impressions which sensible objects make upon the mind, and may be compared to the impression of a seal upon wax: the impression is the image or form of the seal, without the matter of it; in like manner, every sensation is the image or form of some sensible quality of the object. This is the reasoning of Aristotle: and it has an evident tendency to materialize the mind and its sensations.

The Cartesian, on the contrary, thinks that the existence of body, or of any of its qualities, is not to be taken as a first principle; and that we ought to admit nothing concerning it, but what, by just reasoning, can be deduced from our sensations; and he knows that, by reflection, we can form clear and distinct notions of our sensations, without borrowing our notions of them by analogy from the objects of sense. The Cartesians, therefore, beginning to give attention to their sensations, first discovered that the sensations corresponding to secondary qualities, cannot resemble any quality of body. Hence, Des Cartes and Locke inferred, that sound, taste, smell, colour, heat, and cold, which the vulgar took to be qualities of body, were not qualities of body, but mere sensations of the mind.* Afterwards, the ingen-

* Des Cartes and Locke made no such inference. They only maintained (as Reid himself states) that sound, taste, &c., as sensations in us, have no resemblance to any quality in bodies. If the names, therefore, of sound, taste, &c., were to be employed univocally—*i. e.*, to denote always things the same or similar—in that case they argued that these terms, if properly significant of the sensations, could not be properly applied to the relative qualities in ex-

ious Berkeley, considering more attentively the nature of sensation in general, discovered and demonstrated, that no sensation whatever could possibly resemble any quality of an insentient being, such as body is supposed to be; and hence he inferred, very justly, that there is the same reason to hold extension, figure, and all the primary qualities, to be mere sensations, as there is to hold the secondary qualities to be mere sensations. Thus, by just reasoning upon the Cartesian principles, matter was stripped of all its qualities; the new system, by a kind of metaphysical sublimation, converted all the qualities of matter into sensations, and spiritualized body, as the old had materialized spirit.

The way to avoid both these extremes, is to admit the existence of what we see and feel as a first principle, as well as the existence of things whereof we are conscious; and to take our notions of the qualities of body, from the testimony of our senses, with the Peripatetics; and our notions of our sensations from the testimony of consciousness, with the Cartesians.

ternal things. This is distinctly stated both by Des Cartes and Locke. But Des Cartes and the Cartesians observe that the terms in question are equivocally used; being commonly applied both to that in things which occasions the sensation in us, and to that sensation itself. Nay, the Cartesians, to avoid the ambiguity, distinguished the two relatives by different names. To take colour, for example: they called colour, as a sensation in the mind, *formal* colour; colour, as a quality in bodies capable of producing the sensation, *primitive* or *radical* colour. They had likewise another distinction of less importance—that of *secondary* or *derivative* colour; meaning thereby that which the coloured bodies impress upon the external medium. Thus, again, *primitive* or *radical* sound was the property of a body to determine a certain agitation in the air or other medium; *secondary* or *derivative* sound, that agitation in the medium itself; *formal* sound, the sensation occasioned by the impression made by the radical sound mediately, and by the derivative immediately, upon the organ of hearing. There is thus no difference between Reid and the Cartesians, except that the doctrine which he censures is in fact more precise and explicit than his own.—H.

3. I observe, That the modern scepticism is the natural issue of the new system; and that, although it did not being forth this monster until the year 1739,* it may be said to have carried it in its womb from the beginning.

The old system admitted all the principles of common sense as first principles, without requiring any proof of them; and, therefore, though its reasoning was commonly vague, analogical, and dark, yet it was built upon a broad foundation, and had no tendency to scepticism. We do not find that any Peripatetic thought it incumbent upon him to prove the existence of a material world; but every writer upon the Cartesian system attempted this, until Berkeley clearly demonstrated the futility of their arguments; and thence concluded that there was no such thing as a material world; and that the belief of it ought to be rejected as a vulgar error.

The new system admits only one of the principles of common sense as a first principle; and pretends, by strict argumentation, to deduce all the rest from it. That our thoughts, our sensations, and every thing of which we are conscious, hath a real existence, is admitted in this system as a first principle; but everything else must be made evident by the light of reason. Reason must rear the whole fabric of knowledge upon this single principle of consciousness.

There is a disposition in human nature to reduce things to as few principles as possible;† and this, without doubt, adds to the beauty of a system, if the principles are able to support what rests upon them. The mathematicians glory, very justly, in having raised so noble and magnificent a system of science, upon the foundation of a few axioms and definitions. This love

* When Hume's "Treatise of Human Nature" appeared.—H.

† See "Essays on the Intellectual Powers," p. 656, sqq. 4to edition.—H.

of simplicity, and of reducing things to few principles, hath produced many a false system; but there never was any system in which it appears so remarkably as that of Des Cartes.* His whole system concerning matter and spirit is built upon one axiom, expressed in one word, *cogito*. Upon the foundation of conscious thought, with ideas for his materials, he builds his system of the human understanding, and attempts to account for all its phænomena; and having, as he imagined, from his consciousness, proved the existence of matter; upon the existence of matter, and of a certain quantity of motion originally impressed upon it, he builds his system of the material world, and attempts to account for all its phænomena.

These principles, with regard to the material system, have been found insufficient; and it has been made evident that, besides matter and motion, we must admit gravitation, cohesion, corpuscular attraction, magnetism, and other centripetal and centrifugal forces, by which the particles of matter attract and repel each other. Newton, having discovered this, and demonstrated that these principles cannot be resolved into matter and motion, was led, by analogy and the love of simplicity, to conjecture, but with a modesty and caution peculiar to him, that all the phænomena of the material world depended upon attracting and repelling forces in the particles of matter. But we may now venture to say, that this conjecture fell short of the mark. For, even in the unorganized kingdom, the powers by which salts, crystals, spars, and many other bodies, concrete into regular forms, can never be accounted for by attracting and repelling forces in the particles of matter. And in the vegetable and animal kingdoms, there are strong indica-

* We must except, however, before Reid, among others, the system of Spinoza, and, since Reid, those of Fichte, Schelling, Hegel, &c.—H.

tions of powers of a different nature from all the powers of unorganized bodies. We see, then, that, although, in the structure of the material world, there is, without doubt, all the beautiful simplicity consistent with the purposes for which it was made, it is not so simple as the great Des Cartes determined it to be; nay, it is not so simple as the greater Newton modestly conjectured it to be. Both were misled by analogy, and the love of simplicity. One had been much conversant about extension, figure, and motion; the other had enlarged his views to attracting and repelling forces; and both formed their notions of the unknown parts of nature, from those with which they were acquainted, as the shepherd Tityrus formed his notion of the city of Rome from his country village:—

> "Urbem quam dicunt Romam, Melibœe, putavi
> Stultus ego, huic nostræ similem, quo sæpe solemus
> Pastores ovium teneros depellere fœtus.
> Sic canibus catulos similes, sic matribus hœdos
> Nôram: sic parvis componere magna solebam."

This is a just picture of the analogical way of thinking.

But to come to the system of Des Cartes, concerning the human understanding. It was built, as we have observed, upon consciousness as its sole foundation, and with ideas * as its materials; and all his followers have built upon the same foundation and with the same materials. They acknowledge that Nature hath given us various simple ideas. These are analogous to the matter, of Des Cartes's physical system. They acknowledge, likewise, a natural power, by which ideas are compounded, disjoined, associated, compared. This is an-

* There is no valid ground for supposing that Des Cartes meant by ideas aught but modifications of the mind itself. That the majority of the Cartesians did not, is certain. The case is, however, different with regard to Malebranche and Berkeley. But of this again.—H.

alogous to the original quantity of motion in Des Cartes's physical system. From these principles, they attempt to explain the phænomena of the human understanding, just as in the physical system the phænomena of nature were to be explained by matter and motion. It must, indeed, be acknowledged, that there is great simplicity in this system, as well as in the other. There is such a similitude between the two, as may be expected between children of the same father; but, as the one has been found to be the child of Des Cartes, and not of Nature, there is ground to think that the other is so likewise.

That the natural issue of this system is scepticism with regard to everything except the existence of our ideas, and of their necessary relations, which appear upon comparing them, is evident; for ideas, being the only objects of thought, and having no existence but when we are conscious of them, it necessarily follows that there is no object of our thought which can have a continued and permanent existence. Body and spirit, cause and effect, time and space, to which we were wont to ascribe an existence independent of our thought, are all turned out of existence by this short dilemma. Either these things are ideas of sensation or reflection, or they are not; if they are ideas of sensation or reflection, they can have no existence but when we are conscious of them; if they are not ideas of sensation or reflection, they are words without any meaning.*

Neither Des Cartes nor Locke perceived this consequence of their system concerning ideas. Bishop Berkeley was the first who discovered it. And what followed upon this discovery? Why, with regard to the material world, and with regard to space and time, he admits the consequence, That these things are mere ideas, and have

* This dilemma applies to the *sensualism* of Locke, but not to the *rationalism* of Des Cartes.—H.

no existence but in our minds; but with regard to the existence of spirits or minds, he does not admit the consequence; and, if he had admitted it, he must have been an absolute sceptic. But how does he evade this consequence with regard to the existence of spirits? The expedient which the good Bishop uses on this occasion is very remarkable, and shows his great aversion to scepticism. He maintains that we have no ideas of spirits; and that we can think, and speak, and reason about them, and about their attributes, without having any ideas of them. If this is so, my Lord, what should hinder as from thinking and reasoning about bodies, and their qualities, without having ideas of them? The Bishop either did not think of this question, or did not think fit to give any answer to it. However, we may observe, that, in order to avoid scepticism, he fairly starts out of the Cartesian system, without giving any reason why he did so in this instance, and in no other. This, indeed, is the only instance of a deviation from Cartesian principles which I have met with in the successors of Des Cartes; and it seems to have been only a sudden start, occasioned by the terror of scepticism; for, in all other things, Berkeley's system is founded upon Cartesian principles.

Thus we see that Des Cartes and Locke take the road that leads to scepticism, without knowing the end of it; but they stop short for want of light to carry them farther. Berkeley, frighted at the appearance of the dreadful abyss, starts aside, and avoids it. But the author of the "Treatise of Human Nature," more daring and intrepid, without turning aside to the right hand or to the left, like Virgil's Alecto, shoots directly into the gulf:

> "Hic specus horrendum, et sævi spiracula Ditis
> Monstrantur: ruptoque ingens Acheronte vorago
> Pestiferas apent fauces."

4. We may observe, That the account given by the new system, of that furniture of the human understand-

ing which is the gift of Nature, and not the acquisition of our own reasoning faculty, is extremely lame and imperfect.*

The natural furniture of the human understanding is of two kinds: First, The *notions* or simple apprehensions which we have of things; and, secondly, The *judgments* or the belief which we have concerning them. As to our notions, the new system reduces them to two classes—*ideas of sensation*, and *ideas of reflection*: the first are conceived to be copies of our sensations, retained in the memory or imagination; the second, to be copies of the operations of our minds whereof we are conscious, in like manner retained in the memory or imagination: and we are taught that these two comprehend all the materials about which the human understanding is, or can be employed. As to our judgment of things, or the belief which we have concerning them, the new system allows no part of it to be the gift of nature, but holds it to be the acquisition of reason, and to be got by comparing our ideas, and perceiving their agreements or disagreements. Now I take this account, both of our notions, and of our judgments or belief, to be extremely imperfect; and I shall briefly point out some of its capital defects.

The division of our notions into ideas of sensation,† and ideas of reflection, is contrary to all rules of logic; because the second member of the division includes the first. For, can we form clear and just notions of our sensations any other way than by reflection? Surely we cannot. Sensation is an operation of the mind of which we are conscious; and we get the notion of sensation by reflecting upon that which we are conscious of. In like manner, doubting and believing are operations of the mind whereof we are conscious; and we get the notion

* The following summary refers principally to Locke.—H.

† It must be remembered that under *Sensation* Locke and others included *Perception proper* and *Sensation proper*.—H.

of them by reflecting upon what we are conscious of. The ideas of sensation, therefore, are ideas of reflection, as much as the ideas of doubting, or believing, or any other ideas whatsoever.*

But, to pass over the inaccuracy of this division, it is extremely incomplete. For, since sensation is an operation of the mind, as well as all the other things of which we form our notions by reflection, when it is asserted that all our notions are either ideas of sensation or ideas of reflection, the plain English of this is, That mankind

* I do not see how this criticism on Locke's division can be defended, or even excused. It is perfectly evident that Reid here confounds *the proper ideas of sensation*—that is, the ideas of the qualities of matter, about which sensation (perception) is conversant—with the *idea of sensation* itself—that is, the idea of this faculty as an attribute of mind, and which is the object of a reflex consciousness. Nor would it be competent to maintain that Locke, allowing no immediate knowledge of aught but of mind and its contents, consequently reduces all our faculties to self-consciousness, and thus abolishes the distinction of sensation (perception) and reflection, as separate faculties, the one conversant with the qualities of the external world, the other with the qualities of the internal. For, in the *first* place, it would still be logically competent, on the hypothesis that all our knowledge is exclusively of self, to divide the ideas we possessed, into classes, according as these were given as representations of the *non-ego* by the *ego*, or as phænomena of the *ego* itself. In the *second* place, Reid's criticism does not admit of this excuse. But, in the *third*, if the defence were valid in itself, and here available, the philosophy of Reid himself would be obnoxious to a similar criticism. For he makes perception (consequently the object known in perception) an object of consciousness; but consciousness, in his view, is only of the phænomena of mind itself—all consciousness is to him *self-consciousness*. Thus, *his* perception, as contained under *his* consciousness, is only cognisant of the *ego*. With all this, however, Reid distinguishes perception and consciousness as special and co-ordinate faculties; perception being conversant about the qualities of matter, as suggested—that is, as represented in the percipient subject—consciousness as conversant about perception and the other attributes of mind itself.—With the preceding observations, the reader may compare Priestley's "Examination," p. 38, and Stewart's "Philosophical Essays," Note N.—H.

neither do nor can think of anything but of the operations of their own minds. Nothing can be more contrary to truth, or more contrary to the experience of mankind. I know that Locke, while he maintained this doctrine, believed the notions which we have of body and of its qualities, and the notions which we have of motion and of space, to be ideas of sensation. But why did he believe this? Because he believed those notions to be nothing else but images of our sensations. If, therefore, the notions of body and its qualities, of motion and space, be not images of our sensations, will it not follow that those notions are not ideas of sensation? Most certainly.*

There is no doctrine in the new system which more directly leads to scepticism than this. And the author of the "Treatise of Human Nature" knew very well how to use it for that purpose; for, if you maintain that there is any such existence as body or spirit, time or place, cause or effect, he immediately catches you between the horns of this dilemma; your notions of these existences are either ideas of sensation, or ideas of reflec-

* I may here notice—what I shall hereafter more fully advert to—that Reid's criticism of Locke, here and elsewhere, proceeds upon the implication that the English philosopher attached the same restricted meaning to the term Sensation that he did himself. But this is not the case. Locke employed *Sensation* to denote both the *idée* and the *sentiment* of the Cartesians—both the *perception* and the *sensation* of Reid. To confound this distinction was, indeed, wrong, but this is a separate and special ground of censure, and, in a general criticism of Locke's doctrine, the fact that he did so confound perception proper and sensation proper, should always be taken into account. But, waving this, what is gained by the distinction in Reid's hands? In his doctrine, space, motion, &c., as perceived, are only conceptions; only modifications of self, suggested, in some unknown way, on occasion of the impression made on the sense; consequently, in the one doctrine as in the other, what is known is nothing beyond the affections of the thinking subject itself; and this is the only basis required by the idealist and sceptic for the foundation of their systems.—H.

tion: if of sensation, from what sensation are they copied? if of reflection, from what operation of the mind are they copied?

It is indeed to be wished that those who have written much about sensation, and about the other operations of the mind, had likewise thought and reflected much, and with great care, upon those operations: but is it not very strange that they will not allow it to be possible for mankind to think of anything else?

The account which this system gives of our judgment and belief concerning things, is as far from the truth as the account it gives of our notions or simple apprehensions. It represents our senses as having no other office but that of furnishing the mind with notions or simple apprehensions of things; and makes our judgment and belief concerning those things to be acquired by comparing our notions together, and perceiving their agreements or disagreements.

We have shewn, on the contrary, that every operation of the senses, in its very nature, implies judgment or belief, as well as simple apprehension. Thus, when I feel the pain of the gout in my toe, I have not only a notion of pain, but a belief of its existence, and a belief of some disorder in my toe which occasions it; and this belief is not produced by comparing ideas, and perceiving their agreements and disagreements; it is included in the very nature of the sensation. When I perceive a tree before me, my faculty of seeing gives me not only a notion or simple apprehension of the tree, but a belief of its existence, and of its figure, distance, and magnitude; and this judgment or belief is not got by comparing ideas, it is included in the very nature of the perception. We have taken notice of several original principles of belief in the course of this inquiry; and when other faculties of the mind are examined, we shall find more, which have not occurred in the examination of the five senses.

Such original and natural judgments are, therefore, a

part of that furniture which Nature hath given to the human understanding. They are the inspiration of the Almighty no less than our notions or simple apprehensions. They serve to direct us in the common affairs of life, where our reasoning faculty would leave us in the dark. They are a part of our constitution; and all the discoveries of our reason are grounded upon them. They make up what is called *the common sense of mankind;** and, what is manifestly contrary to any of those first principles, is what we call *absurd.* The strength of them is *good sense,* which is often found in those who are not acute in reasoning. A remarkable deviation from them, arising from a disorder in the constitution, is what we call *lunacy*; as when a man believes that he is made of glass. When a man suffers himself to be reasoned out of the principles of common sense, by metaphysical arguments, we may call this *metaphysical lunacy*; which differs from the other species of the distemper in this, that it is not continued, but intermittent: it is apt to seize the patient in solitary and speculative moments: but, when he enters into society, Common Sense recovers her authority.† A clear explication and enumeration of the principles of common sense, is one of the chief *desiderata* in logic. We have only considered such of them as occurred in the examination of the five senses.

5. The last observation that I shall make upon the new system, is, that, although it professes to set out in the way of reflection, and not of analogy, it hath retained some of the old analogical notions concerning the operations of the mind; particularly, that things which do not now exist in the mind itself, can only be perceived,

* See Note A —H.

† No one admits this more promptly than the sceptic himself. See Hume's "Treatise of Human Nature," Book I., Part iv., §7, and "Enquiry Concerning Human Understanding," § 12, Part II. —H.

remembered, or imagined, by means of ideas or images * of them in the mind, which are the immediate objects of perception, remembrance, and imagination. This doctrine appears evidently to be borrowed from the old system; which taught that external things make impressions upon the mind, like the impressions of a seal upon wax; that it is by means of those impressions that we perceive, remember, or imagine them; and that those impressions must resemble the things from which they are taken. When we form our notions of the operations of the mind by analogy, this way of conceiving them seems to be very natural, and offers itself to our thoughts; for, as everything which is felt must make some impression upon the body, we are apt to think that everything which is understood must make some impression upon the mind.

From such analogical reasoning, this opinion of the existence of ideas or images of things in the mind, seems to have taken its rise, and to have been so universally received among philosophers. It was observed already, that Berkeley, in one instance, apostatizes from this principle of the new system, by affirming that we have no ideas of spirits, and that we can think of them immediately, without ideas. But I know not whether in this he has had any followers. There is some difference, likewise, among modern philosophers with regard to the ideas or images by which we perceive, remember, or imagine sensible things. For, though all agree in the existence of such images,† they differ about their place; some placing them in a particular part of the

* That is, by *representative entities different from the modes of the mind itself*. This doctrine, I have already noticed, is attributed by Reid too universally to philosophers; and is also a comparatively unimportant circumstance in reference to the Idealist and Sceptic. See Note C.—H.

† See last note. Berkeley did hold the hypothesis of ideas as understood by Reid.—H.

brain, where the soul is thought to have her residence, and others placing them in the mind itself. Des Cartes held the first of these opinions ;* to which Newton seems likewise to have inclined ; for he proposes this query in his "Optics :"—"Annon sensorium animalium est locus cui substantia sentiens adest, et in quem sensibiles rerum species per nervos et cerebrum deferuntur, ut ibi præsentes a præsente sentiri possint?" But Locke seems to place the ideas of sensible things in the mind ; † and that Berkeley, and the author of the "Treatise of Human Nature," were of the same opinion, is evident. The last makes a very curious application of this doctrine, by endeavouring to prove from it, That the mind either is no substance, or that it is an extended and divisible substance; because the ideas of extension cannot be in a subject which is indivisible and unextended.

I confess I think his reasoning in this, as in most cases, is clear and strong. For whether the idea of extension be only another name for extension itself, as Berkeley and this author assert ; or whether the idea of extension be an image and resemblance of extension, as Locke conceived ; I appeal to any man of common sense, whether extension, or any image of extension, can be in an unextended and indivisible subject. But while I agree with him in his reasoning, I would make a different application of it, He takes it for granted, that there are ideas of extension in the mind ; and thence infers, that, if it is at all a substance, it must be an extended

* An unqualified error, arising from not understanding the ambiguous *language* of Des Cartes; who calls, by the common name of *ideas*, both the organic motions in the brain, of which the mind, in his doctrine, necessarily knows nothing, and the representations in the mind itself, hyperphysically determined on occasion of those motions, and of which alone the mind is cognizant. But of this under the "Essays on the Intellectual Powers."—H.

† Locke's opinion on this point is as obscure and doubtful as that of Des Cartes is clear and certain. But Reid is probably right.—H.

and divisible substance. On the contrary, I take it for granted, upon the testimony of common sense, that my mind is a substance—that is, a permanent subject of thought; and my reason convinces me that it is an unextended and indivisible substance; and hence I infer that there cannot be in it anything that resembles extension. If this reasoning had occurred to Berkeley, it would probably have led him to acknowledge that we may think and reason concerning bodies, without having ideas of them in the mind, as well as concerning spirits.

I intended to have examined more particularly and fully this doctrine of the existence of ideas or images of things in the mind; and likewise another doctrine, which is founded upon it—to wit, That judgment or belief is nothing but a perception of the agreement or disagreement of our ideas; but, having already shewn, through the course of this inquiry, that the operations of the mind which we have examined, give no countenance to either of these doctrines, and in many things contradict them, I have thought it proper to drop this part of my design. It may be executed with more advantage, if it is at all necessary, after inquiring into some other powers of the human understanding.

Although we have examined only the five senses, and the principles of the human mind which are employed about them, or such as have fallen in our way in the course of this examination, we shall leave the further prosecution of this inquiry to future deliberation. The powers of memory, of imagination, of taste, of reasoning, of moral perception, the will, the passions, the affections, and all the active powers of the soul, present a vast and boundless field of philosophical disquisition, which the author of this inquiry is far from thinking himself able to survey with accuracy. Many authors of ingenuity, ancient and modern, have made excursions into this vast territory, and have communicated useful observations: but there is reason to believe that those who have pretended to give us a map of the wnole, have satisfied themselves with a very inaccurate and incomplete survey. If Galileo had attempted a complete system of natural philosophy, he had, probably, done little service to mankind: but by confining himself to what was within his comprehension, he laid the foundation of a system of knowledge, which rises by degrees, and does honour to the human understanding. Newton, building upon this foundation, and, in like manner, confining his inquiries to the law of gravitation and the properties of light, performed wonders. If he had attempted a great deal more, he had done a great deal less, and perhaps nothing at all. Ambitious of following such great examples, with unequal steps, alas! and unequal force, we have attempted an inquiry only into one little corner of the human mind—that corner which seems to be most exposed to vulgar observation, and to be most easily comprehended; and yet, if we have delineated it justly, it must be acknowledged that the accounts heretofore given of it were very lame, and wide of the truth.

INDEX.

Addison, conception of color, 178–9.
Agnolonius, hiso ptics, 254.
Analogy, 339.
Analysis, of the human faculties necessary, 75–6.
Anatomy, mental, 72–3.
Anepigraphus, J. R., 206.
Animal spirits, theory of, 280.
Animals, laws of vision in, 246.
Apprehension, simple, 95, 95 H.
Aquapendens, 284.
Aristotle, on primary and secondary qualities, 140, 156; on imagination, 182 H.; compared with Bacon, 335; definition of the soul, 342–3; referred to, 344; materialistic tendency of his system, 346.
Association of ideas, 332–3.

Bacon, his services, 334.
Belief, Locke's theory of, criticised, 95 sq.; Hume's theory of, criticised, 96 sq., 330; cannot be defined, 96 sq.; in human testimony, 323 sq.; in the continuance of the present course of nature, 328 sq.; an ingredient of mental operations, 137 sq., 228, 330.
Berkeley, relation of his philosophy to scepticism, 81 sq., 86 sq., 349, 353; ideas and spirits, 102, 186; natural signs, 139 H.; primary and secondary qualities of matter, 140; qualities of matter not resembling sensations, 138 sq., 153, 158; his solution of certain phenomena of vision examined, 218, 220 sq.; noticed, 148, 160, 186, 199 H., 267, 272, 310, 312, 316, 345.
Body, its qualities, how apprehended, 181 sq.
Borrichius, 210.
Brain, 223, 224.
Briggs, Dr., 254, 279.

Cæsalpinus, 284.
Cause and effect, 332.
Cheselden, case of couching, 172, 194, 271 sq.; on double vision, 270.
Cold, 129sq.; *see* Touch.
Color, 162 sq; *see* Seeing; a blind man's notion of, 165 sq.
Common sense, the root of all philosophy, 81; principles of, 100, 358; practically acknowledged by the idealists, 104; contrasted with the ideal philosophy, 132 sq., 358.

Conception, distinguished from perception, 289 H.
Consciousness, Des Cartes' view of, 345 H., 350.
Credulity, 325.
Custom, 265 sq.

Democritus, on the qualities of matter, 140, 157, 180, 180 H.
Des Cartes, his doubt, 77, 345; misapprehended by Reid, 77 H.; scepticism the natural issue of his system, 86 sq., 349; on primary and secondary qualities, 140, 157, on seeing objects erect by inverted images, 215, 216; the father of the new philosophy of mind, 341; remarks upon the Cartesian system, 345 sq; noticed, 72, 82, 84, 103, 148, 154, 155 H., 160, 184.
Dimerbroeck, 284
Distance, how computed by the eye, 304 sq.
Divine veracity, 155 H.

Effluvia, 90.
Ἐντελέχεια, 343.
Epicurus and the Epicureans, on primary and secondary qualities, 140, 157, 180; theory of perception, 344.
Experience, 323.
Experiment, 71.
Extension, notion of, 141–7, 187–91; *see* Seeing, Sight, Touch; Reid's and Kant's theories contrasted, 141 H.; possibility of an *a posteriori* perception of, 147 H.
Eyes, parallel motion of, 211 sq., 265 sq; concentration on one object, 263 sq.; *see* Seeing.

Fabricius, 210.
Fichte, idealism, 152 H.
Figure, how perceived by the eye, 315.
Folkes, Martin, 269.
Foster, case of, 269, 270.

Galen, 239.
Gassendi, 239.
Genius, adulterates philosophy, 76.
Geometry of visibles, 199 sq.; *see* Seeing.
Grew, Dr. N., 121.

Halley, Dr., 165.
Hardness, 131, 139 sq; *see* Touch.
Hearing, 122 sq.
Heat, 129; *see* Touch.
Hobbes, on imagination, 182 H.; noticed, 84.
Hume, his Treatise of Human Nature considered, 81 sq.; reduces Berkeley's system to scepticism, 86, 353; his theory of belief examined, 96 sq, 330; his theory of mind, 100 sq.; confession, 135, 358 H.; noticed, 139, 150, 160, 184, 186, 345, 349 H, 356.

Idea, how used by Reid, 93–4; by Des Cartes, 351, 360.
Idealism, 151–2 H.
Ideal philosophy, 87; the theory of sensation, memory, belief, and imagination introduced by it considered, 96; psychological history of, 100 sq.; remarks on, 153 sq.
Ideas, doctrines of ancient philosophers about, 343 sq.
Identity, Locke's account of, considered, 79.
Image, Reid's use of the term, 93.
Imagination, how accompanied, 93 H.; view of

Aristotle and Hobbes, 182 H.; distinguished from perception, 289 H.
Impressions, in reference to sensations, 298 sq.; on the mind, the peripatetic theory of, 347.
Inductive principle, 328 sq.
Instinct, instinctive beliefs, 291 sq.; belief in the constancy of nature, *see* Inductive principle.

Jacobi, on perception, 302 H.
Jurin, Dr.,

Kant, relation to Hume, 66 H.; held the notion of extension to be *a priori*, 141 H., 147 H.
Kepler, on seeing objects erect by inverted images, 215, 216.

Laertius, 83.
Language, imperfection of, impediment to the study of mind, 74 sq.; natural, etc., considered, 124-8, 136.
Laws of nature, their character, 225, 230 sq., 239 sq.; belong to mind as well as to matter, 225.
Light, 162; *see* Seeing.
Locke, his theory of personal identity considered, 79; his definition of knowledge criticised, 97 sq; quoted, 152; his doctrine of primary and secondary qualities discussed, 157, 179, 185; not the originator of these terms, 185 H.; misinterpreted by Reid, 347 H.; noticed, 79, 82, 103, 148, 160.
Lucretius, 344.

Malebranche, his doctrine of primary and secondary qualities, 140, 157, 184, 186; his theory of perception, 343-4; noticed, 79, 82, 103, 148, 160.
Mariotte, 251.
Memory distinguished from perception, 330; defined, 94.
Metaphysic, 88.
Mind, importance of the study of, 70; how to be studied, 71, 72; impediments to our knowledge of, 72-6; the systems of Des Cartes, Malebranche, and Locke, considered, 76-80; of Berkeley and Hume, 81-6; its existence, how inferred, 105 sq.; in sensation, active or passive?, 116-17; operations of, two ways of treating, 338; names of operations borrowed from sensible images, 341.

Nature, the works of, 85; our belief in the uniformity of, 328 sq.
Nerves, theory of, 279.
Newton, Sir Isaac, his regular philosophy, 71; on color, etc., 119; his query on single vision, 246, 282; attracting and repelling forces, 218, 350; followed Bacon's rules of inductive reasoning, 335; concerning species, 360; noticed, 113, 162, 351.

Optic nerve, 222, 336, 279.

Perception, in general, 287-303; distinguished from sensation, 288, 298; law of the manifestation of sensation and perception, 287 H.; distinguished from imagination, 289, 289 H.; from memory, 289; what it implies, 289;

original and acquired, 293 sq.; involves no exercise of reason, 295; perception of objects, the result of what, 297–303; the true object of, immediate, 298 H.; analogous to testimony, 320–37.
Peripatetics, on species, 344; their tendency to materialize mind, 346; noticed, 183, 187.
Phantasms, 344
Philosophers, their notions concerning the soul, 341.
Plato, his system of ideas, 343 sq.; noticed, 104.
Platonists, their notion of the soul, 344.
Porta, Baptista, 239.
Porterfield, Dr., on vision, 226, 231 239, 253, 261, 272 sq.
Pyrrho, the Elean, 83.

Qualities, primary and secondary, the distinction of, 140, 157, 185sq.; 185H.

Reason, in connection with common sense, 79 sq, 149; inaccurate use of term by Reid, 79 H., 149 H.; in relation to our belief in testimony, 327.
Reflection, 338; Locke's account of, 355–6.
Retina, how rays of light affect, 194–237; *see* Seeing; how objects fall upon, 240.
Rousseau, 336–7.

Saunderson, N., 145, 165, 188, 220.
Scepticism, in philosophy of Des Cartes, Malebranche, Locke, and Berkeley, 82, 86 sq, 349 sq.; animadverted on, 290, origin of, 351–2.
Scheiner, experiments on the eye, 231.
Seeing, in general, 162 sq.; color, 173–81; visible figure and extension, 187–91; geometry of visibles, 199–211; certain phenomena of vision examined: the parallel motion of the eyes, our seeing objects erect by inverted images, seeing objects single with two eyes, 211 sq.
Sensation, indefinable, 96; belongs to a sentient being, 107, what it suggests, 106; does not resemble qualities of body, 181–7; distinguished from perception, 288, 298; sensation and reflection as the sources of ideas, considered, 354 sq.
Sensations, distinguished from qualities causing them, 109 sq., 114 sq, 129 sq., 132 sq., 157, 173 sq, 177.
Sense, testimony of, 320–37.
Senses, systems concerning, 156–61; do not deceive, 319.
Sensorium, defined, 222; theories concerning, 280–5.
Sight, *see* Seeing.
Sign, connection of, with thing signified, 135 sq.
Smelling, in general, 89–116; the sensation considered abstractly, 90–2; compared with the remembrance and imagination, 92–5; as a quality in bodies, etc., 109–11; the name of smell, to what it belongs, 115–16; in sensation, the mind active or passive?, 116–17.
Smith, Dr., his system of optics, 216, 246, 262, 267, 268, 269, 270, 272, 275, 279, 310, 313, 314, 316.

Softness, 131; *see* Touch.
Soul, opinions regarding its nature, 341 sq.
Sound, *see* Hearing.
Species, sensible, theories of, 180, 344.
Squinting, *see* Seeing.
Strabismus, 277.
Suggestion, explained, 107 sq., 107–8 H.

Taste, 118–21.
Tertullian, 108 H.
Testimony, evidence of, compared with that of sense, 320-37.
Touch, analysed, 129 sq.; heat and cold, 129 sq ; hardness and softness, 131 sq.; hardness and other primary qualities, 139 sq· extension, 141 sq.; existence of a material world, 148 sq.
Truth, an innate principle, 324.

Valverda, 284.
Vesalius, 284.
Virgil, quoted, 351.
Visibles, geometry of, *see* Seeing.
Vision, *see* Seeing.

Winslow, quoted, 284.
World, material, existence of, a first principle, 148–56, 348, 357 sq.

Zeno. 84,